P9-DHG-455

305.2422 Burge, Kimberly.
BUR
        The born frees.

DISCARD

$26.95

DATE			

Penfield Public Library
1985 Baird Rd.
Penfield, NY 14526

BAKER & TAYLOR

THE TORN PAGES

THE BORN FREE

THE BORN FREES

WRITING WITH THE GIRLS OF GUGULETHU

KIMBERLY BURGE

W. W. NORTON & COMPANY

New York | London

Copyright © 2015 by Kimberly Burge

Excerpts from "A Rock" and "Motherhood" from *Please, Take Photographs*,
copyright © 2009 by Sindiwe Magona. Used by permission of Modjaji Books.

PARADISE ROAD: Words and Music by Patric William Van Blerk and Fransua Roos.
Copyright © 1979 Gallo Music Publishers. All Rights Administered by Warner/Chappell
Music Publishing. All Rights Reserved. Used By Permission of Alfred Music.

All rights reserved
Printed in the United States of America
First Edition

For information about permission to reproduce selections from this book,
write to Permissions, W. W. Norton & Company, Inc.,
500 Fifth Avenue, New York, NY 10110

For information about special discounts for bulk purchases, please contact
W. W. Norton Special Sales at specialsales@wwnorton.com or 800-233-4830

Manufacturing by Quad Graphics
Book design by Chris Welch
Production managers: Louise Mattarelliano

ISBN 978-0-393-23916-4

W. W. Norton & Company, Inc.
500 Fifth Avenue, New York, N.Y. 10110
www.wwnorton.com

W. W. Norton & Company Ltd.
Castle House, 75/76 Wells Street, London W1T 3QT

1 2 3 4 5 6 7 8 9 0

For Harry, Patricia, and Kvn Burge,

and for the girls of Amazw'Entombi,

with gratitude and love

To the youth of today, I also have a wish to make: Be the scriptwriters of your destiny and feature yourselves as stars that showed the way towards a brighter future.

—NELSON MANDELA

I am a rock
Sturdy and strong.
I am a rock
Damn hardy; do not forget.
Were it not so,
I wouldn't be here to tell the tale.

—"A ROCK," SINDIWE MAGONA,

FROM *PLEASE, TAKE PHOTOGRAPHS*

CONTENTS

PART THREE

UBUNTU IN ABUNDANCE: GUGULETHU, TWO YEARS LATER

DRAMATIS PERSONAE

THE WRITING CLUB

Amazw'Entombi, "Voices of the Girls"
[ah-MAHZ-way en-TOHM-bee]

THE LOCATION

J. L. Zwane Presbyterian Church and Community Center
[ZWAH-nay]

THE TOWNSHIP

Gugulethu
[goo-goo-LAY-too]

THE GIRLS

Annasuena
[an-na-SWAY-na]; Eighteen years old

Olwethu
[ol-WAY-too]; Nineteen years old

Sive
[SEE-vay]; Sixteen years old

Sharon
Twenty years old

Ntombizanele ("Ntombi")
[en-TOHM-bee-za-NAY-lay]; Eighteen years old

Gugu
[GOO-goo]; Sixteen years old

Mandlakazi
[mand-lah-KAH-zee]; Sixteen years old

THE BORN FREES

In My Own Being

State of Mind

The state of the mind gets oppressed.
The longer it takes, the quicker you
Break. Choose to let the wind blow.
The foretelling of time spelled unknown.
I still don't know why continuously I
Feel alone. The bare feet have nowhere
To go. And I've lost my way home.

Count from one to ten to please my
Soul yet inside remains a big hole.
When I'm in the most or the warmest
I still feel the brush of the cold, the
Urge to have someone to call,
For I'm the one who didn't have it all.

—Annasuena

Some days, Annasuena simply longed to be a girl. She couldn't say what her ideal girlhood looked like, and she did not need *ideal* anyway. If she could re-create her past, she would locate herself in a time before she knew the troubles that now consumed her.

She would reconstruct her family life. Her mother would be alive and Annasuena would grow up living with her, and with her brothers and sister. They would all stay together in the same home. She didn't have to live with her father, but she would know who he was. She would have the chance to meet him, to know what he looked like, to see whether she inherited her deeper complexion from him.

Cape Town or Johannesburg—she didn't care which city the family lived in. They didn't have to be rich and their house need not be large. For all she cared, it could be a concrete, three-room, government-issued house in a township. But something more than a shack, more than plywood walls and plastic tarps, the roof a corrugated iron sheet held down by old tires and heavy rocks to keep the winds from whipping it away. At night, instead of lying awake listening to the rats crawling under her bed, she would snuggle down with her little sister under a soft pink blanket that smelled flowery, like frangipani, from her mother's perfume when she leaned down to kiss her girls good-night. After her sister had fallen asleep, Annasuena might keep a light on late into the night as she wrote poems in a diary.

As she grew older, her elder brothers would turn protective and look out for her. None of her other male relatives would so much as leer in her direction.

She did not have to attend private schools, but she would attend school, every year, uninterrupted. She would study hard and earn good marks, except maybe in mathematics, which she would never understand. She would sing in the choir. Before she knew it, she would be entering Grade 12, her Matric year. For learners in South Africa, high school culminates in Matriculation exams. Their exam results determine whether they earn a high school diploma, and whether they qualify to attend university.

Most students of her generation do not stay in school long enough to take Matric, or do not pass their exams. But Annasuena knew that if she made it as far as Matric, she would certainly pass.

To celebrate her accomplishment, if she and Phelo were still together, she would allow him to escort her to her school's Matric Dance. She would wear a long satin dress, in purple. It would drag along the ground even if she wore her highest heels. Her hair would be in long, thin auburn plaits, and she would wear crystal earrings that dangled nearly to her shoulders. This might be the first night she would sleep with Phelo, though honestly, they probably would not have waited this long. But it would be her choice. And if they had sex, they would be careful.

She would be HIV negative, and she would stay that way.

Truth be told, whatever advantages Annasuena had inherited as she began life remained unrealized. As a young South African, she was one of the "Born Frees." Finally, her country now granted freedom to everyone with her skin color. But freedom implies choice. Annasuena had already seen her life, her future, even her own body altered by choices made by other people. What could freedom mean for her? What had it meant to be born to a mother who was a famous singer, when what a girl needed was a mother?

If she could have had the girlhood she dreamed up, Annasuena thought she might have had a very nice life. But she had this life. Orphaned at ten, looking out for herself. Growing up from place to place, with family or family friends. House to shack, township to township. Struggling to finish Grade 9. HIV positive and terrified of falling ill. Eighteen years old.

I met Annasuena soon after I arrived in South Africa in January of 2010. I was to live there for a year as a Fulbright Scholar and lead a creative writing club for teenage girls at J. L. Zwane Presbyterian Church and Community Center in Gugulethu, a black township about ten miles outside Cape Town. She became one of the first members of the club, which we named Amazw'Entombi. In Xhosa, it means "Voices of the Girls."

Annasuena and all the other girls who joined Amazw' Entombi were part of the Born Frees, the first generation of black South Africans born after apartheid and coming of age in a newly democratic nation, following the 1994 elections that made Nelson Mandela South Africa's first black president. Apartheid, an Afrikaans word with Dutch origins, means, literally, "separateness, or a state of being apart." For nearly fifty years, it was the government-approved and enforced law of racial segregation throughout South Africa. Apartheid classified and ranked people according to their skin color and one of four assigned racial categories.

Whites were people of European origin, predominantly Dutch and British. Whites make up 8.9 percent of the country's population today. Below whites on the racial ladder came Indian South Africans, people of Indian descent, only 2.5 percent of the population and primarily centered in the city of Durban. Then, so-called "coloured" people, those of mixed race, a melting pot of European, Bantu, Asian, Khoikhoi, and San blood, and a term some people find offensive. "Coloureds" make up the majority of the population in Western Cape and Northern Cape Provinces, including Cape Town, although this group only comprises just under 9 percent of the population nationwide.

Finally, on the bottom rung, were blacks, known then as Bantus, natives, Africans. The vast majority of South Africa's population—almost 80 percent—is black.

Under apartheid, blacks and "coloureds" could not vote. Under apartheid, your race determined everything. Where you lived, traveled, went to school, if at all, and what you could study. Where you worked and what kind of work you did. Whom you could marry. Where you worshipped God. What toilets you used, what beaches or parks you visited. What benches you sat on as you waited for a taxi, and which taxi you could take. In which graveyards you could bury your dead.

After the end of apartheid, these restrictions were lifted. But now, along with freedom, the Born Frees were inheriting a country awash in contradiction. Democratic South Africa has one of the most progressive constitutions in the world. Discrimination is prohibited—whether based on race, gender, sex, pregnancy, marital status, ethnic or social origin, color, sexual orientation, age, disability, religion, conscience, belief, culture, language, or birth. The constitution set up the Commission on Gender Equality on behalf of women and girls, one of six state institutions intended to promote democracy and a culture of human rights in the republic.

South Africa also has one of the world's highest levels of violence against women, second only to the war-torn Democratic Republic of the Congo, and has been called the rape capital of the world. More than a third of girls have experienced sexual violence before the age of eighteen. Levels of child rape, including that of infants, are likely underreported. The country has the world's highest number of people infected with HIV, an estimated 5.6 million. Young women are particularly at risk. Of South Africans aged fifteen to twenty-four who are infected with HIV, three-quarters are women.

The Rainbow Nation has the third-highest level of income inequality in the world, a yawning gap between rich and poor, greater now than during apartheid. A quarter of South Africans live on less than $1.25 a day; 85 percent of whites are relatively wealthy, 85 percent of blacks, relatively poor. Some call it economic apartheid. Since the educational system also remains steeply inequitable, the young are becoming increasingly unemployable and unable to escape generational cycles of poverty. One report estimated that seven out of ten of the Born Frees who have reached age eighteen did not remain in school through Grade 12 or did not pass the Matriculation exams.

These were facts I learned about South Africa as I prepared to live there. I saw the implications of all those statistics as I got to know some of the Born Frees through Amazw'Entombi. The lives of these girls embodied the complicated and brutal history of their country, its present struggles, and all the promise it yet holds. Numbers receded; names took their place.

Girls like Ntombizanele, whose name means "No more girls." Like Annasuena, she lost her mother at too early an age. She wanted to earn her Matric by retaking the exams she had already failed once, but untreated depression threatened to overcome her. For Sharon, her dreams were not hers alone. She carried the weight of her family's expectations: to succeed and provide for them materially, to earn an income that could help to build an additional room onto their overcrowded house or buy a car. Orphaned by AIDS and HIV positive herself, Olwethu sometimes appeared resigned to her fate. Worse, she seemed to tempt it, skipping out on school and finding an older boyfriend who turned abusive. As Olwethu floundered, her younger sister, Sive, excelled at a boarding school for orphans forty miles from Gugulethu. Olwethu had trouble articulating what she wanted for her life, even more difficulty in recognizing her own worth.

Then there was Annasuena, the girl I came to know best of all. Brimming with moxie and excuses, her expectations for her life changed from day to day. She knew well her strengths and occasionally recognized her faults. She saw most clearly where other people had failed her, and she learned she could depend on no one but herself, and sometimes not even that.

The Born Frees and democratic South Africa entered adolescence together, and the growing pains have been ragged and sharp. For all these girls, adulthood muscled its way into their lives years before any birthday declared them of age. While their fellow South Africans attempted to characterize their generation, these burgeoning young writers discovered that they held a particular power in their own hands—the ability to define themselves with a pencil, a notebook, and a circle of listeners.

They all had their own big stack of cake.
Two slices and a cup of Coke was all
I had to take and in my own sense
Of quiet, pain thunders upon the content
Of conscience releasing moments of my sub-
Conscious and the claims that declare
Me obnoxious.

You could only see me in the settings
Of the sun, webbed in dark places
That hide me. I long not to be noticed.
But know that I still exist, that I
Am human in my own being.

—Annasuena

PART ONE

VOICES OF THE GIRLS

1

Our Pride

My Hometown Gugulethu

Gun shots, BANG! the door,
Running, running from who?
The policemen and the dogs.
That was the life in Gugulethu
During the apartheid era.

Seven people lost their lives,
Yes, the Gugulethu Seven.
People shouting, mothers crying.
Everyone outside like ants in summer.
Yep, that's Gugulethu.

Today, in the liberated year 2010,
All of that is now gone but
Remains in our hearts.
Today's Gugulethu,
Still the same as it was back then.
A little changes here and there.

Today I would look at my township,
The chilly, windy and unclear skies of Gugulethu.
Of course, it's the Cape Town weather.
During windy silent days,
I would look at
Children coming home from school,
Or young men chasing their hats across the street.

During hot summer days I would
See girls in miniskirts,
Loud music from the car.
I would ask myself,
Is this the lost generation?
Maybe.

Gugulethu my township
And the people of my township.
I would miss the smile and happiness
Of my people.
People who are in joy and feel liberated.
Gugulethu my hometown.
I'm proud to come from Gugulethu.

—Thulisa

Tourist literature hails Cape Town as the Mother City, though initially it was not meant to be a city at all. When Jan van Riebeeck docked in Table Bay in 1652 with three ships full of sailors, he arrived with clear instructions from the Netherlands: Build a fort that can serve as a refreshment station. Ships of the Dutch East India Company spent months traveling this trading route between Europe and East Asia, rounding the

Cape of Good Hope, thirty miles down the peninsula from Table Bay. Sailors afflicted with scurvy were of no use, so there needed to be a site for a layover on the route, to take on vegetables, fruits, meats, and fresh water.

Some sailors were released from their employment contracts and allowed to establish farms in this new land to supply the needed provisions. A settlement grew up. The settlers imported any goods they needed, along with a labor source—slaves brought in from the lands now known as Indonesia, Malaysia, Madagascar, Angola, Mozambique. The settlement became first a town and then the Cape Colony, with van Riebeeck serving as its first commander. Later on, the British arrived and wrested control of the colony from the Dutch. But the Dutch stayed on, eventually becoming known as Afrikaners. Some remained in the Cape Colony and some began a journey eastward as *Voortrekkers* (pioneers), intent upon laying claim to more land and their God-given right to it, their expression of Manifest Destiny in southern Africa.

To think of Cape Town as the Mother City, though, is to elevate these arriving offspring, to presume that the mothering done there was for the benefit of the European colonists. Such a nickname disregards the notion that this piece of land had long been nurturing those already living upon it.

The Khoikhoi, the original pastoral inhabitants of this southwestern portion of the African continent, had another name for Table Bay that predated the sailors' arrivals. They called it *Camissa* (Place of Sweet Waters). They were the first people displaced by the new arrivals, as the Dutch farmers took over the most fertile areas of land. Initially the Khoikhoi had a decent relationship with the settlers, exchanging cattle and sheep for some of their imports. But as the colonists gained power, they increasingly brutalized the indigenous people. When suspected of theft, Khoikhoi were sent to an island seven miles out in Table Bay—and Robben Island first began to play its role as a prison.

The Khoikhoi also had a name for what remains the dominant emblem of Cape Town. What the settlers called Table Mountain, the evocative name that has stuck, they called *Hoerikwaggo* (Mountain of the Sea). At 3,558 feet, it stands as both beacon and sentry, part of the sandstone mountain range that forms the spine running down the Cape Peninsula. Devil's Peak flanks Table Mountain to the east; to the west stands Lion's Head. When the wind blows southeasterly up the mountain, the flat plateau forms its own cloud cover, a billowing white overlay referred to as the tablecloth. Sometimes a waterfall of clouds cascades down the mountain's slope.

On the other side of the mountain, the land soon turns harsh and inhospitable, a low-lying area that is prone to flooding when the winter rains arrive. Fierce winds, which blow all over Cape Town in winter and summertime both, constantly shift a layer of sand scattered above a deeper layer of shale, forming unstable sand dunes and poor soil unfit to grow much. This area, the Cape Flats, remained largely uninhabited into the 1950s, three hundred years after van Riebeeck's arrival.

In 1948, the National Party, dominated by Afrikaners, came into power in the general election. Blacks were not permitted to vote. The new government immediately began to institute apartheid, meant to formalize separation of the races and to consolidate political, economic, and social control by the country's white minority. One of the first pieces of legislation passed was the Group Areas Act of 1950, dictating what racial groups could live where in urban areas, while maintaining the nicest and most developed parts of the cities for whites only.

Before apartheid, Cape Town was South Africa's most cosmopolitan urban area, with mixed-race communities such as District Six, located near the City Bowl. Under the Group Areas Act, such communities were forbidden. Families were forcibly removed to areas where they were permitted to live only with others of their same racial designation. The scrubby landscape of the Cape Flats became the obvious place to settle nonwhites. Africans were sent to one of the existing blacks-only areas, Langa or Nyanga; "coloured" families were assigned to their own segregated areas. South African historian Dr. Sean Field likened the maneuver to an amputation. "Imagine the community and surrounding landscape you grew up in, that surrounded you throughout your formative childhood years. What if you and your family were forcibly removed because you did not comply with an externally imposed racial identity category, which decreed that you could no longer live in the spaces and interact with the people you regarded as your community? . . . How would your life change after the moment of amputation?"

When the existing townships grew too crowded, new townships were built, including, in 1960, a place called Gugulethu. The name, in Xhosa, means "Our Pride." The government promised to provide houses for the families installed in the new townships, but in oral-history interviews, early residents of Gugulethu told Dr. Field what sort of housing they found when they arrived: "[A] concrete shell. No ceiling. No internal doors. No proper floor. No electricity. No hot water. No internal toilets. . . . Justifiably, they felt tricked." The Cape Flats came to be known as apartheid's dumping ground.

———

From the base of Table Mountain, Klipfontein Road runs out through the Cape Flats, splitting Gugulethu at NY 1, the township's main road. Just before that intersection stands a small strip of shops housed in old shipping containers: Jet Car Wash, a hair salon, Mama Lady's Little Restaurant Take Away, a "spaza" convenience shop to buy cooldrinks (a South African word for soft drinks) and mobile-phone airtime. The smell of smoke and grilled meat hangs in the air as vendors *braai* (barbecue) over homemade steel-drum grills, selling chicken and *boerewors* (sausages). An AIDS ribbon outlined in unlit Christmas lights dangles above the intersection.

There's little grass in Gugulethu—or Gugs, its nickname— and few trees. Yards are dirt and sand that coat everything in a fine grit when the wind blows. But there are unexpected bursts of color everywhere—faded and weatherworn like spring's last blossoms—in the paint on homes and the shipping-container shops. About half the households in the township live in formal dwellings, those original concrete homes, now well settled and sometimes expanded. Some residents in Gugulethu have added second floors and satellite dishes to their roofs, giving homes something of a middle-class feel.

Then there are the "informal settlements." The phrase makes the shacks sound temporary, but they are not. They are home to thousands of people. Wooden planks unevenly nailed together serve as the shack's walls. Faded and flaking paint from whatever the planks used to form hint at reconstruction and resourcefulness. Plastic tarps stretched to their limits offer little insulation or protection from the winter rains. Several shacks dangerously share electrical wires spliced from the source. There are communal toilets and one water pump outside for hundreds of homes. A wide swath of shacks, in a subdivision known as KTC, extends along Klipfontein, across the road from the sprawling Gugulethu Cemetery. Funerals are no longer held here. The graves are full.

Before the shacks and the cemetery, a left turn from Klipfontein onto NY 1 leads past two memorials that commemorate painful events in Gugulethu's history. Farthest away stand seven large granite pillars. Each contains the life-size cutout of a man with arms raised, legs in motion, giving an impression of running or dancing or taking to the streets in protest. This is the memorial to the Gugulethu Seven. In 1986, seven young men, anti-apartheid activists between the ages of sixteen and twenty-three, were ambushed, shot, and killed in the streets by the South African security forces. They were suspected of being members of *Umkhonto we Sizwe* (Spear of the Nation), the military wing of the African National Congress, an organization outlawed under apartheid. Police claimed the seven were plotting an attack on a police van.

Cynthia Ngweu, the mother of one of the Gugulethu Seven, testified before the Truth and Reconciliation Commission (TRC) in 1996 about seeing her son on television: "I said to my kids, 'Let's watch all this on TV, because we don't really know what happened, maybe they will have it in the story on TV.' While we were still watching the seven o'clock or six o'clock news, I saw my child. I actually saw them dragging him, there was a rope around his waist, they were dragging him with the van. I said, 'Switch off the TV, I've seen what I wanted to see. Just switch it off.'" The Gugulethu Seven memorial was erected in 2005.

Not far away, positioned on a sidewalk in front of a petrol station, a smaller granite cross bears the distinct logo of the Fulbright Program. In 1993, a twenty-six-year-old American Fulbrighter, Amy Biehl, was killed at this spot. An anti-apartheid activist while a student at Stanford University, she had been working to register voters for the first democratic elections the following year. Three days before she was to return to the United States, she drove three friends home to Gugulethu. A mob coming from a political rally saw the driver's white skin, assumed she was South African, and attacked, shouting the slogan, "One settler, one bullet!" They dragged Amy from her car and stoned and stabbed her to death as her friends pleaded for her life, crying that she was a comrade to black South Africans. In the late 1990s, Amy's parents also attended TRC proceedings, where they publicly forgave the four men imprisoned for her killing. They were granted amnesty and released from prison. One of them went on to work for the Amy Biehl Foundation that her parents established in Cape Town.

Back on the other side of Gugs that lies across Klipfontein Road and off NY 1, about a mile away from the Gugulethu Seven memorial, J. L. Zwane Presbyterian Church and Community Center sits upon a slight rise, at the corner of NY 7 and NY 11. All roads in Gugulethu are named this way, NY with a number following. NY stands for Native Yards, what apartheid's architects intended the townships to be: places to contain "the natives."

The church's large brick-and-concrete building, enclosed within a fence, appears spotless even when the sand blows. Outside J. L. Zwane's front doors, visitors are greeted by a large framed poster of the Preamble to the Constitution of the Republic of South Africa, adopted in 1996:

We, the people of South Africa,

Recognize the injustices of our past;

Honor those who suffered for justice and freedom in our land;

Respect those who have worked to build and develop our country; and

Believe that South Africa belongs to all who live in it, united in our diversity.

We therefore, through our freely elected representatives, adopt this Constitution as the supreme law of the Republic so as to—

- Heal the divisions of the past and establish a society based on democratic values, social justice and fundamental human rights;
- Lay the foundations for a democratic and open society in which government is based on the will of the people and every citizen is equally protected by law;
- Improve the quality of life of all citizens and free the potential of each person; and
- Build a united and democratic South Africa able to take its rightful place as a sovereign state in the family of nations.

May God protect our people.
Nkosi Sikelel' iAfrika. Morena boloka setjhaba sa heso.
God seën Suid-Afrika. God bless South Africa.
Mudzimu fhatutshedza Afurika. Hosi katekisa Afrika.

That ending prayer blesses South Africa in Xhosa, Sesotho, Afrikaans, English, Tswana, and Tsonga—six of the country's eleven official languages. (People also speak Zulu, Ndebele, Venda, Northern Sotho, and Swati.)

South Africans are rightfully proud of their hard-earned constitution. Its Bill of Rights lays out the right to housing, food, water, health care, social assistance, education. There is a whole section devoted to the rights of children. Children are guaranteed the right to a name and nationality; to family or parental care; to basic nutrition, shelter, health care, and social services; and to be protected from mistreatment and abuse. They should not be required or permitted to perform work inappropriate for their age. They should not be detained except as a last resort. They should not be used in the military or armed conflict. Above all, "A child's best interests are of paramount importance in every matter concerning the child." As with any official document that aspires to an ideal, however, guarantees often fall short of realities.

Inside J. L. Zwane, the church's sanctuary resembles a modern art gallery or performance space rather than a place of worship, even less for a Christian denomination with austere Scottish roots. Colors saturate the walls in rich shades of orange, purple, yellow, blue. White wooden beams crisscross and brace the ceiling. Large abstract paintings decorate the perimeter, created by a German artist who donated his time and work. Chairs for the congregation are wood and metal, linked together in fours and eights, able to be cleared away so the sanctuary can perform multiple functions. On the raised stage of an altar, the plain wooden podium is draped with a crisp white banner embroidered with the words "J. L. Zwane Cares," arcing like a raised eyebrow over a crimson AIDS ribbon.

Words are everywhere at J. L. Zwane. Text written on the walls accompanies the artwork. Sometimes the words *are* the art. They come from Scripture and from sayings.

Lord, I believe; help my unbelief.

When a door closes, a window opens.

We must learn to invite, embrace, include, and engage the unwanted.

Verses from Matthew 25, lettered in careful calligraphy in English, Xhosa, and Afrikaans, fill a space from ceiling to floor: *For I was hungry and you fed me, I was thirsty and you gave me a drink. . . .* Behind the altar, above an expansive painting in swirls of ocher, orange, and black, words appear in English and Xhosa: *The light shines in the darkness but the darkness has not understood it.* A passage from the first chapter of the Gospel of John, when, for Christians, Word became Flesh. This building itself speaks to all who enter, even when silence greets visitors, when the sanctuary is empty of minister and believers.

J. L. Zwane Presbyterian started out as a one-room church, small but active in the anti-apartheid movement. The church's current pastor, Reverend Spiwo Xapile, arrived in 1989, a serious man with a compact build, intense gaze, and reluctant smile. After South Africa won its freedom, the pastor wanted the church to turn its focus toward the needs of the community. The end of apartheid did not mean the end of suffering for South Africa's black citizens. Substandard housing and education persisted, along with limited employment opportunities. Blacks had been denied work or relegated to inferior positions for more than three hundred years. Freedom did not—could not—quickly erode inequality this entrenched.

Reverend Xapile traveled widely to build partnerships with

churches in the United States and Europe to raise money for
J. L. Zwane's efforts. The Rainbow After-School Program
started first, held in an old shipping container behind the church.
It offered tutoring and a meal to children who might otherwise
go to bed hungry. The little church grew in the size of the congregation and its facilities, until this pristine and expansive new
sanctuary and community-center building opened in 2003, in a
service attended by then–Deputy President Jacob Zuma.

Just as the church was expanding its outreach ministries, the
AIDS crisis overtook South Africa. Faith communities worldwide were woefully late to minister to people with HIV and
AIDS, reluctant to speak of sex, gay or straight, of condoms
and needles and drug use. That unwillingness helped to create
the isolation and stigma faced by people living with HIV/AIDS,
turning them into modern-day lepers.

J. L. Zwane became one of the first faith communities in
Cape Town to address the disease openly. A support group for
people living with HIV and AIDS met each afternoon at the
center, where people received a hot meal and, once a month, a
parcel of food. St. Luke's Hospice worked with the church to
provide end-of-life care. J. L. Zwane formed a musical group,
Siyaya, to perform AIDS-education songs throughout the community, singing about condoms and knowing one's HIV status.

More boldly, Reverend Xapile brought the topic right into
the worship gathering itself. He encouraged people who were
HIV positive to tell their life stories during the Sunday service,
an effort meant to educate churchgoers but also to counter
stigma and prejudice. That moment of witness has continued
to be part of each Sunday worship service, right after the choir
and congregation sing together one of the few hymns sung in
English. The hymn's title is the same as the words painted

above the sanctuary doors where the congregation exits after the service has ended, words they carry with them into their weekly lives.

Never Give Up.

I came to J. L. Zwane and Gugulethu for the first time in 2007, directed there by a former work colleague who had lived in Cape Town in the mid-1990s when his wife was a pastor at the church. For fifteen years, I had built a career in nonprofit communications in Washington, DC, working with organizations fighting poverty on both a domestic and a global scale. Now I wanted a new challenge, a chance to live abroad, specifically in Cape Town, and time to devote to writing in my own voice, detached from any organization's aims or constraints. I applied for a Fulbright and was turned down. Then I tried again, my second application based on an idea I blurted out while speaking to Reverend Xapile on my visit to Gugulethu.

"Maybe I could hold a creative writing club for girls while I'm here."

"I would welcome that work," said the pastor. "We do not have any programs for the girl-child. But we need them."

Many people were turning their attention to the girl-child, as girls are called across Africa. Poverty scholars and policy experts call it "the Girl Effect" and have begun to trumpet this approach as the key to development and poverty eradication. Today's youth generation is the largest in history—1.2 billion adolescents aged ten to nineteen—and half of them are girls. The Girl Effect promotes the belief that, when girls are educated, healthy, and financially literate, they will play a key role in ending generations of poverty. Girls who stay in school and stay healthy gain skills that enable them to support themselves and their families. When women in developing countries earn an income, 90 percent of those wages are reinvested in the family, compared with 30 to 40 percent of wages earned by men. Educated women also marry later and have fewer children. On YouTube and at girleffect.org, a punchy animated video about the power of girls has received more than two million views.

In 2005, the United Nations Foundation and the Nike Foundation formed the Coalition for Adolescent Girls, which now includes more than thirty leading international organizations. Promoting gender equality and empowering women was one of the Millennium Development Goals, a set of eight goals generated by the United Nations in 2000 that formed a blueprint agreed to by all the world's countries and leading development institutions. In the United States, women and girls have moved to the forefront of international development policy at the State Department and at the U.S. Agency for International Development. The Obama administration also established the White House Council on Women and Girls to coordinate federal policy on issues both domestic and international that particularly affect the lives of women and girls.

Yet, despite these initiatives, an adolescent "girl gap" has persisted. International development programs frequently target young children or women, overlooking the critical years from twelve to twenty. The Coalition for Adolescent Girls has found that participants and beneficiaries of youth programs are predominantly males, sometimes by as much as 80 to 90 percent. "Adolescence is a critical period, when a girl's future potential and opportunities can flourish through education, economic opportunities, and psychosocial support," the coalition says. "Or, that potential can be stunted and stifled by the irreversible effects of child marriage, early pregnancy, HIV, and other preventable hardships. Fulfilling the rights of adolescent girls—to health, education, and protection from violence and abuse—ensures they have the chance to achieve their physical, emotional, and social potential, and can go on to become empowered women who can support their families, communities, and countries."

This future-focused rationale is compelling. For sub-Saharan Africans, however, graver factors and present-day realities must also be considered. In a special issue of *Buwa! A Journal of African Women's Experiences* that focused on what it means to be a young woman in southern Africa, Alice Kanengoni writes, "The young women's position is that they do matter and need to be included in planning and actions today, as these affect them today as well as tomorrow. Most are very much against the notion that young women are the leaders of tomorrow, and would rather be recognized as leaders of today! In my opinion, this is a reasonable demand in a region where (if nothing is done as a matter of urgency) the majority of these young women may never see their 'tomorrow' since life expectancy has fallen significantly in most [sub-Saharan African] countries in the past two decades." This is true of South Africa as well as the poorer nations; life expectancy has fallen to fifty-two years, primarily due to AIDS. Kanengoni also points to the need to develop and expand spaces where girls can connect with one another, to "meet and share strategies," places that can be kept "safe for young women to freely explore possibilities, create dreams together, and encourage one another to fly high."

That's what I imagined I might do with girls in Gugulethu.

I would not be undertaking a development project. My efforts would be on a small scale, directed toward any girls at J. L. Zwane Presbyterian Church interested in a creative writing club. As I wrote about their lives, I wanted to help them write their stories themselves, discover what they had to say, listen for their own voices.

2

OVCs

Who Am I?

I am a writer by birth
A vocalist by choice
An expressionist by nature
And an instrument by voice.

I pledge to speak my mind
And utter the words that define
My solitude, senses, and space.

I pledge to provoke all existing
Thought and explore every and
Any feeling and emotion of all
Human race.

—Annasuena

The first time I met Annasuena, she declared herself a poet. She came into J. L. Zwane Community Center on a Tuesday afternoon during my second week in Cape Town. I knew nothing about her, though I had heard about her friend, Olwethu, who accompanied her this day. The girls had come

for the orphans' support group that met every Tuesday afternoon. As I sat in a small, spare office at J. L. Zwane, waiting to
attend the orphans' group myself, Mel popped her head into
the doorway and asked whether I would like to meet the girls.

Reverend Mel—most people just called her Mel—grew up
in Florida and graduated from Duke University and its Divinity
School. I had met her six months earlier in Washington, where
she spent a month working at Walter Reed Army Medical Center, a prelude to her upcoming career as an Army chaplain. Mel
was twenty-six years old, a Presbyterian minister who expected
to be deployed to Afghanistan when she returned to the United
States. First, however, she was finishing up an eighteen-month
volunteer position as an assistant pastor at J. L. Zwane, a stint
that grew out of her previous travel to South Africa while in
college. When she visited church members at their homes in
Gugulethu, Mel usually wore her black-and-white clerical collar, a simple white blouse, and a black skirt. The rest of the
time, she wore a lot of pink. Her voice rang with the precise and
chirpy tones of a Disney heroine. She often sang out loud, pop
songs and hymns and Broadway numbers. Yet I had no trouble
picturing her petite frame in camouflage fatigues and scuffed
Army boots. Mel seemed dauntless and indefatigable. She knew
her way around Gugulethu's unmarked streets better than I
expected I ever would. She had promised to help me get accli-
mated to Cape Town and to the J. L. Zwane community.

The girls awaited us in the foyer. Mel introduced them to me
and we took seats in the church's small visitors' lounge on low
sofas with orange cushions and metal frames, a modernist style
that coordinated with the sanctuary's artwork. Olwethu stood
a head taller than her friend. Both girls wore their hair cropped
short, and Olwethu's appeared to be dyed with an auburn rinse.

Annasuena was dressed in skinny jeans and a gauzy top embroidered with flowers in a shimmery gold thread. Olwethu, who had come from school, was still wearing her uniform of gray trousers, white cotton blouse, and navy vest.

South Africa's school year begins in January and follows the calendar year. Seventeen children from J. L. Zwane had just begun their first year living and studying at Bridges Academy, a boarding school for orphans out near Stellenbosch in the Cape Winelands area, about an hour from Gugulethu. Olwethu's sister, Sive, was one of those students; she was fifteen and starting Grade 9 at the school. Mel had known these girls for more than a year, since her early days at J. L. Zwane. A few days earlier, when I had accompanied Mel out to the school to see how the children were adjusting, I had had the chance to meet Sive. Now Olwethu had come early before orphans' group to hear how her sister was adjusting. They lived with their aunt and cousins in Gugulethu.

The sisters had been orphaned when they lost their mother seven years earlier. Olwethu was twelve then, Sive nearly nine. Both were shattered by her death. One of the churchwomen told Mel about the scene at the cemetery. The little girls tried to climb down into the open grave to lie on top of their mother's casket. One of them—the churchwoman could not remember which—cried out, "Mommy, don't leave us! Who's going to care for us now?" Family members had to pull them back from the grave.

Mel talked about our trip out to Bridges, how Sive was settling in, how happy she seemed even as she missed home and Gugulethu. Slumped back against the sofa, Olwethu sat with her arms loosely folded. She listened without asking any questions, only replying with "Oh" and "*Ja*" a few times in a low voice without any inflection, raised eyebrows the only thing animating her features. She was nineteen, enrolled in Grade 11 at a school in Cape Town's city center. She had not wanted to apply to the boarding school. Her skin appeared dull, and dark circles beneath her eyes made her look as though she had not had a good night's sleep in a long time. Just when she seemed about to smile, she changed course and quickly pulled her upper lip down over the bottom one, or held one hand across her mouth. Mel told her that Sive mentioned specifically how much she missed her sister. Olwethu pressed her lips together and nodded, then reached up to rub her eyes, which had suddenly begun to water. When Mel stroked her shoulder, Olwethu seemed to flinch almost imperceptibly. We all sat there quietly for a few moments.

"Annasuena, what's with the jeans? You should be in a uniform, too," Mel said, to break a silence that had grown uncomfortable. "What's happening with school?"

Annasuena leaned back against the sofa and rolled her eyes. "*Sjoe*! I'm still waiting for my cousin-brother. He has to go sign the forms. But whenever I make a plan to go with him, he doesn't turn up."

"Is that who you live with?" I asked, assuming a cousin-brother to be a cousin who had taken on a brotherly role in her life.

"With him and my aunt, *ja*. They're my guardians. Though I've been staying at my boyfriend's quite a bit as well." She glanced at Mel rather sheepishly at this admission. "My cousin-brother and my aunt get the grant for me so one of them has to sign. And there's no way my aunt's taking time to come to my school."

"What grade are you in?"

"I'm not sure where they'll put me, I've been in and out of school so much. I think I'm ready for Grade 9. I'm *not* going back to Grade 8 here in Gugs, because I'd be in the same grade as my little cousin. Plus, I'd rather go to school in Cape Town, where Olwethu goes. But I'd need transport money for taxis."

Annasuena tilted her head and looked at me with a curious smile. She had a heart-shaped face, a wide forehead, and tiny ears that pressed back against her head. "Are you a pastor like Mel?"

"Oh, no, I'm not. I'm a writer."

"A writer? Really?"

I told them that I had come to Gugulethu to lead a creative writing club for girls their age. I said that I hoped they would both come to it when we started up in a few weeks.

"I'll be there," Annasuena said without hesitation. "I love to write. I'm a poet, actually." She pulled her shoulders back and sat up straighter on the sofa as she said this, as comfortable with the title as if she had just introduced herself by her given name.

"Excellent. I hope you'll come too, Olwethu." I dipped my head down to try to catch her eye.

"Yes, I'll come, too." She dried her damp cheeks with the back of one hand and nodded at me, smiling tightly once more.

"Annasuena, let me know if your cousin doesn't take you this week," Mel said. "Maybe I can go along to the school and see if there's a way to get you enrolled. You need to be back in school!"

"I know I do! I'm so *bored* every day by myself."

Annasuena hummed with a restless energy. Unlike Olwethu, who did not appear very interested in engaging in conversation, Annasuena looked as though she was holding herself back from speaking too much.

"Are you coming for orphans' group today?" Mel asked.

"I'd like to, yes," said Annasuena. "This will be my first time there."

"Good. Let's go downstairs now and I'll introduce you to Milly."

When a crisis acquires its own abbreviation, two or three letters to be explained in a glossary or acronym list, a distancing process inevitably occurs. Numbers gain traction and individuals fade away. In international development parlance, aid workers talk about OVCs, shorthand for orphans and vulnerable children. In South Africa in 2010, there were 3.7 million of them. About half that number had lost one or both parents to AIDS. One out of every five children in South Africa is an orphan. By 2015, that number was expected to climb to 5.7 million—one-third of all the children in the country.

The word *orphan* retains a faint Victorian air, visions of a towheaded and tousled Oliver Twist holding up his empty gruel bowl to beg, "Please, sir, I want some more." In this century, a web search for images of orphans turns up strange subcategories. Clumped together are American orphans, white orphans, movie posters for *Orphan* ("There's something wrong with Esther"), sad orphans, happy orphans, crying orphans, and the casts of various productions of *Annie*. But most of the photographs show African orphans. In their photos, these children are happy, sad, crying, smiling, waving for the camera and tumbling over one another to crowd into the shot, playing soccer with Britain's Prince Harry in Lesotho, looking up, looking away, looking straight at you with impossibly large eyes and little expression. They wear ripped and filthy secondhand clothing and no shoes, especially if they live in a rural area. If they're staying in a children's home—an orphanage—they might be pictured tidied up, neatly dressed, and looking playful enough to attract the eye of potential "voluntourists." These short-term volunteers from abroad spend a week or two, maybe a month, helping to care for the children before or after their sightseeing visits, between the safari and a drive along the Garden Route. It is a popular enough phenomenon that social science researchers have coined a term for it: *AIDS orphan tourism*.

The Born Frees are the first generation to be orphaned in large numbers by AIDS, as the disease decimated their parents' generation and approached pandemic proportions beginning around 1995. Yet South Africa's orphans and vulnerable children do not neatly mirror the online image of the African AIDS orphan. Familial roles—who's related to whom in a home and whose job it is to care for the children living there—create complicated relational webs and terms like cousin-brother. It was this way, though, even before the onset of HIV/AIDS.

"Family life in South Africa has never been simple to describe or understand," observed the South African Institute of Race Relations in a 2011 report, *First Steps to Healing the South African Family*. "The concept of the nuclear family has never accurately captured the norm of all South African families."

During apartheid—even before that, going back to the late-nineteenth-century discovery of precious minerals to be mined—black South Africans were subject to a system of imposed migrant labor. Men were sent to work in the mines, the cities, or wherever their labor was needed. They lived in overcrowded hostels with other men, forbidden to bring their wives and families to live with them. Families had to remain in the rural homelands, where they were assigned to live according to ethnic group, such as the Transkei and the Ciskei, the areas designated for the Xhosa people. The South African government claimed these homelands were independent states and self-ruled; in reality, they were meant to keep the population contained to try to minimize unrest. Sometimes wives did join their husbands in urban townships, living illegally with them in the hostels and leaving their children to be cared for by grandparents and extended family in the homelands. Sometimes men created second families with women they met in the areas where they were sent to work. Either way, the system brought about fractured families for multiple generations.

Enforced migrant labor officially ended after 1994, yet this system created a precedent for absentee fathers and single-parent households that has continued, and, in fact, has increased post-apartheid. Single-parent households now are the norm in South Africa. Only 35 percent of children in 2008 lived with both biological parents. Some 40 percent lived with their mother only, 2.8 percent with their father only. That left 22.6 percent who lived with neither of their biological parents, including 8 percent of children living in a "skip generation"—households with grandparents, great-aunts or great-uncles—and most of the rest with younger relatives. Caregivers—guardians raising a child who is not their own by birth—receive a foster child grant from the South African Social Security Agency.

There is a belief that AIDS has created an explosion of child-headed households, where all members are younger than eighteen. In South Africa, this is not really true, although there are 122,000 children living this way, certainly a not-insubstantial number. Parenting younger siblings—feeding them breakfast and preparing them for school, seeing to household chores, providing food, basic necessities, and affection—can interfere with a young person's efforts to complete her or his own education. Yet the majority of these children are not orphans: 92 percent had one or both parents alive; 81 percent had a living mother. The most

likely explanation for these child-headed households was that parents were leaving their children to travel to other provinces in search of work. Drug addiction and alcoholism were also cited as factors in the 2011 report from the South African Institute of Race Relations. Even some children in the children's homes were sent there not because they were orphaned, but because they lived in desperately poor families who could no longer provide for them. There has been an increase in the number of residential group-care children's homes, especially unregistered and unregulated ones, not only in South Africa but also across sub-Saharan Africa. But that's spurred, too, by the money that voluntourists leave behind for the opportunity to help out in an orphanage—an experience that undoubtedly enriches the volunteers but can also leave behind children who face adverse emotional and psychological effects from one abandonment after another.

Some call the family situation in South Africa "a crisis of men." Many agree that it brings up difficult issues of parental responsibility, attitudes toward monogamy, and lack of commitment to relationships. It is also the sort of condition that becomes cyclical and entrenched. Children in dysfunctional families are more likely to create dysfunctional families themselves. The Born Frees will need to confront this crisis as they begin to have children of their own.

At J. L. Zwane, Annasuena, Olwethu, Mel, and I descended into a chaotic scene. In a classroom on the ground floor, thirty or forty children gathered in a circle of seats, from small ones in the early years of primary school to tall boys wearing high school uniform track suits. They shouted in Xhosa across the room to their friends. One thin young boy ran laps around the

outside of the circled chairs until an arm reached out and cor-
ralled him.

"Lifa, enough running! Sit down in your chair. Everyone
sit! It's time to get started so we can get your school supplies
handed out to you."

Milly, the volunteer organizer of J. L. Zwane's orphans'
group, was a tall and tanned woman in her sixties, though
she looked younger. She wore a white tank top, long white
cotton skirt, funky eyeglasses, and wedge sandals. Highlights
streaked through her dark blonde hair. She and her husband,
Ian, owned an electrical company now, but she had been a
schoolteacher many years earlier and still possessed a voice
that could make itself heard instantly above a din. They lived
in Durbanville, in Cape Town's northern suburbs, about a half-
hour's drive from Gugs.

"Right," Milly began, "we'll see who's here and then we'll pray."
She began reading out children's names from a roll book.
Voices both soft and strong answered, until there was silence
after one name. Milly lifted her glasses into her hair and looked
around the circle, her expression approaching a glare. "It's only
the second week and already some aren't showing up. I have
children on a waiting list, and I only have room for fifty spots
in this group. No more. Tell the ones who don't show up that
they're taking a place away from another child in need."

There was no clever name for this weekly gathering; everyone simply called it orphans' group. Every week the children
returned to their homes with bags of food that Milly, Sheila-
Ann, and Jo, the volunteer helpers from her Presbyterian
church in Durbanville, collected as donations from Woolworths and Pick n Pay grocery-store chains. Whatever fruit and
vegetables were available went into the parcels, along with one

loaf of bread, mealie-meal (ground corn used to make a thick porridge called *pap*), maybe canned fish or beans, and, some weeks, tea or coffee.

After she finished calling roll, Milly shushed the children again and read from the Bible, Psalm 46:

> God is our refuge and strength,
> an ever-present help in trouble.
> Therefore we will not fear, though the earth give way
> and the mountains fall into the heart of the sea,
> though its waters roar and foam
> and the mountains quake with their surging.

"We've all seen on TV about that terrible earthquake in Haiti. We need to pray for those people suffering there." Then Milly prayed aloud for the children and adults in Haiti, as the children of Gugulethu bowed their heads and squirmed in their seats, feet kicking rhythmically against chair legs. She also prayed about the crime and corruption, the alcohol abuse and the poverty in their own country. She prayed to keep each child in the room safe throughout the school year.

After prayers came school supplies. Donated notebooks, pencils and pens, calculators and flip files with plastic sleeves to hold handouts—all were given out according to the needs of each grade and learner. Jo and Sheila-Ann measured children's feet in front of a row of black oxford shoes lined up on the floor against the wall. Along with the Durbanville volunteers, three women from the J. L. Zwane congregation, Rose, Nancy, and Johanna, helped with orphans' group. I had met Johanna on my previous trip to Gugulethu. She was in her early fifties and volunteered weekdays at the center as a sort of community outreach worker, visiting homes and assessing people's needs. When I saw her again at church on a Sunday morning, she remembered me as the writer. She had told me on my first trip that she enjoyed writing and wanted to write her own life story. I wished I would have the time to hold a writing club for women at the church, too, but the girls were my focus first.

Noise in the room grew loud again as the kids gathered their school supplies and food parcels into cloth recycled bags smudged with dirt and crumpled from frequent use. I watched Annasuena and Olwethu sitting and whispering together as they waited their turn. When Olwethu laughed one time, she neglected to cover her mouth. I realized then that she was missing most of her front teeth. There was a wide emptiness where the upper row should be. She glanced up and saw me, and I smiled at her, an automatic response to catching the notice of this new acquaintance. Immediately she snapped her mouth closed and looked down at her hands in her lap. Her lips pressed tightly together, curled into her mouth as if she were trying to disappear inside herself.

Milly walked over to the girls and stood with hands resting on her hips. She spoke to Olwethu. "Okay, my girl, are you back at school now?"

"Yes." Olwethu remained seated and shifted uncomfortably in her chair.

"Are you going every day?"

"Yes, I am."

"How's your health?"

"It's fine. It's good."

"Are you taking your tablets?"

"Yes."

"Every day?"

"Every day."

"Good." Milly nodded briskly.

Mel introduced Annasuena. Milly towered above the girl even after Annasuena respectfully stood up from her chair to meet her elder.

Milly then plunged in without preamble. "Are you willing to commit to this group?"

"I will, yes." Annasuena nodded and glanced down to the floor, then back up to Milly again. She rocked nervously from one foot to the other.

"Will you come every week?"

"Yes."

"Will you focus on your studies and finish your education?"

"Yes."

"Okay. Then give Jo your details and she'll add you to the book."

When Milly walked away, Annasuena looked after her with wide eyes and then began to laugh—from apprehension, it seemed, rather than disrespect.

Mel and I walked out of J. L. Zwane with the two girls. Annasuena turned to me and said, "If you'd like, I can bring you my diary. I've got some poems in there you can read. If you'd like." She shrugged one shoulder in a gesture that looked both casual and hopeful. I told her I would love to read them.

After the girls left, I asked Mel about Olwethu's health. The previous year, she had spent large portions of time in and out of hospital, battling tuberculosis. The frequent hospitalizations caused her to miss too much school, so now, at nineteen, she was repeating Grade 11. Olwethu was also HIV positive, as was Annasuena.

3

Disclosure

To me, writing is . . .

To me, writing is me.

*It is me listening
to what I have to say,
to what I want to say,
to what my heart says.*

*To me, writing is not
my strong point, but
it is my strength.*

*My strength to write down
my thoughts and feelings.
This is done by my hands,
by my writing.*

*That is why writing,
for me,
is the best gift God has
ever given to me.*

—Gugu

To recruit girls for the creative writing club, I asked Reverend Xapile whether I could make an announcement to the congregation during a church service. I was not certain how much interest such a club would generate among teenage girls in Gugulethu. Many township children and youth are hungry for organized activities and respond enthusiastically, especially to performing arts programs. The Amy Biehl Foundation sponsors extracurricular programs in township schools across Cape Town. Their creative arts program teaches drama, visual and fine arts, and dance, including ballet, modern, and *kwaito*, a popular South African music similar to hip-hop. In their music program, instructors train students in music theory and choral music, on recorder, violin, brass and stringed instruments, and marimbas. Broadway in South Africa had also paid several visits to J. L. Zwane. This New York–based cross-cultural organization brings performers from the States to hold arts workshops and empowerment programs for disadvantaged youth. Improvised skits are also popular. They are frequently performed at youth gatherings, for both fun and education, by young actors who seem entirely comfortable working without a script. But I hadn't heard of any creative writing projects that had reached township youth.

Books and the written word seemed to be a luxury. Across South Africa, 80 percent of all state-run schools have no library. This is one of the many lingering disparities in South Africa's educational system. In 1982, with apartheid-era educational spending, the South African government spent R1,211 per white child, R771 per Indian child, R498 per "coloured" child, and R146 per black child. (South Africa's currency is the rand; in 2014, the exchange rate was eleven rand to the dollar.) These expenditures reflected the philosophy that it was pointless to educate blacks, as proclaimed by Dr. Hendrik

Verwoerd, the prime architect of apartheid, who conceived of and implemented the country's segregationist policies first as minister for native affairs and, later on, as the country's prime minister. Verwoerd announced, "There is no place for [the Bantu, or black] in the European community above the level of certain forms of labor. . . . What is the use of teaching the Bantu child mathematics when it cannot use it in practice? That is quite absurd. Education must train people in accordance with their opportunities in life, according to the sphere in which they live."

It was clear in which sphere Verwoerd intended for blacks to remain. They did not appear even to be children to him. Why should a black child learn mathematics, he asked, when *it* would have no opportunity to use that knowledge? This dehumanization of Africans, the belief that they were savages to be subdued by others—a task taken on, with heavy paternalistic sighs, as the white man's burden—had driven colonialism and brutality across the continent.

Since 1994, the South African government has been playing catch-up in the educational system, with disappointing results. Schools receive a government grant toward operational costs, such as school upkeep, teacher and administrator salaries, textbooks, and extracurricular activities. Most schools supplement the government grant with other forms of income, such as school fees paid by parents, fundraising events, and donations. So the best schools are the ones where parents have the means to pay higher school fees; those schools can hire more and better qualified teachers and provide better facilities, including libraries. Education is now stratified, in large measure, by class.

The Born Frees had begun to make noise about the subpar

conditions of their schools. In 2009, thousands of schoolchildren marched to City Hall in Cape Town in their school uniforms. Among their demands: libraries and librarians. "We want more information and knowledge," Abongile Ndesi, a ninth grader, said to a reporter from the *New York Times* in coverage of the march. The protest was organized by Equal Education, a movement founded in part by Zackie Achmat, the campaigner best known for his stubborn activism to gain access to antiretroviral medications (ARVs) for AIDS patients through the Treatment Action Campaign. HIV positive himself, he went public with his status in the late 1990s and announced he would not seek treatment until the South African government made ARVs available in the public sector. He began his treatment shortly before they did so in 2003. Now, with Equal Education, he had turned to the state of the nation's schools. The organization brought together learners, parents, teachers, and community members to advocate for quality and equality in schools. In one effort, they gave students in Khayelitsha disposable cameras to document problems in their high schools. The youth returned with photos of leaking roofs, cracked desks, and children crowding around a single textbook.

I knew these girls had steep educational obstacles to overcome, hurdles I would barely, if at all, be able to help them with. I wasn't teaching an English class. I wanted to see them claim their voices, find out what they believed, how they saw themselves, their country, their generation. I wanted to get to know the girls and for them to know one another, to create a safe space to tell their stories. I wanted them to understand the power in telling their own stories. Most of all, I wanted us to have fun. So I found myself on a Sunday morning nervously practicing my Xhosa greeting to the congregation and praying that a cough I had developed in the previous days would subside before I stood in front of several hundred church members.

A small choir led the a cappella singing, the only instrumentation an occasional thump of a hand slapping against a small plastic pillow that one of the choir members held and struck percussively. Except for "Never Give Up"—the hymn sung before the AIDS moment of witness each Sunday—the songs, the Bible readings, and the sermon were primarily in Xhosa, with a few English words peppered in. When Reverend Xapile called me forward, I only caught my name and "Fulbright Scholar" in his Xhosa introduction.

I stayed planted behind the podium—speaking to crowds makes my knees and hands tremble, sometimes noticeably—and stood tall so I could reach the microphone. "*Molweni. Igama lam ngu* Kimberly." The congregation responded with politely appreciative murmurs and chuckles for what I imagined was my botched pronunciation effort.

I made my pitch to girls between the ages of thirteen and twenty, knowing their English skills would be stronger by this age. I told them there would be no homework and no marks given, that this club was more about discovering what they had to say than learning where to place the commas. Many older women in the crowd—the congregation was largely composed of women—nodded along as I spoke. I kept it short, and when I had finished, Reverend Xapile asked girls who were planning to attend the club to stand up. A dozen girls rose. As I looked around, one girl in particular caught my eye for a moment before she glanced away. She looked to be in her late teens and grinned like she was in on a joke.

"Ten years from now," Reverend Xapile said to the girls,

"you'll be able to say, 'In 2010, I learned to be a writer. I learned from Kimberly.' And then you'll be a better writer than Kimberly. Because the best professors produce students who outdo their work."

After the service, I lingered in the back of the sanctuary to talk with anyone who had questions. To any girl who walked past me, I smiled and said or nodded hello, greetings returned both shyly and easily. The one I'd noticed when the girls stood up now approached along the edge of the crowd exiting the church. "I'm glad you'll be there," I said to her.

"*Ja*, thanks."

"Tell me your name?"

"It's Sharon."

She wore the same inscrutable smile I'd noticed, though it widened as she spoke. I wondered about her, whether she was genuinely interested or whether she would be the sort of girl who attends something like a writing club only to mock it. A ridiculous worry, maybe, but I began to feel like a teenage girl myself that morning, with the pangs of anxiety that strike when you are in a new place, when you want to prove yourself cool enough to hang around. Middle school insecurities take a long time to shed.

Another girl came up to me then, tossing a handful of long, thin braids back over one shoulder as she walked. She had a tiny frame, high cheekbones, and resembled a porcelain doll. I asked her name, too; it was Gugu.

"Can my friend please come join us?" she asked in a pleading voice. I was ready to say, "Of course!" when she gestured to her friend nearby, a boy, around sixteen. He looked nervous and held up one hand in a small wave in our direction.

"I think we're going to keep it to girls for right now."

"Does it help to tell you he's very in touch with his feminine side?" She looked so hopeful.

"I'm glad he is." I fought back a smile. "But I want girls to get to know each other and feel comfortable to write what they want in the club first."

"Okay," she said, as her head bobbed a little in affirmation. "I can accept that."

"Thank you for understanding."

A dozen girls; that would be a great number for the writing club. I hoped they would all show up when we started in two weeks.

A deep rattle, low and raspy, came in through the open window at the J. L. Zwane office. Fighting a lingering bout of bronchitis myself, I registered that same painful barking sound. Glancing outside, I saw Annasuena slowly climbing the stairs to the church's front doors. Her head was turned, mouth pressed against one shoulder to absorb the cough. She wore a short dress that was too big for her, mostly black with a patchwork-pattern bodice, and black flats. The outfit seemed to shrink her already diminutive body even further. From this angle above her, she looked as though she might have to stand on tiptoe to reach the door handle. I stood up at the window and waved to catch her eye. When she lifted her head, she spotted me and her pinched face opened into a surprised smile. She had not been in church on the Sunday I announced the writing club, and I was eager to see her again.

As I walked out to the foyer, a coughing fit nearly doubled me over. When the spasms passed, I looked up and Annasuena stood there, her high forehead creased in commiseration.

"We sound like quite the pair," I said ruefully.

"Are you ill as well?" she asked.

"Yes, but I think it sounds worse than it is. I *hope* it does. I get this cough every year or so, since I was a kid. I keep waiting to outgrow it."

"*Ja*, I know. Last week, I had to go to hospital because I couldn't breathe. I had asthma as a child, but I thought I'd outgrown it too. I'm worried this might be TB."

She pressed a palm against her chest as if to shield it from the mere mention of the disease. For me, a persistent cough meant discomfort, some sleepless nights, annoyance. To Annasuena, or Olwethu, or anyone with an immune system compromised by HIV, a cough warned of much graver possibilities. A bout of untreated tuberculosis could rapidly kill her. Worldwide, TB is the leading cause of death among those with HIV.

"Did they test you for it?" I asked.

"They did. They did a . . . oh, what d'you call it?"

"A sputum test?"

"That's it."

"Have they given you the results?"

"Not yet."

She shook her head and took a shallow breath after she spoke. I reassured her that the test would most likely come back negative. The almost imperceptible nod of her head and wary smile revealed a girl who wanted to believe that, and also one who knew I could promise her no such thing.

Annasuena should have been sitting in mathematics and English classes like other learners on this weekday, but she was still having difficulty re-enrolling in high school. She had already fallen several grades behind, held back not because she failed to keep up with her studies but because of poor attendance and shifting school enrollment, as she moved between family homes after her mother died. Now tired of waiting for her cousin-brother to act on her behalf, she had taken her education into her own hands and, with Mel's help, was wrangling with school secretaries and paperwork in order to enter Grade 9. In the meantime, without school, she had nowhere to go each day. She had wandered over to J. L. Zwane early for orphans' group that afternoon.

Like Annasuena, I didn't quite know what to do with my days. While planning for the writing club, I felt lost in my transition from a nine-to-five office job in Washington to setting my own daily schedule as I learned my way around a foreign city. I had come out to Gugulethu in the morning to practice my driving—I was also learning to drive on the left side of the road with a stick shift—and to help with orphans' group. I wanted to make myself useful at the center, become a part of the community, but I wasn't quite sure how to do that yet. When another cough seized Annasuena, a thought occurred to me.

"Are you hungry?" I asked after her coughing subsided. She shrugged one shoulder, but her raised eyebrows and suddenly attentive expression answered the question more definitively. "Come with me." She followed me into the kitchen.

The J. L. Zwane Community Center staff prepared meals each day for the fifty or so members of the HIV/AIDS support group that meets every afternoon. Seventy-five to a hundred children would also show up soon after school for a meal and tutoring, as they did each weekday. Church staff also ate lunch at the center. Apparently that now included me, since on the days I came in, someone would bring me a large plate of food on a tray covered by a cotton cloth in a traditional African textile pattern, rich swirls of cornflower blue and sunny yellow. In the kitchen, I asked Nomzamo, the head cook, whether she could prepare an extra plate for Annasuena, to whom I gestured, by way of introduction. Nomzamo said, "Oh, okay," but she looked none too pleased about the request and spoke to Annasuena in Xhosa. The girl lowered her eyes respectfully and answered. I had no idea what they were saying. I did not want to upset the daily routine. I didn't want to be the woman who arrived from America and quickly made special demands of everyone. But if this girl was ill and hungry, I wanted her to eat.

"*Enkosi*," I said, to thank Nomzamo as we retreated from the kitchen. Then I turned to Annasuena. "You haven't had lunch, have you?" She caught my tone of voice, the note that sought approval for my request, and smiled a reassurance.

"It's fine, *ja*. Lunch would be good."

Nomzamo brought us plates filled with diced carrots, stewed spinach, potatoes mixed with meat I did not recognize, and some *pap*. This Xhosa staple is a maize porridge, dense and flavorless, filling in the winter but too heavy for this warm day. We ate to the muffled sounds of multipart harmonies, electric guitar, and drums. Siyaya, the church's musical group, was rehearsing downstairs.

I asked Annasuena what she thought of Jacob Zuma, South Africa's president, whose private life was making news, and not for the first time.

"*Ag*, him!" she said, shaking her head in disgust as she raised a glass of tropical fruit juice to her lips. "You *know* he's not practicing safe sex because these women are falling pregnant. Then he goes on to the next wife after he's been with the others."

President Zuma is a polygamist, which he defends as part of his Zulu culture. The practice is legally allowed in South Africa. He had just publicly acknowledged the birth of his twentieth child. The girl was born not to one of Zuma's three current wives—he has had five wives in total—but to the daughter of Irvin Khoza, chairman of the World Cup organizing committee. In a few months, South Africa would bask in a global spotlight as the first country on the continent to host one of the world's most-watched sporting events. This news was not especially welcome in advance of that celebration.

The president initially maintained that this was strictly a personal matter. His political party, the African National Congress (ANC), supported that position, while critics countered that his actions belied his public calls for everyone to practice safe sex in the nation with the world's largest number of HIV-infected people. In his statement, the president failed to recognize any contradiction: "I said during World AIDS Day that we must all take personal responsibility for our actions. I have done so. I have done the necessary cultural imperatives in a situation of this nature, for example the formal acknowledgement of paternity and responsibility, including the payment of *inhlawulo* to the family. The matter is now between the two of us, and culturally, between the Zuma and Khoza families."

In the Zulu practice of *inhlawulo*, if the father of an out-of-wedlock child refuses to marry the mother, he pays money to her family for "damages" incurred by the pregnancy. The payment in this instance was symbolic rather than financially necessary. Soccer had made Irvin Khoza a wealthy businessman, and his daughter Sonono was not a young girl but a thirty-nine-year-old woman with two older children. Shortly after his initial statement, Zuma amended his stance to apologize for fathering the child: "I deeply regret the pain that I have caused to my family, the ANC . . . and South Africans in general." He then reaffirmed his commitment to "the importance of the family as an institution."

This was not the first instance when Zuma's behavior clashed with his public health policies. In 2005, he was charged with raping the thirty-one-year-old daughter of a prominent ANC family. Zuma maintained that the sex was consensual, defending his actions because the woman wore a *kanga*, a traditional wraparound skirt. Zuma told the court that this provocative dress indicated her arousal, and Zulu culture dictated that a man could not leave a sexually aroused woman unsatisfied. The woman was also known to be HIV positive, yet Zuma admitted in court proceedings that he did not use a condom. Instead, he said he took a shower afterward to cut his risk of contracting HIV. At the time, he headed up the National AIDS Council. The court dismissed the charges, ruling that the sexual act in question was indeed consensual. But health experts and AIDS activists excoriated his grossly misguided actions, while others mocked what seemed to be willful ignorance. South African political cartoonist Zapiro began to draw Zuma with a shower-head sprouting from the crown of his head.

All Zuma's notions of family, personal responsibility, and shower-taking riled Annasuena. Her words began to leap out between bites of lunch in a dizzying verbal hopscotch: "Doesn't matter what he *says* about safe sex. Men see him and they say, 'If the president can go without a condom, why can't I?' Then *they* won't be safe. It's awful. It's bad for gender equality. *Sjoe!* Men in power. Or who think they have power."

Then she told me about the night the police officers stopped her. She and her elder brother were walking together after dark along NY 3. It was not so late, not the middle of the night, but most people had already retreated into their homes, to what little protection these structures offered against the crime that runs rampant in Gugulethu and in every other township. They were just taking a walk to escape from a home overcrowded with their aunt's new boyfriend and his drinking buddies who had stumbled in from the nearby *shebeen*, a township tavern.

A police car pulled up beside them. Two officers emerged and began tossing out questions to the siblings. What are your names? Where do you stay? Where are you going? Why are you outside after dark?

"We're just taking a walk!" Annasuena insisted.

She did all the talking while her brother kept quiet, cowed perhaps by previous encounters with the police. He dressed like a gangster. Just to be fashionable, she said; he didn't really run with the gangs. He had other problems, yes, but he wasn't a *tsotsi*; she was certain of it. But he looked enough like one that the police had stopped him previously for random searches. Now these men wanted to search Annasuena, too.

They had no right to search her, she told them. "We were just walking. There's no law broken here!"

One officer pulled her aside, away from where the other stood with her brother. He leaned down close to speak to her and then she smelled the alcohol on his breath, hot against her cheek. She refused to retreat from what she knew to be her right over her own body. "I will *not* be searched by a male officer. If you want to search me, I'll go to the station to a lady officer. But I won't do it here. I know what happens."

Her forthright resistance must have addled the policeman. He backed down and away from her, returning to his partner who was searching her brother. They found nothing. Then they told them to go home and stop walking about after dark.

As she told this story, she waved a fork above her plate like a conductor leading the symphony through a tricky passage.

Then she noticed my own fork that had been poking cautiously around the untouched meat as I listened to her talk.

"Do you not like it?" she asked in surprise.

"I'm not sure what it is."

"It's spiced mince. Don't you eat that at home?"

I tried to recall the contents of English mincemeat pies, whether mince is organ meat. I took a small bite with a large helping of potato and was carried back across miles and years to family dinners growing up, main course provided by Hamburger Helper.

"Yes, I do know this." The seasonings here were not familiar, and they were salty rather than particularly spicy, but the mince was not bad.

"Are you a picky eater, hey?" Her smile was teasing, like that of a younger sister who knows how to goad.

"Pickier than I should be at forty."

"What? You're *forty*?"

I laughed at her undisguised astonishment, her gaping mouth and wide eyes. She spoke as freely with her eyes as she did with her words. "Forty-one, actually," I said. "Why does that shock you?"

"You don't seem forty."

At eighteen, Annasuena occupied that murky borderland in life—not fully a woman, yet no longer a girl-child. As she held forth with her stories over lunch, I tried to picture her as a child. Some things about her made that easy to do. Her small stature. An alertness for any person or situation she found funny, with a ready laugh that alternated between a high giggle and a snicker that lodged in the back of her throat. I could imagine her having a curious nature, being a girl who asked questions. *Too* many questions, I'm sure she was told. But she also showed glimpses of a hard-bitten veneer that seemed disproportionate to her age. Her body was petite, but even with that brutal cough, nothing about her was fragile. Given that she had been orphaned at the age of ten, it was not surprising that she would have learned to protect herself. I did not yet know all the ways she'd had to try, in her eighteen years, to keep herself safe, to guard body and soul, and from whom.

"Were you afraid?" I asked. "That night with your brother and the police?"

Her eyes grew large again, as if considering for the first time her own boldness, and she laughed nervously. "*Ja*, I was, a bit." Then her expression darkened. "But I was angry more than I was afraid. They can't just *do* things like that, even if they are the police."

Looking across the table at this girl now finishing off the last bites of her mince and *pap*, I wondered when and how she learned to plant herself in the soft ground between preservation and outrage.

I reminded the young poet that she had said she would bring in her diary so I could read the poems she had already written. "Shame, I'm having trouble finding it. I lose everything, or people take things that don't belong to them. That's probably what happened to it. People are always looking for things to use against you or take from you. That's why I keep these papers close. I *can't* lose these."

She gestured to a smudged plastic bag that no longer zipped shut. She had placed the bag on the table beside her plate when we first sat down to eat. It contained her South African ID book, with a small black-and-white headshot and her thumbprint on the first page. These IDs replaced the pass books of apartheid days. During that era, every black South African was required to carry a pass book and could be arrested for failing to produce the pass when traveling outside of areas designated for blacks only, such as white neighborhoods, where they were allowed only if and when they worked for white families. Any white person—even a child—could demand that a black person show his or her pass. The plastic bag also held a copy of her mother's death certificate, folded and unfolded so many times that the creases were threadbare, the paper disintegrating from the center outward. This death certificate proved her status as an orphan.

"I can remember by heart some of the poems I wrote. I'll write them down again and bring them in for you. When does the writing club start?"

"Two weeks," I said.

"Ah. Good."

Even after we had both finished eating, we sat there and continued talking—or, rather, Annasuena did. Moving on from Jacob Zuma and drunken, lecherous police officers, she began to tell me about her boyfriend. She had been dating Phelo, who was twenty-three, for three years. She spent most of her time living with him in a shack behind his mother's house. The woman did not like her and didn't want them to date. Still, better to stay there than with her own family, in a shack behind the house occupied by her cousin-brother. This was the family house where she had stayed sometimes when she was ten, when her mother was dying. Now her cousin-brother shared it with his girlfriend and did not want anyone else staying there. So she and her Aunt Lillian stayed in a two-room shack out back, but she did not like that arrangement. Her aunt drank and gambled and sometimes brought men home to the bed that Annasuena shared with her.

"Why doesn't Phelo's mom like you, do you think?" I asked.

"She thinks I'm not good enough for him, that I'm not edu-cated and will only bring him down." She swatted one hand through the air as if trying to fend off a pesky fly.

"Can you talk with her at all?"

"I tried, hey? I tried to be mature and talk about some of the difficulties in my life, why I'm where I'm at. I even told her about the rape. And then she went and spread that around to the neighbors, and now I have to face their stares, too. It's ridiculous."

She said all this so matter-of-factly, no shift in tone, in the same rapid flow of conversation we'd been having. I was not sure I had heard her correctly for a moment. Maybe I'd misun-derstood her accent, though I'd had no problem understanding her so far. She kept talking without pause, without explana-tion, and before I could formulate any response or question to ask, before I could pair that violent word *rape* with this ani-mated girl, her conversation outpaced my thoughts and she had moved on.

"Thank God I didn't disclose my status to her at least."

I had already heard this phrase multiple times in Gugulethu. AIDS treatment and prevention programs encourage those who are HIV positive to disclose—tell the people in their lives that they are infected—to help break down the stigma still associ-ated with the disease. But while that stigma persists, disclosing remains difficult and dangerous for anyone to do. It's harder still, and even more risky, for a young woman to disclose her status to a gossip who disliked her already.

"Anyway, I'm not sure how much longer I'll be with Phelo."

"Why's that?"

She shrugged one shoulder and sighed. "I love him, and he's

been there for me when no one else has. But I can't take his pos-
sessiveness. He's cross with me now because I've made friends
with his neighbor from Zimbabwe. He thinks it means I want
to be with this man instead of him. I told him I just like *talking*
to people. Learning about other countries and cultures. I don't
understand why he can't understand that."

Now Annasuena took up the serviette, swiped at her mouth,
and set it down unfolded beside her plate. She inhaled deeply
and, with a grim face, on the exhale held up her right hand in an
oath.

"And I swear—on the grave of my mother—I'm staying single after this. I don't *want* another man."

After orphans' group, Milly cornered Annasuena. "Right.
What's happening with your schooling?"

Annasuena explained her situation yet again, saying that
she awaited word about whether nearby Cathkin High School
would take her into Grade 9. She showed Milly the bag of
paperwork she carried with her and Milly nodded approvingly.

"Good. I'm glad to see you taking this seriously. We'll help
you here, but first you must help yourself."

When Milly turned away, Annasuena looked at me and
mouthed, "She *scares* me, hey?"

I laughed and whispered back, "She really wants to help you."

"I know. But she's scary."

Annasuena was not wrong. Milly was formidable and I found
her a bit daunting as well. But it was clear that she loved these
children; her commitment to them was fierce. Before the kids
scattered with their groceries, Milly gathered everyone in
a circle to pray, as she did at the beginning and end of every
orphans' group. "Lord, I lift up these children to you. I pray

for the grannies and the aunties who are trying to raise them well. I pray for these learners as they begin this new school year. That they will not be happy with an inferior education and bad teaching, but will demand good teachers and a good education for themselves." After the prayer was finished, I told Annasuena I'd want to keep Milly on my side.

I asked whether she wanted a ride back to Phelo's. "If you're brave enough. I'm still learning to drive and no one's actually ridden with me yet, except for the driving instructor."

"What, you don't know how to drive?"

"I know how to drive automatic cars but not manual. I'm learning here. And you drive on the other side of the road than we do. So I'm just warning you that you'll be my test passenger. Okay?"

"*Ja*, okay." Her hand half-covered her mouth to stifle either a cough or a laugh.

We walked out behind the church to the small parking lot and my rented 1997 Volkswagen Polo, in candy-apple red. Annasuena halted so abruptly I nearly bumped into her. "Kim?" she said in a low voice, with a horrified look.

"What's wrong?" I looked quickly around the parking lot to see what had frightened her but saw nothing.

"Kim, you *must* wash this car."

She shook her head reproachfully and squeezed her lips together in a distasteful pout. I thought she might be too embarrassed to get inside. I looked back at the car.

"Seriously? It's dusty, I know. But it's not *that* bad. Is it?"

"It is. People in Cape Town keep their cars *very* clean."

Annasuena would brook no argument, even though I had seen plenty of unwashed cars in the city. Phil, the Belgian owner of Penny K's Auto Hire, where I leased it, told me that cars pick up a lot of dirt and grime when the Cape winds blow. He also said, in a sadder voice, that Americans and Europeans constantly scratch up the wheels by hugging the curb too closely. I had already added my share of black marks to the Polo's silver hubcaps.

"I promise I will wash it before you ride with me again." She finally conceded to climb inside.

As I carefully put the car into gear and eased down the slope of the church's driveway onto NY 2, I noticed her unfastened seatbelt and asked her to buckle in.

"Are you serious?" Her head whipped to the right and she stared at me openmouthed.

"Hello? American driver!"

She laughed, a lovely sound that was growing familiar to me. I liked this girl.

Twice she told me to turn left when she meant right. "Girlfriend," I said, "you need to learn which hand is which."

"I forget! I'm sorry."

A taxi swerved around us the second time it happened and hooted its horn, as South Africans say. Annasuena glared at the driver. "*Eish*! People here are just plain rude."

She kept up her chatter in the car and told me her mother had been a well-known singer, that I should try to find her recordings. I asked what her mother's stage name had been.

"Anneline Malebo. But look for the name of her group, Joy."

I promised to look her up as soon as I got the chance.

When we arrived at Phelo's house, boys playing soccer in the street stopped their game and watched as I pulled the car to the curb and parked. I smiled and waved at them; they waved back and then threw the ball into play again. An older woman standing in the doorway of a house across the street stared too, and I waved at her. She raised a hand, returning the gesture without a smile, then disappeared into the house. I seemed to get these stares frequently in Gugs.

"Thank you for lunch, Kim."

I stopped going by this nickname when I went away to college, when I encountered three other Kims living on my dormitory floor. Only family and childhood friends used it now. It usually irritated me when others shortened my name. But hearing it from Annasuena did not sound jarring at all.

"You're welcome. I mean, it's a pleasure. Isn't that what people say here after thank you?"

"Yeah, it is. Now you just need to work on your Xhosa."

"I'll do my best, *sisi*."

"That's good, hey! That's a start."

Our embrace, when I leaned over to hug her goodbye, was awkward because of the steering wheel, and entirely comfortable.

"Take care of that cough."

"*Ja*, you do the same."

Annasuena walked away slowly, like an animated toy abruptly winding down, her shuffling feet kicking up sand and pebbles. One hand carried the bag of groceries she received at orphans' group while the other gripped the dirty plastic dossier.

4

Amazw'Entombi

The day of the first writing club session arrived with a swelter. The temperature climbed to ninety-five degrees that Saturday in late February, the hottest day since I had landed in Cape Town. I had spent the previous day buying items for the club. Thin spiral notebooks with powder-blue covers, pages blank and crisp and promising, and pencils and erasers from Walton's Stationery. Name tags with plastic holders and clips to attach to clothing. Colored markers for the girls to write their names, and dry-erase markers for the classroom whiteboard. Five packages of cookies, liters of juice and cooldrinks—Coke and Stoney's Ginger Beer—along with plastic cups and paper serviettes.

I had rushed through getting myself ready in my eagerness to get out to Gugulethu early, with plenty of time to set up chairs in the classroom and take a few deep, steadying breaths to calm what felt like first-day-at-a-new-school nerves. Once I'd started toward Gugs, as I felt my back grow damp pressed against the hot car seat, I realized I had forgotten to apply deodorant after my shower. I needed to stop at a Clicks drugstore. On our very first day together, I didn't want the girls to see me sweat.

I arrived at J. L. Zwane an hour before our starting time, only to find the door to the church locked. I had told Reverend

Xapile that the writing club would begin this day. I thought I understood that the Methodist Women's Guild met on Saturday afternoons as well, so I expected other people to be around, but the church stood dark and empty. As I plotted Plan B, wondering whether the girls and I could form a circle and sit on the hot sand behind the church, Reverend Xapile's wife, Zethu, walked out the front door of the manse, the parsonage on the other side of a low brick wall behind the church. I had not seen the pastor's Volvo parked in front of the manse, as it usually was when he was present, so I thought they were away.

Zethu invited me inside the manse foyer and went to call for *umfundisi*, the Xhosa title of respect for a pastor. Curtains were drawn and lights turned off to keep the rooms cooler. Reverend Xapile soon appeared and asked me to take a seat on the velvet couch in their lounge as he made a phone call to get someone to open the church. Several minutes later, Zethu entered with tea on a tray—two cups of woodsy-tasting *rooibos*, along with a small pitcher of milk and a sugar bowl.

"Kimberly," said Reverend Xapile, pronouncing my name in a lilting voice, "I would like to come over and address the girls first when they arrive."

"Of course."

I did not quite feel comfortable yet around Reverend Xapile. His demeanor tended toward commanding and stern. When I spent time at the church and community center during the week, I noticed that his presence could set people on edge, as the boss will. As I was trying to find my place at J. L. Zwane, he seemed unsure what to do with me as well. At the church offices, he always looked a bit surprised and slightly guarded when he saw me. He would say hello and add, "We really must talk soon," before retreating into his office and shutting the door.

Stembele, a young man about twenty, soon arrived, jangling a large ring of keys in one hand. I had seen him at church on Sundays, stacking chairs in the sanctuary after the service. He would unlock the church and classroom doors for me, Reverend Xapile said, and then he himself would come over to talk with the girls at the 2 p.m. start time.

As we walked outside the manse, the pastor said, "Don't leave her alone over there, Stembele. She's very pink." A glimmer of a smile cracked his grave expression.

The writing club would be held in a classroom with walls painted in the same rich colors as the church's sanctuary— purple, orange, and yellow. Stembele helped me to arrange the chairs in a circle. During the week, J. L. Zwane's AIDS support group met in this room. Posters with AIDS education messages hung on the walls. "Let's talk about nutrition and HIV." "AIDS is not spread through everyday contact," printed above drawings of a toilet, a public phone, and a hand reaching into a bowl of popcorn. "*Siyaphila La*. We are living," and underneath, "99 Faces. Thousands of Lives Saved." Each face pictured was about the size of a third of an index card. These were people in rural South Africa now receiving ARVs.

On a small table beside the door, I laid out the name tags and colored markers. I wanted the first writing task to be painless yet revealing. When each girl entered the room, I asked her to write her name and its meaning on a name tag. While some choose English names, most Xhosa parents give their children Xhosa names with significance attached to them. Meeting each girl, I wanted to learn something about her. Her place in her family. What dreams or healing she brought along when she entered the world. What hopes and expectations lay ahead for her. I knew pronunciations would take me a while, but at least I would have impressions to pair with faces.

Gugu arrived first. "Do you remember me?" she asked, pursing her lips in an exaggerated worried pout.

"Of course I do. I'm glad you're here, Gugu."

"Me too!"

She hugged me with abandon. This one bubbled, a champagne fizz of a girl. I showed her where I had set up the cookies and drinks, the name tags and notebooks. We chatted before the other girls arrived, and I learned that she was sixteen, in Grade 11, and that Gugu means Precious. Sharon came next, with Samantha, another older girl I hadn't seen before. Both of them were nineteen, both studying at a business school. Then came Portia, Ayanda, Wendy, Queen, Best, Anelisa, and Bonani. Connie flashed me a peace sign when she arrived. She wore the dressiest outfit, a ruffled blouse in dusty rose, with a black pencil skirt covered in small pink polka dots and a wide black belt encircling her tiny waist. I had the feeling that she was not coming from or going to another event, that this was simply the way Connie dressed. All the other girls looked more casual and outfitted for the hot weather, with T-shirts and layered tank tops, jeans and cropped trousers, strappy sandals and *takkies* (athletic shoes). They could have been a group of girls gathered for an afternoon at a high school in Washington. And they kept coming—alone, in pairs, and in larger groups. I tried to greet each one but fell behind with names; at least fifteen girls had arrived.

At ten minutes past our 2 p.m. start time, Reverend Xapile appeared in the doorway. "Kimberly, is everyone gathered?"

"I think most are probably here, but a few are still trickling in." I tried to joke about having expected arrivals on "African time," as Europeans and Americans tended to call the more relaxed approach to timekeeping and punctuality they found on the continent. Reverend Xapile did not return my smile.

"We do not follow African time here at this church," he said.

I asked the girls to take seats in the circle of chairs. Reverend Xapile came into the room with another man, Zukile, one of the church leaders whom I'd met briefly before, and we three joined the circle. Before I had a chance to say anything, Reverend Xapile spoke.

"As you become writers . . . ," he began addressing the girls in English and then switched to Xhosa. I had no idea what he was saying. He looked around the circle and the girls seemed to avert their eyes when he looked at each one. I was not sure whether that was out of respect for an elder, because of nerves, or some other reason I could not understand. When he paused in his speech, Zukile spoke up, also in Xhosa. He added, though, in English, "This is your opportunity. Do not waste it." I appreciated his words but wondered why it required two men to address these girls.

With a pointed look in my direction, Reverend Xapile spoke again in English. "You must be on time. I hear that people think they can come around on *African time*. There is no such thing at J. L. Zwane. I have never been late for an appointment in twenty-one years as pastor of this church. If you participate, you show up when expected."

He switched back to Xhosa for a few more minutes, and then, with a single nod in my direction, he seemed to finish.

"*Enkosi, umfundisi*," I said, to thank him, and the men left the room.

I looked around at the girls' faces. Some looked anxious, one girl positively frightened; most looked bored already. I had not intended to begin the writing club with a lecture. I asked them to go around the circle and say their names and the meanings, and to be patient with me as I repeated after them.

Olwethu showed up. Her name means Ours.

Xolelwa. Peace.

Keneuwe. Given.

Nompumelelo. Success.

Anathi. They are with us.

Mandlakazi. Power.

Onele. Enough girls.

"How many girls came before you?" I asked, chuckling a bit.

"Two before, one after," answered Onele patiently, as though she had been asked the question before.

A few girls later in the circle, I met Ntombizanele. This combination of two names also means "No more girls"; it seemed to be a common theme when naming a girl-child in a family that had more than one. "You can call me Ntombi," she said in a low voice that was difficult to hear. Altogether, twenty-two girls showed up.

Annasuena arrived around half past two, while we were in the middle of introductions. I could tell that she noticed that I noticed how late she was, after all her assurances that she would be at the writing club. She glanced at me with an expression halfway between a grin and an apologetic grimace, then sat down in the empty seat next to me.

When it was time to name the club, I asked for a volunteer to help me write on the whiteboard. Keneuwe, Olwethu and Sive's cousin, offered to help. I asked the girls to throw out words related to writing and to what we wanted this club to be. I wrote the English words on the board, and Keneuwe wrote the Xhosa translations.

Girls. *Entombi.*
Writers. *Ababhali.*
Thoughts. *Iingcingo.*
Opinions. *Langazelela.*
Emotions. *Imizwa.*
Voices. *Amazwi.*

Then the girls arranged the words in different combinations, sounded them out to check the fit. Annasuena was the one who put together *Amazwi* and *Entombi.* It received resounding approval from the circle. Keneuwe had been seated as we talked, so I wrote it on the board, *Amazwi Entombi.*

"Not like that!" one of the girls exclaimed.

"Like what, then?"

Gugu rose, took the marker from my hand, and made several corrections. She dropped a vowel, added an apostrophe, and made the name one word, to adhere to grammatical rules in isiXhosa, the proper name for the language.

Amazw'Entombi. Voices of the Girls.

I explained how the club meetings would work. Each week we would do a freewrite. I would give them a prompt—a word or phrase, a question, sometimes the beginning of a sentence, a poem, or song lyrics—to get them going. Then everyone would write for a set amount of time, whatever came to mind, wherever the prompt led.

"I don't like deadlines," Gugu fretted with a creased brow.

"These deadlines are just to keep you from thinking too much," I said. "Just turn off your brain and write."

We started with an undemanding three-minute freewrite. For the first prompt, I took advantage of the World Cup fever already enveloping South Africa. In a few months, the country would be the first on the continent to host the soccer championship, an event that sends much of the world into spasms of excitement every four years. Early welcome signs and massive construction had greeted me at Cape Town International Airport, and 2010 had become a buzzword for anticipation, for progress, for showing off to the world the new South Africa.

I wrote the prompt on the board: "In 2010, I believe I will . . ."

"Just keep your hand moving for three minutes. Keep putting words on the page. Don't worry about whether you're doing it right. It won't be perfect or complete. It doesn't have to be."

I set the timer on my watch and said, "Go!" I wrote too, as I told the girls I would do each week. When I checked my watch around the two-and-a-half-minute mark, I looked up to see twenty-two girls' heads bowed over their notebooks, hands scribbling furiously. For a moment, my breath caught at their level of concentration, at my vision come to life of all these girls eager to be heard.

When time was up, I asked whether anyone wanted to read aloud what she wrote. "It really helps you find your voice if you actually *hear* your own voice reading your own words. But I also know it's scary, reading aloud at the first gathering. So who's brave enough to try it?" Several hands rose into the air at once.

Some lines stood out to me as the girls read:

> *2010 marks the rest of my future, the end of my childhood, the beginning of new things, new challenges, new experiences, new friends, a new me.*

> *I'm looking forward to the World Cup and believe it will do South Africa good and will make history for the years to*

come. I've also come up with ideas of what I would like to do in order to make money.

In 2010, I believe that in this country crime, poverty, piracy and unemployment will come to an end.

I believe I will give back to people less fortunate than I am, because they deserve a lot more and are all equal to us more fortunate people.

Through whatever struggles, obstacles, and life's challenges, I believe that I will succeed at the end of it all.

In 2010, I believe I will be a better and a strong person. I believe I can make it through even if it takes fighting temptations. I believe a new change has just begun.

About a third of the girls chose to read, and we all applauded after each reading.

"Are *you* going to read?" Annasuena asked me. A smile danced round her mouth and her voice held the hint of a challenge.

"I can, if you all want me to." Nods and yeses from around the circle, and so I read.

In 2010, I believe I will enjoy living in South Africa. It's far from my home, but I've waited a long time to come here. I believe I will meet some wonderful people. I have already. I believe I'll find some words of my own, to tell others back home what I'm seeing, who I'm meeting. I believe the girls of

*Amazw'Entombi will teach me a whole lot more than I will
teach them. I believe I'll feel lonely sometimes. I have already.
But I believe that words can break through loneliness.*

"Why were you lonely?" Annasuena asked when I had finished. She looked at once confused and concerned.

"I haven't made many friends here yet. It's only been a few
weeks. And I'm living alone, so I'm spending a lot of time by
myself."

"What? *All* alone?"

"All by yourself?"

"Where do you stay?"

As they began to pepper me with questions, I realized I had
not told the girls much about myself during the introductions,
only that I had come to South Africa from Washington to live
here for a year and lead this writing club.

"I'm staying in Pinelands, in a cottage that's attached to a big-
ger house where an older couple lives. Their kids are all grown.
So there are people nearby, but yes, I'm staying all alone."

Pinelands was conveniently situated halfway between the
City Bowl and Gugulethu, about a fifteen-minute drive out
the N2 highway from each place when the traffic wasn't heavy.
Pinelands is also very suburban and overwhelmingly white. For
both reasons, I felt torn about taking the cottage. I love city
living, being able to walk to places I need to go, but flats in the
heart of the city were prohibitively expensive on my Fulbright
stipend. Mel had told me that living in Gugulethu as a white
woman alone was not an option.

Sixteen years after the end of apartheid, Cape Town still
contained deep pockets of segregation, by race and mother
tongue both. The southern suburbs, where Pinelands is

located, are primarily white and English speaking; the northern suburbs are white and "coloured," with both groups speaking Afrikaans. Out on the Cape Flats, Gugulethu, Langa,
Nyanga, and Khayelitsha are almost exclusively black and
primarily Xhosa speaking. Manenberg and Mitchells Plain
are "coloured" townships on the Cape Flats. The Atlantic
Seaboard and the South Peninsula leading down to the Cape
of Good Hope are their own distinct communities as well.
There are a few mixed neighborhoods, like Rondebosch, next
door to Pinelands and home to the University of Cape Town.
I looked at several flats there, none too impressive and one
downright gloomy.

I'd found the cottage through my friend Rebecca, who
lived in rural Mozambique doing HIV/AIDS education for
the Anglican Archdiocese of Southern Africa. Rebecca was a
friend of the daughter of my landlords, Peter and Martli, who
were warm and welcoming, yet respectful of my privacy. The
cottage was not elaborate, just one bedroom with a combined
lounge and kitchen area, and a small bathroom with a shower.
French doors that served as my private entrance framed a view
of Devil's Peak and opened out to a small garden where I could
sit beneath a bottlebrush tree with scarlet blooms. For me,
it was the perfect writer's cottage, a room of one's own, and
a place that felt safe. High levels of home burglaries mean
that most houses in South African suburbs tend to be small
fortresses, with alarm systems and high walls topped with
barbed wire enclosing house and gardens and often a pool.
Homes in Pinelands are beautiful, but they can also feel isolated and besieged.

This cottage where I lived alone was larger than the homes
and shacks some of these girls shared with multiple family

members. Why would someone need more than one room to live alone? Why live alone at all? Meeting these girls, I felt like I needed to try to explain why, for myself perhaps more than for them.

"I really need time where I can be by myself, to write and to think sometimes. Being alone doesn't mean you're always lonely. But this week, for some reason, being alone did feel lonely. Honestly, I didn't know I would write that when we started writing. I didn't expect that to come up. You'll find you surprise yourself at times in your own writing. Anyway, sometimes I can feel loneliest when I'm surrounded by people. Does anyone else ever feel that way?"

A couple of heads nodded, but some of the younger girls looked as though they were puzzling the idea over in their minds, as though they could not grasp how anyone could be lonely in a crowd. Then I heard, "*Yes!*" a quiet explosion that came from Ntombi. It sounded as though she had been holding her breath for a very long time. We locked eyes and I smiled encouragingly, hoping she might say more. She pressed her lips tightly together, trapping in any more outbursts, and her mouth curled upward the tiniest bit to return my smile.

"Would you like to say anything else about that?" I asked.

"No."

The smile vanished. She did not look as though she could be coaxed and I didn't want to pressure her, especially on this first day. Ntombi had not volunteered to read aloud. During introductions, her voice sounded like she was getting over a sore throat.

"Okay. No worries," I said. "Does anyone else have any other questions for me? Anything about my life you'd like to know?"

"Miss Kimberly, how many children do you have?" asked one

girl. I couldn't recall her name and couldn't read her name tag from the distance across the circle.

"No children. You can just call me Kimberly, if you like."

"None back in America?" asked another with surprise.

"Not that I'm aware of." Several girls laughed, though a couple didn't seem to get the joke.

"Do you have a husband?"

"No husband either." Eyes darted left and right as some of the girls looked to one another to see how to interpret this information. This was not the first time I had encountered questions about my status, marital and maternal, in Africa. In any travel I'd done on the continent, these were almost always the first questions people asked. My responses often generated undisguised confusion and sometimes a blunt follow-up: "Why not?" Even with marriage rates in decline in South Africa, marriage remained the ideal and children the assumption.

I saw Sharon grin and give a subtle bob of her head. Something about her perpetual mysterious smile, which I'd first noticed that Sunday morning when I announced the writing club, had made me wonder whether she would be a mean girl. Now I began to think she might simply be someone quick to find the humor in life.

Next question: "Have you ever met Oprah?" This girl's tone ascended in a desperately hopeful note.

"I have not met Oprah, I'm sorry. I've met Bono, when he's been in Washington meeting on Capitol Hill for Africa. That was exciting. I've loved U2 since I was your age." I pointed to a girl I guessed was fourteen. Polite chuckles, which made me realize that U2 probably was not a musical passion these girls would share. "And I saw Queen Latifah in Macy's Department Store the day before President Obama's inauguration."

"*Really?*"

"In the lingerie department. I think everyone was buying long underwear because it was going to be freezing, standing outside watching the ceremony the next day."

"Did you speak with her?" Annasuena asked, her mouth agape.

"No! You don't talk to a woman when she's buying underwear!"

Annasuena's cackle rose above the chatter that had now started up. I told the girls we would leave it at that for the day. I thanked them for coming and said I hoped to see them all the next week. Looking around the circle, I said, "You are all here because you're writers already. If you give up your Saturday afternoon to come to a writing club, that means you're a writer. You have something to say and you're ready to say it. Even if it's only to yourself."

Twenty-two faces looked back at me. They looked proud, uncertain, amused, anxious, ready to get the hell out of there so they could wander around Gugs and meet up with their friends for the rest of this hot afternoon. Twenty-two beautiful faces.

Before Annasuena left, I asked her to make herself a name tag with her name and its meaning, since she had arrived late and missed doing it earlier.

"But you know my name already."

"Yes, I do, but not all the other girls know you, do they? And who knows, we might have visitors at some point."

"I don't *know* my meaning," she said, becoming slightly agitated. "It's Portuguese. My mother came up with the name." As she spoke, one of her hands fluttered about like a darting hummingbird.

"Well then, you can just . . ."

"I know!" she exclaimed.

She grabbed a red marker and scrawled out two words in a girlish flourish. *Annasuena. Unique!*

"That works," I told her. She laughed with delight and raised one hand to offer a high five. Her short fingers lingered to entwine with my own.

After all the girls had left, I collected their notebooks, which would stay with me so none would get lost from week to week. As I cleaned up the empty packages of cookies and the plastic cups to leave the room tidy, I felt exhilarated and exhausted. Our session had lasted two hours. *Twenty-two girls.* That so many had shown up at all, and that so many had demonstrated their enthusiasm right from the start, thrilled me. But I had not anticipated a group this large, and now I worried I'd never learn all those names, so many of them unfamiliar to me.

My exhausted side craved solitude, but I also wanted to celebrate the day's success. I knew Mel had plans this evening, and, as I had told the girls, I didn't know anyone else well enough yet to call and ask them to join me somewhere. So I drove to Sea Point alone, to stroll its long promenade by the ocean, to savor the perfect views of the sunset, maybe have a glass of chenin blanc. Sundowners, South Africans call their happy hours, of which they partake freely.

The suburb of Sea Point lies along the Atlantic a couple of miles away from the City Bowl on the other side of Signal Hill. During apartheid, Sea Point was a whites-only community, and only whites were permitted to swim at its beaches. Now it is one of the more diverse areas of Cape Town. It also draws many expats who settle into high-rise flats with stunning ocean views. On a summer Saturday evening like this one, when the day's heat had eased and breezes off the Atlantic brought a welcome chill, the promenade drew everyone, Capetonians and tourists alike, skin tones of every hue. Now it was a snapshot of the Rainbow People of God, as Archbishop Desmond Tutu once christened the citizens of South Africa.

Walking the promenade, I noticed people in clusters, in pairings and groups. A young couple spooned against the seawall, waiting for the sun to dip into the sea. An older couple power walked alongside their two yellow Labradors on leashes. What looked like a grandmother, a mother, and a daughter posed for a photograph, three pairs of hands clasped together, laughing faces peeking through their *hijabs*. A father raced his small son away from the water and across the grass to a swing set. The solitude I needed when I drove away from Gugulethu slipped away with the sun, and a hollowness settled in. Thinking about the girls' questions—what they asked about my life, what they left unasked, and what I had written myself—all unnerved me. No girl had asked what brought me to their country, really, beyond a writing club. Why South Africa? Why now?

The first question was easy. I had long thought of myself as an activist. From an early age, faith, music, books, and pop culture had fired protest-charged passions within me, even more so than dreams of being a writer. As a teenager in the 1980s, I learned about South Africa and apartheid in three ways: from scenes on the evening news, when troubles in the townships erupted into violence; from Peter Gabriel's song "Biko," about slain Black Consciousness leader and anti-apartheid activist Steve Biko; and by watching the music video for "Sun City," a song that urged Western artists to boycott performing at South Africa's most exclusive resort in protest of the country's racist policies. The video showed black marchers facing off against white policemen equipped with guns, whips, and snarling dogs.

It offered a glimpse of a determined-looking man, small in stature and draped in purple robes, a heavy gold cross hanging from his neck. His face shone in the sun like a raven's glossy wing. Archbishop Tutu linked arms with other marchers, an undulating crowd that jogged in perfect unison down a dusty township street to the video's background music: ". . . 23 million can't vote 'cause they're black, we're stabbing our brothers and our sisters in the back. . . . It ain't that far away, Sun City. . . ."

Although South Africa felt enormously far away, I tried to engage with its struggle throughout my four years at college. I wrote letters on behalf of South African prisoners of conscience through Amnesty International. I wore a button on my denim jacket that read "Dismantle Apartheid," though when others boycotted Coca-Cola for doing business with South Africa, I could not bring myself to give up Diet Coke. I celebrated when Nelson Mandela walked free from prison with one arm raised in triumph. From the distance and safety of my American home, I learned about Fulbrighter Amy Biehl's story and her death; she was only a year older than I was. I envied her bravery, her zeal to go where she went, when she did. It took me a while longer to get there.

By the time I did visit South Africa, in 2002, on my first trip to the continent for my Washington job, it was a different country from the one Amy knew—stabilized in many ways, unsettled in many others. I fell in love with the people and the landscape, and especially with Cape Town. The city seduces you, like a holiday fling that leaves you craving a deeper relationship. I wanted more time there. To spend a year living in South Africa, I realized I did not need bravery so much as determination, and a belief that bold moves are not solely attempted in one's twenties.

Still, why now?

I am someone who, to a large degree, defines myself by the relationships in my life. While I can be perfectly happy alone, I am not a loner. Though I have not lived near my parents and my brother in years, I speak to them on the phone every few days. I have had the same best friend since sixth grade and cherish an expansive circle of longtime girlfriends, in Washington, scattered across the country and around the world. But marriage, a partnership, that seemingly closest of relationships, has eluded me.

I have a young mother; she married my father at seventeen, gave birth to me at twenty, and managed to stay married. "When you get married and have kids," she told me for the first time when I was in high school, "make sure you've lived your life first. Get out and see the world. I love your father. I love you and your brother. But if I had it to do over again, you'd be ten years younger than you are now." As much as any teenage girl is loath to follow advice planted by her mother, roots tunnel down deep and settle in buried places. I listened to her. My life, at forty, in many ways reflected the one I always meant to create for myself. The one notable exception was something my mother's advice had assumed: *when you get married and have kids*. When you form a family of your own. There was never any question. I always saw myself getting married, raising children. I always pictured myself with a daughter.

I had relationships over the years, though not as frequently as I would have wished. Maybe because I could be comfortable in my own company, I never became someone who had to be with a man. Still, I wanted it. For a long time I kept the faith and maintained a belief that my well-lived life would lead to an encounter with the person I wanted to spend the rest of that life with. When it did not, what to do next became trickier.

In America, in Africa, all over the world, people still cling to an ideal of couples. Sometimes I felt that nothing else I did or wanted to do with my life, that neither accomplishment nor ambition nor activism, truly mattered—to others, to myself— until there was marriage. Until someone chose me and I chose him. *I don't know why* is an insufficient answer to skeptics who ask why you're not married. It's an insufficient answer *to me*.

Yet I harbored no illusions that marriage would banish loneliness forever. I knew enough lonely married people to know better than that. And I didn't sit home and regret The Man That Got Away. There was no one in my past I wished I had married. But I knew what it meant to yearn, a feeling familiar and yet uncomfortable, like a worn wool sweater that retains its ability to prickle the skin. My yearning was for a person I had yet to meet. Sometimes it was a yearning for the version of myself I might be with him, a calmer, more consistently confident me.

Motherhood, surprisingly, held a less fraught place in my life. I knew having a child on my own was an option. My mother, in fact, suggested once, and only once, that I adopt, that a grandchild would be welcomed into the family any way it got there. I thought that's what I would do, when the right time came, if the right man did not. But as my closest friends had children, I saw how much work they are, even when you have a supportive partner and involved co-parent. Whatever desire I had to mother a child wasn't strong enough that it could overcome my misgivings that I was ill-equipped to be a single parent. Maybe I wanted the partner more than the child. I did not think of myself as childless anyway. That *-less* implies negative space, a gaping hole that, honestly, most days just was not there. Sometimes I would watch a friend, or a stranger even, cuddle with

PENFIELD PUBLIC LIBRARY

her baby or chase a laughing preschooler and feel a pang of longing then, sharp and centered and unexpected. But those moments happened less often than I might have imagined. Instead, I relished my role as godmother and honorary auntie. I got to be the subversive grown-up presence in a kid's life.

A couple of years before I arrived in Cape Town, I gradually recognized that I was in a rut. Somehow I had stopped living a life I wanted to be living. I knew that feeling was not restricted to single people without children, that the daily grind can wear anyone down. I managed, though, to realize something important about my particular circumstances. With no husband to consult or children to consider, with all this unplanned independence, I could make dramatic changes to my life. I held that power. I could spend a year with the girls of Gugulethu. Together maybe we could discover the writers we wanted to be and the lives we had yet to lead.

PART TWO

YOU STRIKE A WOMAN,
YOU STRIKE A ROCK

5

A Force to Be Reckoned With

Proudly South African

I'm a young black girl
Trying to live life easily.
I'm a youth of today
And also an adult of tomorrow.

I'm the history of this continent
And also the future of this continent.
I am the sister of brothers.
I am a human
Trying to survive.
I may be a victim
But one day I will
Be a survivor.

I'm a young black girl
Who is proudly
South African.

—Olwethu

Over our next few Saturday gatherings, I took individual photographs of each girl wearing her name tag. I hated when I could not identify a girl by name, but the rotating size of the group was making the effort difficult. Portia, one of the older girls at eighteen, had persuaded a half-dozen of her younger cousins to join us. They attended as a faction in an unpredictable manner. They arrived together, they skipped the same Saturdays, and I had yet to sort them out individually. Most of the girls also had ever-changing hairstyles—braids and extensions and lengths that could change dramatically from week to week—which was no help in pairing names with faces. A couple of weeks in, I noticed a small girl I assumed was new. She stood talking to another, her short hair straightened and slicked against her head. I said hello and welcomed her.

"Kim! I'm Gugu!"

"Where did your long braids go?"

"I took them out." She patted the side of her head.

"You can do that?"

Gugu and the girls standing around laughed at my ignorant question. They accessorized with their hair as much as they did with jewelry or shoes. "Well, I've got curls, flat-ironed, a pony-tail, and then I'm out," I said, and they howled.

From the way each girl approached having her picture taken, I learned more than names. Connie jumped in line first. She cocked her head to one side until her chin-length braids brushed against her shoulder, propped a hand on her hip and with the other flashed a sideways peace sign, allow-ing herself only the coolest of smiles. She clearly lived to be photographed. Bonani also posed with a hand on her hip, chin slightly tucked into her chest, with an expression somewhere between amused and dubious. Silindokuhle—her name means

"Waiting for good to come to us"—tugged at one side of her cardigan and helpfully pointed a finger at her name tag. Some girls faced forward, some angled their bodies to feature what they considered their better sides. They beamed, pouted, grinned shyly, uncomfortably, and not at all. Portia tilted her head over one shoulder coquettishly, her luminous dark skin contrasting with the white tank top she wore.

Mandlakazi looked like she was still making up her mind whether to smile or appear serious when the shutter snapped and captured her round baby face. She was wearing a red V-neck sweater pulled over a crisp white-collared shirt, an outfit that made her look like she was heading off to a job interview after the club. The effect was that of a schoolgirl's portrait cut-and-pasted onto a professional woman's body.

"Is that good?" I asked, showing her the screen on my camera. I allowed for retakes if the girls insisted, though few had so far.

"Oh my word!" She opened her eyes wide, pulled the camera closer, and stared at the small screen as if trying to identify the person pictured.

"Is that a yes?"

"Yes!" she said with a nod and a laugh.

Ntombi held back from having her photo taken. "I'm not sure I'm going to keep coming each week. I don't really do clubs." She scrunched her nose in distaste.

"Well, let's take your picture anyway," I said.

In the first attempt, she stood facing forward, arms down, hands held in front of her, smiling with her mouth tightly shut. It was a cute smile; she looked like she was trying hard to hold back a giggle at church during *umfundisi*'s sermon.

"No, I don't like that one," she said in her low voice when she saw the shot. I had come to realize that Ntombi had not had a sore throat the day of our first gathering. Her voice always sounded this way, as rough and gravelly as an unpaved road. She had yet to read her writing aloud, but many of the girls were shy in that regard.

"Okay, let's try another."

For the next one, she again looked straight ahead and this time she did not smile. She looked lonely and lost. This one she hated.

"I agree. That's not a good shot of you."

She took a raspy breath and shook her hands out like she was trying to shake the nerves off, as though she kept getting this assignment wrong. "Hon, it's all right, it's just a picture," I said. "We'll do it till we get something you like. That's the beauty of digital!" She suddenly looked as if she might cry.

"Turn to the side," I directed, and she complied. She tried to smile, but it looked fake and forced even before I held up the camera. "It's going to be a great picture. Look at your outfit. You coordinate with the background."

She was standing in front of the classroom wall painted a shade between purple and cornflower blue, wearing a sleeve-less top with a square neckline and thick straps in a madras pattern, squares of pink and red and white and purple. Her ear-rings were large hoops made of pink wooden beads with purple thread woven through, like a web spun by a particularly crafty spider. My compliment on her clothing did nothing to make her smile any more authentic.

"Ntombi!" Sharon said in a sharply raised voice, and then something else to her in Xhosa. Ntombi had looked over toward Sharon, and whatever she said made Ntombi laugh. I clicked the shutter and got her with eyes glancing sideways, a full-on, teeth-baring grin, skin smooth and cheeks aglow, a wisp of fringe against her forehead. It was the best shot of the day.

"We are *so* keeping this one," I told her.

I walked out with Ntombi at the end of the session. "I don't always like clubs very much myself. But I hope this won't be an annoying club. So maybe you'll want to keep coming."

"Maybe." Her faint smile promised nothing.

Initially I wanted to hold the writing club on Saturday mornings at ten, instead of midafternoon. I thought that hour a convenient time, less disruptive of the weekend for the girls—and for me, to be honest. I hoped to travel around a bit, take weekend getaways to see more of South Africa beyond beautiful Cape Town.

"That won't work," said Edwin, the center director, when I suggested the time to him.

"Why not?"

"Saturday mornings are for funerals."

I saw what he meant when I began driving into Gugulethu on Saturdays. It is a community that organizes its weekends around funerals. They announce themselves on Thursdays or Fridays with a tent hired from local suppliers, who are fully booked every weekend. Red-and-white striped, with a peaked roof, it resembles a shrunken big-top circus tent. Steel poles held upright by sandbags brace each corner against the strong southeasterly that blows across the Cape Flats. The tent will sometimes reach beyond the family's small front yard—the sand and dirt, more rarely scattered tufts of grass—across the sidewalk and into the street. Pedestrians must step off the curb to go around it, and cars flying by swerve into the oncoming lane to avoid it. But no one complains about the tent's placement. People understand what a tent means.

After the service at the cemetery, hired buses return everyone to the family home, where the tent fills with mourners and neighbors expecting a meal that the family must provide. Styrofoam containers overflow with stewed chicken and *pap*, maybe *umngqusho* (samp, similar to hominy, and beans). Everyone tries to keep the sand from blowing into the food. The guests will linger for hours until the food runs out, until some must make their way to the bus station for the trip back home to rural Eastern Cape. Funerals are an elaborate, expensive, and frequent occurrence, often landing families in debt.

Milly had heard the story about the two little girls, Olwethu and Sive, and their grief at their mother's funeral, when they had tried to climb into her grave. She had started to lead orphans' group in the township because of a death as well. She began coming into Gugulethu around 1999 or 2000, when she represented her Presbyterian church in the Presbytery of the Western Cape, the local governing body to which J. L. Zwane also belonged. This was about the time that Reverend Xapile determined that the church needed to confront the AIDS crisis, to care for those suffering, and to educate the community about the causes and the myths surrounding HIV/AIDS. Milly was also seeking to educate herself about the disease and the toll it was taking on her country, which she had only recently seen firsthand in a personal way.

Throughout the 1970s, '80s, and '90s, Milly employed a live-in housekeeper named Lina, a woman who had helped to raise her own daughter and son. During apartheid, black women basically could hold one of three categories of jobs: as domestics, industrial workers, or farmhands. A small number with advanced education were allowed to be nurses and teachers for other blacks. When they obtained such jobs, women tried hard to hold on to them, and Lina was no exception. Sometime in the early 1970s, Milly noticed Lina's figure expanding and told her husband, Ian, that she suspected Lina might be pregnant. She planned to ask her outright, in her straightforward manner. Before Milly got around to the discussion, however, she called home one afternoon on the last day of school to speak with Lina. "I told her I was having tea with a friend and then I was coming around to get Shirley-Ann and take her shopping, to please have her dressed and ready. She says to me, 'But ma'am, I've just had a baby.' You've *what?* I screeched home and there she'd popped this baby out on our kitchen floor! She buried the afterbirth out in the back garden."

Milly took mother and baby, whom Lina named Thelma, to see the doctor; both were fine and healthy. Thelma then lived with her mother at Milly's home until she reached school age and had to return to Khayelitsha—the township where Lina stayed in a shack with family when not working at Milly's—to attend a black school. Eventually Milly helped Lina and her family move into a newly built Habitat for Humanity house.

When Thelma entered her twenties in the early 1990s, at the end of apartheid, she was able to pursue further schooling, which Milly helped to fund. She studied to become a teacher first and then ended up teaching life skills—how to fill out a job application, how to open a bank account—to adults seeking employment and new opportunities for the first time under Mandela's government. Sometime during 1996, Thelma had a baby girl who was ill from birth. Lina did not know what was wrong with her grandchild, and the baby died at just over a year old. At the beginning of 1998, Thelma herself was hospitalized. Lina and Milly learned then that Thelma had AIDS.

"She never told anybody that she was HIV positive," Milly

recalled. "She knew she was positive, but she never told. At that stage, no one was getting the medication." Thelma died three weeks after they learned her status.

"We knew *nothing* about it. AIDS was just this dreaded disease," said Milly. "We thought if you touched somebody who had it, you'd get it."

Milly is a woman of great faith and great practicality, someone who takes literally the biblical injunction to care for the widow and the orphan. Pairing up with J. L. Zwane's fledgling AIDS program, she began to learn about the disease. In 2001, she traveled with Reverend Xapile's wife, Zethu, on a combination fundraising and educational trip to America, to speak at churches and visit public health centers in Maryland, Florida, and Texas. "I was really on fire about this. People weren't getting treated, and it was mostly women who were coming down with the disease, who were the most susceptible. They couldn't refuse sex. Americans didn't understand this when we tried to explain it. They'd ask, 'Why would you have sex with a man without insisting on a condom?' They didn't understand how difficult it was for these women to insist on that with their husbands and partners, especially at that early stage of the disease."

At that stage, too, women who contracted the disease, without access to ARVs—women like Thelma—did not live long. "These mothers were dying fast and furious. And I started to think, what are we going to do for the children they leave behind?" When she returned to Cape Town, Milly began planning J. L. Zwane's orphans' group, which officially began in 2002.

"I fell flat on my face a thousand times," she said, "and I got back up. I'll never forget our first meeting. I brought muffins for the kids. They all kind of tasted it, took one bite and spat it out. That was not in their diets, it was foreign to them. I asked,

'What do you want me to bring you on a Tuesday to eat?' They all wanted white bread with *polony* (a processed meat similar to bologna). So that's what we did."

It also took Milly a while to sort out which children were orphaned and which were kids from the community sent by their parents to collect the food parcels the support group distributed. Rose, Nancy, and Johanna, women who attended church at J. L. Zwane, knew the community, knew who was ill, who was dying, who were orphans. They worked with Milly and the volunteers she brought with her from Durbanville to learn about the children and their family situations. Most lived with extended family, with aunts or grandmothers, or had been taken in by neighbors. When they discovered a child-headed household—only two or three that Milly could recall—Reverend Xapile would help to find adults in the community who could take in those children. With Bible readings and prayer, Milly wanted to make sure the orphans' group attended to these children's spiritual as well as physical needs.

On a weekend when there was a public holiday, Sive came home for a visit from her boarding school and I made plans to meet up with her and Olwethu. We had canceled Amazw'Entombi that Saturday because many of the girls would be with their families, most likely having a *braai* (pronounced "bry"). Short for *braaivleis* (Afrikaans for "roasted meat"), a *braai* is a barbecue—a "bring and *braai*," South Africa's version of a potluck gathering. A tradition that originated with Afrikaners, *braai* has crossed all racial, ethnic, and cultural lines. Archbishop Tutu says, in his usual effusive manner, "We have eleven different official languages but only one word for the wonderful institution of *braai*." He is patron of National Braai

Day, celebrated on South Africa's Heritage Day in September. Gugulethu contains a *braai* hot spot, Mzoli's, a restaurant and butchery opened by local businessman Mzoli Ngcawuzele in 2003. Customers choose their cuts of meat, which are then grilled and brought to them at communal tables. Only meat, *pap*, and beer are sold at Mzoli's. If you want any other food or nonalcoholic cooldrinks, you must bring your own. There is often a live band or DJ playing house music or *kwaito* with deep bass sounds, and local residents have complained of noise levels and public drunkenness around the place. A few daring tourists venture to Mzoli's to get a view of township life. Enterprising car guards hang around to help people find parking spots and offer to look after their cars for tips of R2 or R5 (about twenty cents or fifty cents in U.S. currency).

I arranged to pick up Olwethu and Sive at J. L. Zwane. It was early afternoon and neither the girls nor I had eaten lunch yet. Mzoli's would be crowded and rowdy, so we drove to Gugulethu Square Shopping Center, a large mall on NY 1, another venture built in part by Mzoli Ngcawuzele. It houses two large grocery-store chains, Spar and Shoprite, along with smaller retailers and restaurants. The first time I drove past the mall, I laughed out loud at the sight of a KFC with Colonel Sanders's giant grinning face in their corporate logo prominently featured outside, his shock of white facial hair and black string tie so recognizable.

The mall, only a couple of years old, allowed residents to shop locally rather than having to travel into the city or the suburbs to buy their groceries and clothing. All the stores are national and international chains, however, and the mall is owned by wealthy developers and businessmen. I wondered whether any of their profits were reinvested in the township, to make substantial and much-needed improvements to Gugulethu. Like the gentrification I have witnessed in my own Washington, DC, neighborhood, convenience and lowered prices come at a cost to local merchants, stores, and restaurants.

When I asked the girls where they wanted to have lunch, they suggested pizza. At Debonair's, they chose the Meat Triple-Decker, layers of cheese and ground mince, ham, spareribs, pizza sauce, barbecue sauce, mozzarella, cheddar, and cream cheese. "That sounds like a lot of meat," I said. "Aren't you having a *braai* today too?"

"That's not until tonight," Sive explained in a patient tone, as though I failed to comprehend the need to eat right then.

When I first met them separately, I did not think they looked much like sisters. Now, sitting across from them side by side, I thought they could be twins. Part of that effect was clothing. Both wore faded jeans and denim jackets; their only difference in outfits was on their choices of tops. Olwethu's T-shirt was a camouflage print, Sive's was light blue. Both wore small rhinestone studs in their ears. Unlike Annasuena, who could carry on an entire lunchtime monologue, these girls did not talk much. I asked questions, but even those often got only the briefest of responses. Sive was the more open one. I had been able to see her since our first meeting, when I traveled again out to her school to hold some writing workshops with girls there. She was enjoying the school, doing well in her studies, and had begun writing poetry.

What I knew about Olwethu lately I knew through Milly, who'd had a report from the girl's Aunt Pinky. Apparently Olwethu had a new boyfriend, who was several years older, and Pinky and Milly both suspected she had been skipping school to be with him. Olwethu was already struggling through Grade 11, set back by her earlier hospitalization for tuberculosis.

"Olwethu, what's new with you?"

"Nothing much," she said after a pause to finish chewing. I thought she would continue, but she did not.

"Did I hear you have a new boyfriend?"

"*Ja*." She said this without the smile I would have expected from a girl speaking about a new boyfriend.

"Is he in Gugs or in town?"

"In Gugs."

"Does he go to school?"

"He's out of school."

"Where did you meet him?"

"Just around Gugs."

It was clear she would be offering little information here and now, so I switched topics. I knew the girls had been born in Eastern Cape and asked how old they were when they came to live in Cape Town. Olwethu was five, Sive two. They stayed first at their grandmother's home, while their mother was still alive, before moving in with their Aunt Pinky. I suggested that, after we ate, we could go back to their house and then they could show me around Gugulethu. They agreed.

The girls lost track of how many people lived in their house. "Oh, there's lots," Sive said. There was Aunt Pinky and her husband, her grown daughter Caroline, who was Keneuwe's mother, another one of the writing club girls. Pinky's other grown children came and went, bringing along their own children. The house was one of the older settled ones in Gugulethu, with two bedrooms, a lounge, kitchen, inside toilet. On the outside, it was painted a coral color, faded by the sun; the door was dark wood and elaborately carved. There were few security measures here, unlike in the suburbs. No alarms, only a low metal fence around the grassless yard. We stepped inside so I could say hello to Pinky, whom I had met briefly on a Sunday morning at J. L. Zwane, but she was not at home. Caroline was there, folding laundry in the lounge, watching a television with the volume turned way up. She nearly dropped what she was holding when I walked in the door. I introduced myself and told her how much I enjoyed having Keneuwe in Amazw'Entombi.

"She's grown scarce, I know," Caroline said, with a note of apology. It was true; she had already begun to miss our gatherings. "School is getting more difficult now."

"Sure, that needs to be her priority." I had the feeling that Keneuwe took her schooling as seriously as Sive did. It must have been difficult for Olwethu to have a sister and a cousin, younger but close to her own age, performing well while she struggled so.

As we stood there speaking, a little one came tearing down the hallway toward me. "*Haaaaa!*"

"Hello! Who's this?" I knelt down to the girl, who was about three, her hair wild, her mouth wide open with what looked like remnants of a very recent lunch.

"This is Gugu," Olwethu said.

"Like our Gugu, at Amazw?"

"*Ja.*"

This Gugu did not speak English yet, only Xhosa. I said, "*Molo* [Hello]," and gave her soft belly a quick squeeze. When I started to move away, she pulled me back to her for a longer embrace. Gugu's older sister, Dima, then appeared in the lounge. She wore a white, short-sleeved hoodie printed with an African woman in profile with a colorful head wrap and lips painted crimson in the image. She had the hood pulled up over her head and responded with a muffled "Hello" to my Xhosa greeting. Dima was eight. Olwethu shared a bedroom with these little girls, with Caroline and Keneuwe, with Sive when she came back home, and with any other cousins who might be living there. The small room had only a bunk bed and a twin bed. No one got to sleep alone.

We left the house then, and the girls headed toward my car. "No, we're not driving," I said. "I want to be able to see things. Let's walk around."

"Walk?" Sive looked perplexed.

"Sure. Is your granny's house far from here?"

"Not far," Olwethu said.

"Then let's walk."

The girls kept glancing at one another and snickering none too subtly. I thought I knew why, which the obvious stares from other people also walking along these roads seemed to confirm. White people were rarely seen strolling about in Cape Town's townships. I smiled, nodded, sometimes said hello, greetings usually returned but with a wary hesitation.

"Mel doesn't even walk around Gugs," Olwethu muttered.

An older man staggered along the sidewalk toward us, his head looking away at something across the street. When he turned back and saw us, he stopped for a moment, then continued forward. Just as he was passing, he leaned in and said to me, with a finger raised and the stale smell of beer on his breath, "This is a non-racial country!" Then he kept on walking.

We did not enter the girls' grandmother's house. She had died years earlier, and other family lived there now. I asked them whether they had a favorite memory from this place. Sive could not remember much at all, but Olwethu had an answer at once.

It was Sive's fifth birthday; Olwethu was eight. The family rarely celebrated birthdays with a party. Olwethu herself had never had one. But this time, their mother splurged. There was a cake from a bakery with pink and white flowers, and "Happy Birthday, Sive!" written out in pink icing. There were cooldrinks and chips and balloons. All the family members in Gugs came over to their granny's house to celebrate. Music played on the radio, the children danced, and the adults ate and drank and laughed at all the antics around them. It was the happiest day that Olwethu could ever recall. Even better, their mother promised her girls that, one day, she would throw each of them a fabulous Sweet Sixteen party.

Olwethu and Sive were born in Mthatha, in Eastern Cape. The city was formerly the capital of the Transkei, the apartheid homeland for the Xhosa people, anglicized then as Umtata. It lies not far from Nelson Mandela's home village, Qunu. The girls lived there with their father and mother, Simphiwe and Nomatheba. Sive cannot recall their time in Mthatha at all. As the eldest, Olwethu keeps their memories.

Their parents were a study in contrasts. Nomatheba was talkative and energetic, never slowed down, enjoyed life. She smoked heavily, despite the aggravation it caused her asthma. She did not work outside their home, so when evenings came round and her husband returned, she wanted to go out, to meet up with friends. Simphiwe held a good job at Sanlam Bank. He was tall and quiet, someone who wanted to avoid trouble and a fuss. Go out if you like, he would tell Nomatheba. In the evenings, he wanted time with his girls. Olwethu curled up against her father's side as baby Sive lay across his chest, listening as he read bedtime stories to them, and felt deeply loved.

In looks and disposition, the sisters favored each parent. Olwethu has her father's high forehead, full lips that press tightly together even while at rest, and a reluctance to speak more than is absolutely necessary. Along with her vivacity, Sive inherited her mother's chestnut complexion, round cheeks, and especially her eyes. Nomatheba's eyes glowed.

In 1998 or 1999, the girls and their parents drove to Cape Town for the Easter holidays, a fourteen-hour trip from Mthatha. Nomatheba's mother and her sister, Pinky, lived in Gugulethu. After the holiday, Simphiwe had to return to his job at the bank. Nomatheba and the girls extended their time with the family in Gugs. On his trip back home, somewhere in Eastern Cape, Simphiwe was killed in a car accident. After burying her husband, Nomatheba decided to remain with the girls in Gugulethu. They settled in at her mother's house.

After losing their father so tragically, Nomatheba tried to give her girls some happy memories, such as Sive's birthday party and the assurance of more parties to come. She could make such promises because she had a new source of financial support. Simphiwe had always provided well for his family, and this included a life insurance policy, to care for them in case of his death. But tensions increased in the family after Nomatheba received the money, as they expected her to share from her abundance. That's *ubuntu*.

It is a cherished South African value, an idea that has migrated beyond the country's borders and around the world. In a concise phrase, *ubuntu* means "A person is a person through other persons." My humanity is tied up in yours, as yours is in mine. *Ubuntu* speaks of interconnectedness, a need, a demand to seek out, embrace, and rely upon the greater whole rather than the rugged individual. A reverence for the *we* over the *I*. But *ubuntu* is also an expectation. If you have, you must share.

Nomatheba decided she needed to get away from Cape Town for a while. She traveled to visit friends in East London, a large port city on the Indian Ocean not far from Mthatha, leaving Sive and Olwethu in Gugs with their granny and Pinky. Nomatheba stayed away for a year, and then for another. The girls visited her once. Their mother seemed happy, surrounded by many friends, as she always wanted to be. With money from the insurance settlement, she was comfortable and could throw many parties. After the girls returned to Gugulethu, contact between Nomatheba and her family diminished. Their granny taught them another lesson then. Do not rely on anyone—not even your own mother—to take care of you. You must learn to care for yourself. *Ubuntu* notwithstanding, she expected her granddaughters to learn to be independent.

Months later, friends of Nomatheba in East London contacted Pinky. Nomatheba had taken ill. Her friends could not care for her; she needed family to do that. They put her on a bus back to Cape Town. When Olwethu traveled into town with her aunt and granny, she did not recognize the woman who cautiously descended the bus steps. This woman was thin and frail, with limbs that looked ready to snap in two. Only when Olwethu saw her eyes, saw the way they still glowed, did she believe this shadow of a woman was indeed her mother.

Nomatheba told her family that she had been diagnosed as HIV positive in East London. Now her condition had progressed into full-blown AIDS. Her girls only understood that their mother was clearly very ill. She moved back into her mother's house, where she stayed alone in a small front bedroom. Olwethu, Sive, and their granny moved into another bedroom shared with other family members, to keep some distance from Nomatheba. The family thought they could catch HIV by sharing the same room, so they isolated her, kept her girls away from their mother. She died within the year of returning home.

After their granny died the following year, the girls moved in with Pinky and her family, and all the other family members living in the two-bedroom house.

That was where they remained when I met them.

My Name Is HIV AIDS

I love human beings.
I live in their blood.
I love to make them sick.
I love to make them weak,
Especially those who let me.

You can find me everywhere you go.
I could be in your brother or sister.
I could be in your boyfriend or girlfriend.
And if I get into your body,
I ruin and destroy it.

I love people who let me do what I want.
And when I am doing what I want,
I will kill you.
My name is HIV AIDS
And I am the lover of human beings.

—Sive

One Saturday gathering, I asked the girls to work together in small groups to design posters that displayed, through words and images, what they wanted Amazw'Entombi to be. I brought in poster boards, colored markers and pencils for writing and drawing, scissors, and old magazines if they wanted to cut out photographs and make collages. I wanted the exercise to show them that words and visuals can work in tandem to inspire their writing. I was also eager to hear how they saw the club. After they had collaborated for an hour or so, we would all come back to the circle and the girls would present their posters to the group.

Olwethu arrived late for this session, bringing along her cousins Dima and Gugu. We set Dima up on the edge of the group with some markers and paper, to draw and write whatever she wished. She took to the task with great gusto. Gugu raised her arms and demanded, in Xhosa, that I pick her up. I did, and then carried her to where the other girls were working.

"Gugu," I called out. "Meet Gugu."

Big Gugu gasped with delight. "She's my Mini-Me!" With a gentle hand, she smoothed down the child's shock of hair that sprouted from her head like an untended garden. Her remark made me chuckle but did not surprise me. American movies, music, and television shows permeate South Africa as they do many countries in the ongoing globalization of pop culture.

I propped little Gugu on one hip and walked around the room to observe the girls sprawled out on the floor, huddled over their poster boards and magazine clippings. Sharon turned on her phone's music player, and the voice of Beyoncé filled the room. They concentrated, whispered confidences, and cracked one another up. One poster showed, in profile, two women drawn with luscious lips singing out the words, "Voices of the Girls." On another, an oversize Valentine's heart, layered in pink and red construction paper, awkwardly wore headphones. A sketch of a striped pencil wrote out a caption that explained the image: "Listening to your heart through writing." Photos of Sandra Bullock and Michelle Obama featured prominently on one poster, along with words clipped from a glossy magazine:

"They all start somewhere." Handwritten words appeared on a drawing of an open book: "We are Black like a Bible's cover, like the words written inside it."

Phrases splashed across the posters like graffiti and found poetry. "*Ses'fikile*: We have arrived." "Tiger lilies in the sunshine." "These words are journeys." "Out of their league, in over their heads, and exactly where they want to be."

Annasuena and Wendy worked on an orange poster board. "Amazw'Entombi: The Strong Miraculous Voices" was drawn in fat block letters, edges rounded off, dots and stripes filling them in. Drums and musical notes decorated each corner. When we gathered together again in the circle, Annasuena presented their poster, reading the two lines she had written there in the center: "I am the source that lies within, for I speak the voice of the nation." Even in that short phrase, her reading voice resounded with musicality.

Sharon worked together with Ntombi and Onele. When she stood up in the circle, she read a poem from their poster titled *Amazw'Entombi*.

> *We are a force to be reckoned with,*
> *Women with vision, goals, and dreams.*
> *We have powerful voices,*
> *LOUD ENOUGH*
> *To rouse or stir,*
> *Yet subtle enough to ease the community's pain.*

> *We are*
> *Strong*
> *Focused*
> *Multi-talented*

Multi-faceted
Women
From different areas
Different backgrounds
Different families
But we are still of one blood.

See us.
Hear us.
Feel us.
Fear us.
Understand us.

In this group, the saying is true:
Wathint'abafazi, wathint'imbokodo!

As she read, she gestured with her arm to emphasize words and the rhythm of the poem, picking up speed toward the Xhosa crescendo, after which all the girls erupted in cheers and applause.

"Wait, I don't know what that means!" I raised my voice to be heard above the noise, knowing I had missed the key line. Their cheers turned to laughter.

"It's an old saying from apartheid days," explained Sharon. "It means, 'You strike a woman, you strike a rock.'"

Even before the anti-apartheid movement coalesced, women played a pivotal role in the struggle for equality—of races, and between the genders. Traditional South African tribes such as the Xhosa were patriarchal and, when a man could afford to support more than one wife and family, polygamous. At marriage, women left their families to join their husbands' families at their *kraals* (homesteads). As heads of the family, men built and maintained the *kraal*; owned the cattle and crops; oversaw and controlled the economic means of support. Boys cared for the cattle. Women and girls raised children; planted, tended, and harvested crops; fetched water from the nearest source, carrying large pots atop their heads for miles; maintained the home's interior; cooked and served all meals. The arrival of European missionaries and the conversion of many to Christianity further reinforced strict gender roles and an expectation that men head the household and women remain subservient.

With a shift to urban industrialization, black and white women began working in the textile industry in large numbers in the 1930s. Many organized or joined trade unions to seek better working conditions and wages. Although these unions were legally kept segregated by race, they often banded together for meetings and strategy discussions, an effort that grew more difficult after the Group Areas Act further limited where people could and could not congregate based on race. In 1954, Lilian Ngoyi, president of the ANC Women's League, joined with others—Ray Alexander Simons, a Latvian woman and trade unionist who arrived in South Africa in 1929 at the age of sixteen; Amina Cachalia, a political activist of Indian descent; and Helen Joseph, originally from England, who worked with the Garment Workers Union—to form a multiracial women's organization, the Federation of South African Women (FEDSAW).

At their first conference in Johannesburg, the group drafted the Women's Charter, an extraordinary document that addressed not only the country's racial discrimination but also its patriarchal tradition of treating women as minors in relation to men, their husbands and any male relative. If a woman's husband died, for example, she could be—and often was—driven out of her home by her husband's family without recourse, for only men could own or inherit property. The charter acknowledged that some of these marriage and property law practices originated with "ancient and revered traditions and customs," in a time "in the African society when every woman reaching marriageable stage was assured of a husband, home, land and security." Accordingly, she and the family created with her husband were largely self-sufficient, providing for most of their material needs from the land and supplemented by extended kinship relations. "Men and women were partners in a compact and closely integrated family unit. Those conditions have gone." With loss of tribal land, forced migration of men to work far from home, the growth of urban areas, and the need for wage earners on both farms and in cities, the African family unit underwent a monumental shift. Large numbers of women became the breadwinners and de facto heads of their families, without the appropriate legal rights and societal status for that role being accorded to them.

The charter called for women to unite in working to secure the right to vote and to be elected to public office; for equality with men in employment opportunities and in equal pay for equal work; and equal rights in terms of property ownership, marriage, and children. It also insisted upon free and compulsory education for all children; child care for working mothers; proper homes for all; and the provision of water, light, transport, sanitation, "and other amenities of modern civilization."

Nearly sixty years later, proper homes for all South Africans have yet to be obtained, while shacks in the townships and many rural homes still lack some of these "modern" amenities listed in 1954 as requirements for civilized living. While the Women's Charter documents a historic moment in South Africa's development, its encapsulation of "women's lot" also echoes the lives of the nation's twenty-first-century women.

> We women share with our menfolk the cares and anxieties imposed by poverty and its evils. As wives and mothers, it falls upon us to make small wages stretch a long way. It is we who feel the cries of our children when they are hungry and sick. It is our lot to keep and care for the homes that are too small, broken and dirty to be kept clean. We know the burden of looking after children and land when our husbands are away in the mines, on the farms, and in the towns earning our daily bread.
>
> We know what it is to keep family life going in *pondokkies* [shacks] and shanties, or in overcrowded one-room apartments. We know the bitterness of children taken to lawless ways, of daughters becoming unmarried mothers whilst still at school, of boys and girls growing up without education, training or jobs at a living wage.

Without concerted effort paid to improving the lives of women and girls in the new South Africa, "women's lot" might well portend the lives of future women of the Born Frees, several generations removed from those who drafted the charter.

Two years after its founding, FEDSAW organized massive protests against the government's decision to extend the reviled pass laws to black women. Pass laws were intended to keep the population segregated. They dated back to the eighteenth century, when European arrivals at the Cape Colony enslaved some Africans living there. Slaves were forced to carry passes connecting them to their "owners" and controlling their movements. Pass books designated where nonwhites were permitted to live and work and how long they could remain at such places. They had to be carried at all times and produced upon demand by any white person. Informally people called them *dompas*—literally, "dumb pass."

When FEDSAW requested a meeting with J. G. Strijdom, South Africa's prime minister, the request was denied. On August 9, 1956, the organization led 20,000 women from across South Africa in a peaceful protest at the Union Buildings in Pretoria, the head of the administrative government and the prime minister's office. It was one of the largest crowds ever to demonstrate in Pretoria up to that point. After dropping off bundles of petitions signed by more than 100,000 South Africans, the women remained outside the building, standing in complete silence for half an hour. Then they sang *Nkosi Sikelel' iAfrika* ("God Bless Africa"), the song that became South Africa's national anthem in 1994. In 2000, the government declared August 9 National Women's Day, a public holiday. Marching on their way to the Union Buildings, the women sang another song, composed for that very day's protest: *Wathint'Abafazi, Wathint'Imbokodo.*

You strike a woman, you strike a rock. For the girls of Amazw'Entombi, this mantra from their history fortified their present lives and would need to carry them into the future.

Annasuena hung around to chat with me after our session. Some of the other girls grew timid or uncomfortable when I tried to talk with them one-on-one, but there was nothing shy about this girl. She did not necessarily need responses; she just needed to talk. This day, though, she did have a question for me.

"Did you look up my mom's music?"

"No, I keep forgetting. I'm sorry. I'm still getting settled in and I keep losing track of things I need to do."

"You'd like her, I think." She grinned and tilted her head in a gesture that suggested she was proud but understood she should not show it too obviously.

I thought Annasuena's mother was probably a locally renowned singer, someone who had gained a following in clubs around Cape Town. Later that night, when I Googled Anneline Malebo and the musical group Joy, I found out how famous her mother had been.

6

Paradise Road

I wish someone had told me how life was going to be. That life was not just a garden filled with blooming flowers. I wish someone had told me every morning how beautiful I was. I wish someone had told me I could do anything I wanted to and that I am capable of conquering any situation that may come my way, to tell me what it's like finding yourself in the bushes of life. I wish my mother had told me how much she loved me and how to act as a young lady, to prepare me for my life. I wish someone told me how to prepare for obstacles and trials that may come. I wish someone told me how caring, intelligent, and able I am to do anything.

—Annasuena

Anneline Malebo always intended to be a star. She believed, she *knew*, her talent and drive could take her far away from Gugulethu, maybe even around the world.

The Malebo family was Sotho, an ethnic group usually found farther east in Free State and Gauteng Provinces, rather than in the Xhosa-dominated Western Cape. Anneline's mother originally lived in Athlone on the Cape Flats, until it was declared a "coloureds only" township during apartheid and the family was removed to Gugulethu, then called Nyanga West. Born in 1954, Anneline arrived in the middle of the family's eight children, four boys, four girls. For income, her mother and sisters sold smileys (barbecued sheep heads) grilled on a *braai* behind the family house on NY 46. The Malebo women would purchase the heads in bulk, after they had been severed and bled dry, sitting lined up in the sun on top of a sheet-metal roof. They removed the wool, cleaned them well, and charred them until the skin was blackened and crisp. The name came about because, as the head is grilled, the meat contracts to expose the sheep's toothy grin. Smileys remain popular treats in the townships.

Anneline loved Miriam Makeba, the singer known as Mama Africa, who was the first African performer to popularize music from the continent around the world. She left South Africa to tour in Europe and the United States in the late 1950s. After she spoke out against apartheid, the South African government revoked her passport and would not allow her to return, not even for her mother's funeral in 1960. Makeba remained in exile abroad for the next thirty years, as did many South African artists and anti-apartheid leaders who were banned in their home country. She lived in London, the United States, Brussels, and Guinea, returning to South Africa only after Mandela was freed from prison in 1990.

But this girl, Anneline, was not thinking about politics, only performing. Her younger sister Lillian said Anneline never once suffered from shyness. She blossomed especially on center stage while still at school. She loved to sing with the choir at Fezeka High School and at music festivals in Gugulethu. While studying at Fezeka, she told her mother of her intentions to be a professional singer, explaining that she wouldn't need secondary school for this career. Her mother dragged her down to the local police station for their help controlling her unruly daughter. They could only refer the matter to Children's Court, a policeman told her mother. She was in Standard 7 then, the equivalent of Grade 9 in South Africa's old educational system. A few weeks later, legend has it, Anneline jumped up in class and announced to everyone she'd had enough. She was through with school. She never returned to class.

Whenever and wherever she sang, people took notice of her voice. As she grew older—with a heart-shaped face, large eyes, glowing skin, and lithe body—men simply took notice of her.

"Anneline was just one of those beautiful women that you couldn't miss. Young men and old men used to run around her. And I was one of them who used to fall in line." Fanie Jason grew up in Gugs with Anneline. Both were stumbling upon their artistic passions at the same time. As Anneline molded herself into a singer, Fanie discovered a gift for photography. The two met up often when he was photographing jazz musicians and she began to perform local gigs.

Later on, after Anneline was gone, Annasuena would learn about her mother's allure among Gugulethu's men. Even the father of her boyfriend, Phelo, had dated Anneline for a while at one point—another reason, Annasuena believed, why Phelo's mother could not stand her.

Anneline started out singing with jazz and pop groups with such names as The Flamingos and The Rockets. In the early 1970s, while still a teenager, she got her first big break—a chance to tour South Africa with emerging stars Jonathan Butler and Lionel Petersen. After the tour, instead of returning to Cape Town and Gugulethu, she settled in Johannesburg, the center of South Africa's music industry. There she gave birth to her first child, son Clive, in 1972. She performed regularly at the Pelican, a Soweto nightclub. A few years later, she joined up with Felicia Marion and Thoko Ndlovu to form Joy, an all-girl pop group. In 1980, with one song, Joy exploded over the radio airwaves and onto the pop charts, in a way South Africa had never seen.

> *Come with me, down Paradise Road*
> *This way please, I'll carry your load . . .*

After the opening notes, the first voice lures in the listener with a caressing invitation in a sweet soprano tone. The orchestration is dramatic and rich, with harps and French horns. Then the music swells into the chorus and a different, richer voice sends it soaring, singing in a fiery tone redolent of the lyrics' imagery:

> *There are better days before us*
> *And a burning bridge behind,*
> *Fire smokin', the sky is blazing*
> *There's a woman waiting, weeping*
> *And a young man nearly beaten,*
> *All for love,*
> *Paradise was almost closing down.*

That voice belonged to Anneline Malebo. She held nothing back, hit every high note and held on to each one like a woman clinging desperately to her lover's arm, pleading with him to stay. Promising that things could still turn around, life could get better, once they had made it through the wreckage and out the other side. More than just another lush pop ballad from that era, Anneline's performance made "Paradise Road" memorable. The song's success made history.

Under apartheid, popular music was as segregated as the rest of life in South Africa. With this song, Joy broke through to become the country's first black singing group to score a number-one hit on the "white" pop charts. "Paradise Road" stayed at the top of the charts for nine weeks. It also swept the Sarie music awards, South Africa's equivalent of the Grammy, making Joy the first black group to win Best Album.

Beyond the song's groundbreaking success on the charts, some saw, in these lyrics, a prescient glimpse of where life in South Africa was heading. The members of Joy were singing about their country. In the 1980s, many townships would erupt in flames as they became the focal points of anti-apartheid protests. Clashes between protesters and the South African police force often turned violent and bloody and were covered by the international press corps, which helped to turn public opinion worldwide against the country's racist policies and apartheid government. Tensions and tempers flared; suspicions arose. Within the townships, crowds would turn on anyone suspected of colluding with the police as a secret informant. There was a particularly brutal form of vigilante justice meted out to these people. A rubber tire was placed around the person's neck, doused with gasoline, and set on fire until he burned to death. This torture was called "necklacing."

Before all that, though, what people heard in "Paradise Road" was a song that made them turn the radio up and join Anneline in belting out that chorus. Joy reveled in their success. People began to call them South Africa's version of The Supremes, which would have made Anneline the equivalent of Diana Ross. They toured across the country and then went abroad to the United Kingdom. Anneline had found the fame she always suspected would come her way. Along with that fame came financial rewards that were new to her and to her family. She moved into a nice house in Johannesburg, and sometimes she brought family members from Cape Town to stay with her for a while. Anneline was generous; Annasuena especially remembered that about her mother.

Besides helping out her family, she mentored younger singers, working to bring success to others as well. "Sis'Anneline," people in music called her, a term of respect as for an elder sister. The most notable example of her generosity came when she needed a substitute for herself in Joy. While on tour in London in 1981, she learned she was pregnant with her second son, Linden, and would need to take maternity leave from the band. She recommended a sixteen-year-old singer from Cape Town who had impressed her. Brenda Fassie grew up in Langa, a township near Gugulethu, and was named after the American singer Brenda Lee. She stepped right into Joy, up to the task of taking on a chorus that Anneline's voice had already made iconic. In time, Fassie's fame would eclipse Anneline's. She became known as the Queen of African Pop Music, probably the most renowned female singer since Miriam Makeba. Two years after her unexpected death in 2004 at the age of thirty-nine, brought on by an overdose of cocaine, a life-size bronze sculpture of Brenda Fassie was installed outside Bassline, a Johannesburg music venue.

Annasuena hated that news articles or television reports about Fassie's musical origins rarely mentioned her mother's name or gave her credit for the discovery. She met Brenda once, not long after her mother died. At a Cape Town performance, the singer learned that Anneline's children were in the audience

and summoned them backstage. She told Annasuena that she owed her success to Anneline, and she was sorry they all lost her too young. This acknowledgment years later still brought a small measure of comfort to Annasuena.

Joy never again matched the success they found with "Paradise Road," although the song remained wildly popular. It has been recorded by Ladysmith Black Mambazo and the Soweto Gospel Choir, among other groups. But Joy only recorded one more album together and then split up in 1983. Anneline formed a new band, Shadiii, which featured another teenage singer she mentored, Tsidii Le Loka. But Anneline's star dimmed, and the gigs grew fewer. She went to live for a while in nearby Lesotho, performing at a casino. Mostly she faded from view, as pop stars will.

Annasuena was the third of her mother's four children, born in Johannesburg in January 1992, following her brother Linden by nearly ten years and the eldest, Clive, by twenty. Each of Anneline's children had a different father. Annasuena never knew hers, not even his name. When she grew old enough to ask about him, Anneline would only say that her father was Mozambican and a musician. If the girl pressed for more, her mother responded bitterly.

"He's a scumbag. That's all you need to know. You don't need anything more than that."

Yet Anneline gave her first daughter not a Sotho name, to honor the people she came from, nor an English name, as she did with her boys, but one with a Portuguese inflection, the people who had colonized Mozambique. A gesture, perhaps, to subtly acknowledge the girl's paternity.

Anneline could not tour or perform at gigs easily with

children in tow, so she placed them in the care of other people. Sometimes she sent the boys to Gugulethu to stay with
her family, or brought her younger sister Lillian to Johannesburg to care for them. During Annasuena's first ten years
of life, even while her mother lived, she didn't always know
where her next home would be or when she might land there.
It was difficult to call them homes anyway. Just places to
stay, really, the atmosphere dependent upon caretakers who
accepted the child willingly or grudgingly. She always knew
the difference, could sense where she was wanted and where
she was seen as a burden from the outset. When Annasuena
was still a baby, she was deposited with friends of Anneline's
in Kimberley, in Northern Cape Province. This likely coin-
cided with Anneline's 1992 trip to the United States, to perform in the musical *Sheila's Day*. A collaboration between
South African and American writers and performers, the
play depicted parallel lives of domestic workers in South
Africa during apartheid and in the Deep South during the
American civil rights movement. Anneline was one of four
South African performers who staged the play at the Brook-
lyn Academy of Music.

Of course Annasuena cannot recall that time in her early
life, but she's heard the story. These friends fell in love with
the baby girl and wanted her to live with them permanently, to
raise her as their own. But Anneline had not intended to give
her daughter away. She returned to South Africa and wanted
her back. She had to go to court to reclaim custody and prove
she was the girl's rightful mother, which she did. As Annasuena
saw it, the fact that Anneline went to the trouble of taking the
matter all the way to court showed that her mother was willing
to fight for her, that she really loved her.

The exception to this pattern of disruption was a few years in Johannesburg, from the time she was four until age seven, when Annasuena lived her perfect life. Anneline had a new partner. Vuyisile Dikana fathered her youngest child, Anna- suena's baby sister, Naledi, who came along in 1996. He was another musician, a drummer, from Port Elizabeth, and Anna- suena loved him. Vuyisile had other daughters back in Port Elizabeth, but he treated Annasuena as if she were his own. He fed her, bathed her, tucked her into a bed of her very own at night. He cared for her and for Linden as well as he cared for baby Naledi. In fact, he spent more time tending to the children's daily needs than Anneline did.

Anneline never married. Marriage would have made her a housewife, someone expected to stay at home to cook, clean, and care for a husband. Even a man willing to tend to children, as Vuyisile did, would expect his wife to perform these funda- mental tasks. That sort of life would work on her nerves, she once told Annasuena. Definitely not the life Anneline had in mind years earlier when she fled Gugulethu.

After several years of stability, something happened to frac- ture Annasuena's happy family life. Vuyisile left Johannesburg and took only Naledi to live with him in Port Elizabeth. Anna- suena heard, years later, that he had wanted to take her along as well, but Anneline would not permit it. Instead, shortly after, she sent Linden and Annasuena to Cape Town, to live with her eldest brother and his wife in Gugulethu.

Annasuena spent one year there, a year that was too long a time to live with her uncle. She begged her mother to fetch her and take her back to Joburg.

Anneline did, and she kept her daughter with her for a little while. Then Annasuena was sent off again, back to Cape Town.

First she stayed with her mother's friend, Auntie Shireen, in Mitchells Plain, a predominantly "coloured" township on the Cape Flats. Shireen had daughters around Annasuena's age and the girls bickered frequently. Annasuena was taken along on shopping trips for clothing, but Shireen made purchases only for her daughters.

She didn't remain long in this home and found herself placed out again in Mitchells Plain, in the shack of Anneline's cousin. Auntie Sharon had taken in other children whose mothers had died or could not care for them. Annasuena recalled thirteen children and adults living together at one point. There wasn't always enough food for everyone to be filled, but at least Sharon did not dole it out only to her own blood children. Annasuena felt happy when she lived at this place, and something approaching loved.

The instability, however, began to wear on the girl. As Annasuena remembered it, "At different houses, people have different rules, different morals. So my life had to change to these rules whenever I went to a new place. Then they would change *again*. It makes a person confused about who they are and how they're supposed to be living."

This pattern to Annasuena's upbringing is a phenomenon common enough with the Born Frees that South African sociologist Dr. Sharlene Swartz has named it "partial parenting." Fathers are frequently absent from homes of origin, never present in the first place, or have left or died. Mothers must work when they can, so they leave children with relatives, neighbors, family friends. Children rotate through homes, frequently unsure what role the adult figures play in their lives. Grannies, aunts, friends, any woman really can take on the role of mother. Some of this is a function of the African extended-family structure, but Swartz also recognized the effect of a lack of "face time" with adults on township children and youth. During Swartz's study with youth in Langa, she noted that they soaked up any attention from adults, "like a desert in a rainstorm."

Annasuena longed for that attention, especially from her mother. As Anneline remained an elusive figure, a partial parent, her daughter loved her, praised her, wanted to be like her. But by the time her mother returned to Gugulethu for good, giving Annasuena her first chance to spend significant portions of time with her, Anneline was dying.

Annasuena arrived at orphans' group wearing a school uniform for the first time since I'd met her. "Did you finally start school?" I asked.

"I did! Just today. I'm back at Cathkin High in Heideveld, where I was last year. So I still have some friends there."

"Grade 9, right? Did they move you ahead?"

"*Ja*. Actually, today, there was a test already, in Life Orientation. The teacher said I didn't have to write it, since I'm only starting now. But I told him I wanted to take it. I want to jump in and work hard."

"How did it go?"

"Very well, actually. The teacher called me out to the whole class because my answers were quite good. I'm quite pleased with myself." She tried to layer a sheen of modesty over a proud smile, an expression quickly replaced by defiance. "I know I'm smart. I don't need anyone to tell me that." She said these words as though no one had ever told her any such thing.

"I need to take a photo of you," I said suddenly, reaching for my messenger bag.

"Why?"

"It's your first day of Grade 9. Capture the moment." I pulled out my cell phone. Her mouth dropped open and she rolled her eyes, looking around the room to see whether anyone was watching us. "C'mon!" I said. "Pick up your book bag and pose."

"Okay, all right!"

Annasuena stood there in dark gray trousers, navy sweater with a pointed white collar peeking out, a chunky rectangular book bag slung over one shoulder. Her head was tilted slightly to the side and one hand was curled up where it hung against her thigh. Though she smiled widely, her face was that particularly adolescent mixture of pride and mortification. "You look like a flight attendant," I teased. "Like you're about to jet off to Paris." When she snickered, I realized what that laugh reminded me of. She sounded like Ernie on *Sesame Street*, a *kee-hee-hee* gurgle that caught on the roof of her mouth before she let it loose.

I drove her home to NY 46, and when we arrived, she asked whether I had time to spare. She wanted to show me a magazine with a feature article about her mother. I had time, and I waited in the car, as she requested, for her to retrieve it from the shack she shared with her aunt, Mama Lillian, behind the family home. Annasuena returned with the magazine, its cover missing and the pages disintegrating along the edges. We leaned against my car and looked at it together. The publication was *Drum*, a prominent South African magazine aimed at a black audience that dated back to the 1950s. This issue was from May 2002.

More than twenty years after "Paradise Road" hit the charts, the television show *Idols* (South Africa's version of *American Idol*) revived the song for its female singers to perform. Viewers old enough to remember the song asked, Whatever happened to that singer who belted out the chorus? Where was Anneline Malebo now?

The *Drum* headline told them: "SA's Heartbreak of the 'Paradise' Songbird." Below that: "Anneline Malebo made famous the song women sing on 'Idols' and she's dying in poverty. Sleeping on a concrete floor, her glory days are far behind her." Anneline had returned to Gugulethu because she had no one in Johannesburg to care for her when she fell ill. She did not know what was wrong with her until a visit to a Cape Town clinic confirmed the diagnosis. She was HIV positive, with the disease progressing to full-blown AIDS.

In those years, misconceptions about the disease proliferated, even at South Africa's highest levels of government. The country's president, Thabo Mbeki, professed skepticism that a virus caused AIDS, consulting on the matter with discredited AIDS "denialists," people who maintained that the human immunodeficiency virus—HIV—could not be what caused AIDS. In 2000, at the International AIDS Conference in Durban, South Africa, Mbeki stated that poverty, bad nourishment, and general ill health brought about the collapse of the immune system with AIDS. The solution, he insisted, was not expensive Western medicines but the alleviation of poverty in Africa. His health minister, Dr. Manto Tshabalala-Msimang, infamously championed dietary changes such as an abundance of garlic, lemons, African potatoes, and beetroot to combat the effects of HIV, rather than antiretrovirals. These positions led to South Africa's dragging its feet in the development of a comprehensive public-health treatment approach to AIDS, even as the number of cases soared. Mbeki's government also earned scorn from health care professionals and AIDS activists within South Africa and around the world.

When Anneline returned to Cape Town, she wanted to keep working as a singer for as long as she could. Her only sources of income were a disability grant of R620 a month and her sister Lillian's wages as a domestic worker in Sea Point. She was struggling to afford basic necessities; medications to prolong her life were out of the question. In 2002, ARVs were not distributed widely in South Africa. Besides the skepticism from Mbeki and his health minister, the drugs were prohibitively expensive. There was a pilot treatment program several miles away that provided ARVs to residents in Khayelitsha, but Anneline lived in Gugulethu, so she was ineligible. What money she had left from her performing career remained in a small savings account. She wanted to keep that for her children's care, if the worst happened to her.

Fanie Jason saw Anneline playing with some other musicians in Gugulethu and right away he knew. He might have known even before Anneline really knew, before she had been seen at a clinic. He saw his friend's dramatic weight loss. Her one-time full and shining face was now drawn and skeletal, chin and cheekbones protruding in sharp corners. When people saw her appearance, heard the rumors about her condition, offers of work trickled away.

As Anneline had made a name for herself, so had Fanie. A freelance photographer whose pictures appeared in publications in South Africa and internationally, he worked in fashion, photojournalism, and sometimes as a paparazzi. He tangled in court with Earl Spencer, the late Princess Diana's brother, after photographing him in Cape Town. He had also begun to document the AIDS crisis in the townships after seeing three coffins laid out in a house in Philippi township—mother, father, infant. All died on the same day.

Fanie stopped by to visit and found Anneline without a bed,

sleeping on the concrete floor. Soon after he saw her, Fanie made a proposition: With "Paradise Road" back in people's minds from *Idols*, say what's happening to you. Go public with your status. Help educate South Africans about the disease. A journalist, Raymond Joseph, would interview her, Fanie would photograph her, and they would split their fees with Anneline. She could buy a bed. Anneline wasn't sure. She wanted to preserve her dignity. Necessity quickly overtook pride, however, and she agreed.

Anneline Malebo became the first South African celebrity to publicly declare her HIV status. The article appeared three months before she died.

Four of Fanie's photographs accompanied the two-page spread. The pictures emphasized Anneline's withered body and her destitution. There was a shot of her lying on the floor, eyes open but unfocused, a tattered blanket pulled up to her neck. She wore three different articles of clothing in the photos— orange turtleneck, blue cotton shirt, a housecoat—and all swallowed her shriveled frame. In one shot, a plate sat on her lap, clean and empty save a lone chicken bone. She wore no makeup.

In three shots, Anneline was pictured alone. In the fourth, she sat in a lounge chair, turned to one side, her arm propping up her head. She gazed up at a little girl who hovered above her. The child's eyes focused on something outside the shot. She wore jeans and a green T-shirt with a spray of ironed-on pink and white flowers across the front. An orange bucket hat was pulled back on her head. One spindly arm twisted behind her, the other reached out to grasp the back of Anneline's chair. The face was unmistakably Annasuena's.

"Look at little you!" I exclaimed, and she smiled sadly. "Where were these photos taken?"

"Right here," she said, gesturing toward the family house where she was not allowed to live now.

"Were you living here with her then?"

"No, I was staying in Mitchells Plain. I came here on weekends to look after her. That's the only time I got to really know her. I mean, there was no time to chat, really. And she wasn't open to that, anyway. But I had some time with her."

When Annasuena came to Gugulethu to care for her mother, she was only in Grade 4. Linden, attending high school, looked after Anneline sometimes during the week, but he was not a good nurse and didn't handle the responsibilities well. Anneline's sisters, Joyce and Lillian, helped Anneline when they could, though Lillian worked for a family in Sea Point and usually stayed there for weeks at a time. When Annasuena came to the house, she tried to coax Anneline into eating, but so many things made her ill. Sores covered the inside of her mouth, possibly a case of thrush, an opportunistic infection that her compromised immune system would not have been able to fight. The sores made eating physically painful. Sometimes she could stomach bland soup and *amasi*, similar to buttermilk. Sometimes it would be tea and toast.

Annasuena learned to recognize the medications that her mother had been prescribed to ease her symptoms. After a while, the ten-year-old knew which tablets to administer at what times. There was also a Nigerian neighbor who brought round some home remedies that he thought might help. What Annasuena could not give her mother were the ARVs that might have slowed the progression of her disease.

When Anneline felt up to it, mother and daughter would sing together. She taught Annasuena what she knew about singing. She'd pull her away from the wall whenever Annasuena slouched against it, pushing her daughter to stand in the middle of the room instead. Don't be shy when you perform, Anneline commanded.

"She *never* liked for me to be shy. I would watch her sing and practice and do the same thing she did."

Annasuena remembered other things her mother taught her. Let the air into your lungs. Garlic is good for the throat. "And she was very stubborn. I inherited that. She was funny and didn't take crap from people. She wanted me to be like that, too. She wanted me to be outspoken."

I asked Annasuena whether I could borrow the *Drum* magazine, to read the whole article. I promised to take good care of it. "Of course. It's probably safer with you than with me anyway." She rolled her eyes and added, "I'm surprised my brother hasn't found it and sold it to buy tik yet." *Tik* is Cape Town slang for crystal methamphetamine, the city's main source of drug abuse.

Back home at my Pinelands cottage, I read in the magazine about how Anneline believed she had contracted HIV. Two years prior to the article, at a friend's party in Johannesburg, she was raped in the toilet by a man holding a knife to her throat who warned he would kill her if she screamed.

Afterward, her friends "wanted to call the police, but I told them not to," Anneline said in *Drum*. "I was too ashamed of what had happened and did not have the strength to deal with the police and court cases. Later, I discovered the man's wife was HIV positive but I thought I would be okay. I did not know about AIDS. I thought it was something that happened to others, not me."

When she came to Cape Town and received her diagnosis, she

was devastated and angry. "My whole world crumbled and I did not know what would happen to my kids and me. At first I was ashamed that I had AIDS, but now I believe it is important for people to know I was raped. I was an innocent victim, yet there is such a stigma attached and my friends stay away from me."

Anneline said this with "a sad, wry smile," the writer noted—the same smile her daughter had mirrored earlier as we looked at the magazine together.

Annasuena had been at that Johannesburg party with her mother. This was during the time Annasuena had returned to stay with Anneline for a little while, after she refused to live any longer with her uncle in Gugulethu. She was one of only a few children at the party, left to their own entertainment. At some point, she withdrew from the others and went looking for her mother. When Annasuena asked, no one knew where Anneline was. Some didn't bother to answer the little girl at all.

"The house was crowded and people were getting very drunk, stumbling around," she remembered.

In a dark hallway, she thought she heard her mother's voice, low and distressed, behind a closed door.

"I looked through the, what do you call it? Just below the door handle? The keyhole. I looked through there, because it was just about at my eye level."

She saw her mother pressed against a wall, her head turned to the side, eyes closed. A man stood pushing against her. He held Anneline's wrists in one of his hands above her head. His body blocked the rest of Anneline's thin frame and kept her beyond her daughter's sight.

The scene frightened Annasuena. "I knew something bad was happening but I didn't know what exactly." She ran back to the other children, afraid to tell anyone what she'd seen.

Later on, she remembered her mother crying at the party. Black ovals of mascara ringed Anneline's eyes, and her lipstick was smeared across her cheek. One of her friends held her by the chin and tried to clean up her face.

When they left the party that night, Anneline didn't say anything to Annasuena about what had happened. Annasuena never told her mother what she had seen through the keyhole. Anneline never told her daughter that she had been raped. Annasuena only learned the story when she discovered her aunt's copy of *Drum* and read the article a few years after her mother died.

After the *Drum* article appeared, Anneline's friends and fans tried to rally around her. Cape Town musicians staged a benefit concert to raise money for her care. Annasuena's aunts promised she could attend the show, but they never came to Mitchells Plain to fetch her for it. Anneline did attend. Everyone hoped that she would be able to rally and they could hear her sing along to "Paradise Road" once again. But the activity exhausted her; she left the show before it finished.

With some of the money her friends raised for her, she started on ARVs in July 2002, too late to reverse the effects of the disease. Anneline died in a nursing facility on August 14.

South Africa's minister of arts and culture, Dr. Ben Ngubane, issued an official tribute to her: "The late Anneline Malebo made an immense contribution in promoting music both in South Africa and in the international arena during the 1970s and 1980s. As a result she became an icon of hope, encouraging and educating generations to become seasoned musicians."

Two days later, Nelson Mandela released a letter of condolence to Anneline's four children. He praised her courage for publicly disclosing her HIV status: "This must serve as an example to other people who live with HIV/AIDS. It is only through making their status known that we shall be able to overcome the stigma of HIV/AIDS." Then Mandela added, "We . . . learnt with great sadness that Anneline's economic position made her unable to take antiretrovirals earlier. This again emphasizes the need for us to make treatment available in the public sector and in places accessible to those who cannot afford otherwise." Although he did not mention President Mbeki by name, the statement was widely reported as an indirect swipe at his successor's AIDS policies.

A month earlier, Mandela had spoken at an AIDS conference in Barcelona, Spain, advocating for treatment to be extended to the HIV-infected parents of children. "Many children are orphans today because their parents were not able to get access to treatment for AIDS."

The morning after Anneline died, Auntie Sharon told Annasuena, out in Mitchells Plain, that she would be staying home from school that day, without telling her why. She took the girl to a clinic to meet with a counselor. As Annasuena sat waiting for the counselor, she learned of her mother's death from a television news report playing in the waiting room.

7

You Can Wear Your Gucci or Your Prada, But I Don't Have to Feel Insecure Just Because I'm Wearing My Mr. Price

The Best Thing, The Worst Thing . . .
The Age You Are Now

Twenty, twenty, twenty. Very confusing age, because firstly you're legal, but not really legal. You can drive, drink, and enter clubs. Technically, that is. Doing it is a completely different story, because the legal age at home is twenty-one.

The best thing I'd say is, firstly, wisdom of the ages. With every year comes a new lesson. Secondly, it's interesting to count the amount of boyfriends you've had as you increase in age. The freedom and responsibility I have are sometimes overwhelming but also show me how far I have come to earn those two things. And lastly, I am about to make my own cash, going to be independent, and—who can forget—cash. When I see the age twenty, I see the last time I ask my mom for money. I see the last time I have to listen to a teacher, I see . . . so many last times even if those last times may be my very best ones.

Which then leads me to the worst things about my age. The worst thing about being twenty firstly, it breaks my heart to say it, but what I noticed is that my metabolism seems to have stopped. No, actually, I wouldn't mind if it stopped. My metabolism is going the wrong way. It's moving back. I used to laugh it off when people said, "At my age, I have to watch what I eat." All I can say now is, that line isn't so funny anymore.

My other worst thing about being twenty: I'm not treated like a baby anymore. Now don't get me wrong, I'm not talking about sitting on mom's lap. I'm talking about getting away with murder. When I was younger I'd get away with a smile and crocodile tears. Nowadays, not even "I'm sorry" works. Nowadays I have to work for things, I can't just cry and get them. I literally have to beg that woman. When I argue that when she gave birth to me she made an investment, she counters with, "Even a long-term investment at Old Mutual would have paid out by now." Translate that sentence and it's, "Hell no, you are not getting what you want."

It's sad, really, what age does. Not only do you lose certain privileges, you have to be the responsible one and understand stuff. Who on earth came up with those words, understand and responsible? With my age, I have come to learn that when a parent starts off with either one of those words, she's going to lie and manipulate you. You're going to end up giving her something instead of the other way around.

Be responsible and understand. Agh. I can honestly and openly say those are the two worst things about being twenty. I can say without hesitation that I have heard those words more than I have heard the word "sorry" come out of my mom's mouth. And trust me, it's not because she's never wrong. It's just cause she thinks she knows better. Wisdom is of the ages. At least that's what she says. I think it's actually denial of the ages.

—Sharon

A month into our gatherings, Sharon changed the rules at Amazw'Entombi. From the time we began, I had asked for volunteers to read aloud after we had spent time writing. The same self-assured girls repeatedly raised their hands, while the less-confident ones stared at their notebooks and avoided eye contact. A few made a show of slinking down into their chairs with notebooks held up to cover half their faces, as if that made them invisible. I tried to gently encourage the quieter ones, usually to no avail. One week, Sharon decided she was having no more of this timidity from her peers.

"Come *on*, girls. Stop being scaredy-cats. We all know each other here now. Everyone reads."

She did not offer it as an option. At twenty years old, Sharon was the oldest in the club, no longer a girl really. She had a compact athletic body and, during warmer weather, wore tie-dyed sleeveless tops and denim miniskirts and often painted her fingernails alternating shades of white and metallic green. Her writing showed a solid command of language and a lively personality on the page. In her directive to read out loud, she gave the impression that she would brook no argument because she believed in her fellow writers. Sharon knew every girl was capable of making an effort to write and to read out loud. She dispensed generous praise with an equally ample measure of tough love, which helped to create an atmosphere of mutual respect among the girls.

Ntombi, in her quiet stubbornness, held out the longest this day. She had never volunteered to read out loud, though I noticed her hand always kept moving beyond the point I'd called time, and long after many girls had stopped writing. She sometimes filled multiple pages when other girls struggled to fill half a page. Clearly she did not lack for things to write.

"I can't read. My voice," she said, reaching a hand to her throat. She hated to hear herself speak out loud at all. One of the girls asked her about it once, what was wrong, and Ntombi bristled. "Nothing's wrong. It's just my voice."

Her square face wore two primary expressions. In her more severe look, a piercing gaze took in everything around her even as it allowed nothing to escape from inside. I watched Ntombi watching others, sometimes caught a moment of decision when she had made up her mind about what she saw but would not be saying any of that out loud. I always wondered what this girl was thinking. On rarer occasions, when something genuinely made her laugh, as on the day I took her photograph, her face broke open with the widest smile. It reached up to stretch her eyes back into perfect cat's eyes. Getting a laugh out of Ntombi felt like earning praise from a critical college professor.

Sharon learned how to elicit that response more easily than the rest of us. The two girls had not known one another before Amazw'Entombi began, but their friendship was growing.

"Yes, you've got that voice. We know. We've heard it," Sharon said, waving one hand in exasperation toward Ntombi, who sat on the opposite side of the circle from her. "Doesn't matter. Just *read*, hey?"

Ntombi led all of us in the laughter then. "Okay! Okay, I'll go." She inhaled deeply and audibly through rounded lips and then began. Everyone quieted down so we could hear her well.

The week's writing prompt was "I need to find a place."

I'm not sure if it was after my mother's death or before when I started longing to find a place of my own where I can just be me and have peace all around me. I usually dream about this place that has a need in my soul. I

*always find myself to be the only person that exists in this
beautiful colorful land. Sometimes I feel very happy to be
in this place alone and sometimes it scares the bits out of
me. In this place I feel that this is the way the world was
supposed to be.*

Ntombi did a terrible job of trying to suppress a grin as her
peers applauded wildly. When the noise died down, Sharon
scoffed, "What's that about a voice? Look what you've been
keeping from us. Shame, you should have been reading from
the first week, *sis'*," cutting her friend no slack at all.

Sharon stopped by J. L. Zwane one weekday afternoon when I
was there. The church wanted to reinvigorate its youth group,
and *umfundisi* had asked her to come talk with him about helping out. As she waited for Reverend Xapile to become available,
she sat with me in the small volunteers' office, next door to
Mel's, where I sometimes worked when I came to the church
during the week. I asked how she was enjoying Amazw'Entombi.

"It's great, *ja*. I got excited when I heard there was going to
be a writing club here. I used to love to write, but now it's all
business papers. No time for anything fun."

I asked her to remind me again where she was studying now.
She was finishing a two-year business course at Damelin College, a technical school in the suburb of Mowbray, and she
hated it. "Why did you study business, then?" I asked.

"My mom. Her idea." Sharon said this as though her mother
had not offered the business course as a choice. Her no-nonsense
ability to give orders seemed to be inherited.

"What about your dad? Is he around?"

"Nooo! No. He's *long* gone."

"What would you rather study?" I asked.

"*Yhuu*, I don't know. Maybe . . . ." She paused and tipped her head back to look up to the ceiling, as though her plans hovered overhead. A dreamy smile flickered across her face before she looked back down again. "Maybe psychology at varsity [university]? I'd like to be a life coach. Can people really do things like that?"

"Sure, they can. What's stopping you?"

"Well, this would *not* go over well at home. My grandmother has already asked when's the money coming in."

"Money that you earn, you mean?"

"Oh, yeah. My older cousins already screwed things up. See, this is how it works," Sharon leaned forward in her chair and began to gesture with her hands. "You go down the line, as the kids get older. The adults in the family want them to get jobs and bring the money home. Once one kid messes that up, then all hopes fall on the next in line."

"And now you're next in line."

"Yes, I am." Sharon laughed, shook her head, rolled her eyes. It was not the gesture of a surly teenager but more of an admonishment to herself, for daring even to contemplate escape from arrival at the head of that line of family expectation. "All she wants is to add on to the house."

"Your grandmother?"

"*Ja*. She's going to tell me, enough of this studying! Get a job!"

I could not believe I had initially suspected Sharon of being a mean girl; I couldn't have been more wrong. Watching her interactions in the writing club, I realized that the almost constant smile she wore, the one I first took for insolence, showed her refusal to take herself, and often anyone else, too seriously. It was a lesson she was subtly imparting to the other girls. Her easygoing exterior clearly helped her to carry the weight of responsibility she felt to her family with a large measure of grace and good humor.

I told her how strong her writing was, that she was already producing drafts of personal essays that came full circle. I could pick up her notebook and, without seeing the name written on the outside, know right away the words were hers.

"Really?" She looked genuinely surprised at the compliment. I thought she knew, from everyone's reactions, how much we all enjoyed listening to her read. "I feel weird when it sounds so different from everyone else's."

"No! Not weird. Not at all. You've got a voice in your writing. That's a great thing. That's what every writer wants."

"All right, then." She smiled and glanced at the floor. Praise seemed to make many of the girls bashful, even one as self-possessed as Sharon. I wondered how familiar they were with acknowledgment and acclaim, how often the adults in their lives offered recognition of their efforts and accomplishments.

"I think you should lead a session of Amazw'Entombi."

"Really?"

"Of course. You made everyone read already. They know you can take control."

"*Yhuu*! Everyone knows I don't have a problem there."

"Maybe we should start taking turns each week, with a different girl leading. You should be the one who starts. The girls look up to you as a leader. Would you?"

She laughed in a way that made me think she might refuse the offer. I had learned—from Sharon's interaction with Ntombi—how to spurn her refusal, turn her powers of persuasion back on herself, but that wasn't necessary. "*Ja*, all right. I can do that." She nodded reluctantly, as though she had barely won an argument with herself.

At the school awards assembly at the end of Grade 12, in her pivotal Matric year, Sharon had collected the award for Most Conscientious Reader. The honor went to her for the sheer number of books she had checked out from her high school library—four books each week, every week, for the four years she studied there. Most of the time, these were not books to supplement her schoolwork. They were extracurricular reading material, like the Sweet Valley High young adult series, for her hour-long, twice-daily journeys between Gugulethu and Camps Bay High School.

Gugulethu was the only home Sharon had ever known. She was born in 1990, a few months after Mandela walked free from prison, and had grown up in a corner of Gugs where she loved to play outside as a child, running along the streets and from house to house with other children. In the township at that time, she felt safe and protected by the mamas in her section. Like the two daughters she bore, Sharon's own mother, Kholeka, was born in Gugulethu. But she was born during apartheid, and her family was sent away to the Transkei, the homeland designated for Xhosa people. Kholeka finished high school in the Transkei before returning to Gugulethu to seek employment. Sharon had almost no contact with her father as she grew up. He had started a new family in Butterworth, in Eastern Cape Province (as the Transkei and Ciskei were combined and renamed in the new South Africa). She met him once when she was in Grade 7 or 8, a nice man who stopped by for a visit with the family. Only later did she learn he was her father. She never knew how her parents met.

Their core of three—Kholeka, Sharon, and her sister, four years older—lived with her grandmother, an aunt, an uncle, and assorted cousins, children of the couple, and children of family members who had died and needed taking in. The two-bedroom cement house was always too small. Sharon's grandmother understandably wanted an extension to that crowded home. But any money Kholeka made went first to providing an education for her daughters. They would receive better than Kholeka had been allowed in rural apartheid-era Transkei, and better than what the township schools now provided.

When her girls were ready to start school, Kholeka decided to send them to wealthier areas of Cape Town for their education. Sharon and her sister began primary school in Sea Point and then went on to high school in Camps Bay, a historically all-white, beachfront enclave that has been called South Africa's Malibu. Under the 1996 South African Schools Act, schools may not discriminate against any students based on race; they also may not refuse admission to children who live in the immediate vicinity of the school. However, all schools, including government ones, may charge fees for attendance, except for those in the very poorest areas, which are the townships. At Camps Bay High School, learners have highly trained teachers, smaller class sizes, and an academic support program that is compulsory for students who are struggling with their studies. With all this investment, the school can boast of a Matric pass rate of 100 percent for the National Senior Certificate examination.

Camps Bay's success at Matric—and the accompanying opportunities for future study, job prospects, and overall achievement—comes at a steep price. Annual fees for a school like this are set at around R25,000 (more than $2,200), which does not include books, uniforms, or required outings. Parents at each school help to establish the fees through School Governing Bodies, knowing that increased funding will enable their children to have better facilities and more teachers. Many fee-charging schools provide some financial assistance to students who qualify and show educational promise. Still, Sharon's mother worked multiple jobs as a domestic, a cleaner, in office buildings and in people's homes, so she could pay the fees, buy uniforms and books, and provide taxi fare for her girls' daily travel. Kholeka was still paying off Sharon's school fees after she graduated.

Since it was one of the best government schools in the area, learners traveled to Camps Bay High from locales all over Cape Town, including Gugulethu and Khayelitsha. Sometimes feuds developed among girls coming in from the townships to the school. Tension would heighten on long morning rides around Table Mountain, bodies pressed together in the overcrowded minibus taxi. Girls exchanged taunts with one another over the heads of women who snoozed on their way to work as they ignored the commotion to squeeze in a few extra minutes of rest.

Sharon refused to be drawn into such nonsense. With her placid personality, she chose to view her high school as a relaxed place, chilled, where no one cared where you lived or how far you traveled to attend. On those morning taxi rides, she kept her head hidden away in her latest book. She would not let herself be distracted by petty feuds. She would not squander the opportunity her mother provided for her, as she had already seen her sister do.

Sharon watched her sister skip class whenever she could, forge their mother's signature on exam reports, wear her skirts too short, and hang out with an older crowd she met on the taxi rides. After she left school, she delivered her ultimate insult, marrying a man without her mother's permission or presence at the ceremony. Even worse, her fiancé did not pay *lobola* to Kholeka, the bride-price that Xhosa grooms still traditionally pay for the privilege of marrying a family's daughter. Sharon's sister asked her to attend the ceremony, but Sharon demurred, knowing she could not be present when her mother didn't know anything about it. Whatever her sister did, Sharon vowed to behave differently, to honor her mother's sacrifices, to be the daughter she knew she was expected to be.

When life began to work on her nerves, Sharon wrote, scribbled down her thoughts and feelings and frustrations. As soon as she put words down on paper, she tore the pages into tiny slivers and threw them away, a confetti cloud of her discontent showering the rubbish bin. That way, her mother could not find them, piece them back together, and know her youngest daughter's deepest thoughts.

Weekly attendance at Amazw'Entombi ebbed and flowed but overall grew smaller as the weeks wore on. Connie went to Johannesburg to stay with family there. Portia, taking a gap year between high school and further studies, became involved with a volunteer project that would send her to Mozambique for several months after training in Cape Town. She stopped by when she was in Gugulethu on Saturdays, but those became rarer occurrences. Her crew of cousins also became scarce, except when Sharon ran into them in Gugs and cajoled them to attend. Sharon's young cousin, Mary-Ann, began coming along with her. The youngest in the group at thirteen, Mary-Ann remained silent through the sessions when we talked, reading her short pieces of writing only in a whisper. Another new girl, Thulisa, age sixteen, proved to be a strong and committed writer. She was also eager to show me poetry she had written on her own. I hoped she would come to the writing club consistently, but funerals, schoolwork, caring for younger siblings and cousins, and other family responsibilities could keep many of these girls away from week to week. The core of the group, though—Sharon, Ntombi, Gugu, usually Mandlakazi, sometimes Ayanda—turned up fairly faithfully.

From the beginning of our gatherings, Annasuena's attendance was haphazard. When I saw her after a missed week or two, she apologized and rattled off reasons why she had not been able to make it. She'd had to run errands for her aunt, Mama Lillian. Phelo grumbled that she already spent too much time away from him. Sometimes she just forgot or slept through the afternoon. She told me she always missed the group, when she did not make it, and that she would try to do better. Olwethu, for the most part, abandoned the writing club altogether early on and also began ditching orphans' group. Her Aunt Pinky and Milly again suspected this to be the lure of the boyfriend. They had learned she was still with him, and that he was at least thirty years old. Olwethu was nineteen.

As the girls grew to know and trust one another, conversations opened up among them about more than writing. Now, before the writing started, they wanted to talk about happenings from the week just past. On the Saturday when Sharon was to lead Amazw'Entombi, Gugu had a story she was anxious to tell first.

The previous weekend, she had attended a Matric ball, South Africa's equivalent of a senior prom. Gugu was not in Matric yet but in Grade 11. A boy who was a friend asked her to accompany him to the dance. "It wasn't a date. I'm not dating him. I don't date." She insisted we understand this key element of the story. The boy had some specific requests to make of her, some directives that he knew would make them the swanky couple at the dance.

"So you *are* a couple," Sharon said with her teasing smile.

"No! Not even a pretend one."

Still, this boy felt he could offer his assistance to Gugu about how she should dress. He wanted her to wear a floor-length gown, in gold lamé—a gown that would match his gold suit. Any and all jewelry had to sparkle. She was to dust gold glitter around her eyelids, over her cheekbones, across her cleavage.

"Cleavage? What? *Where?*" Mandlakazi jerked her head around, up and down, to inspect Gugu's petite offerings.

"I know!" Gugu feigned outrage, though not at Mandlakazi's playful jab or at the raucous laughter from the rest of us.

Gugu did not wear a gold dress. She also nixed the boy's suit idea, but she permitted him a shiny gold tie. She would not be photographed with his arm around her. ("Because it wasn't a date!") The boy tried, once, to lure her into feeding him. He handed her a single strawberry from his own plate. Then he bent his head low until it nearly lay on the table, his mouth creeping open wider, and looked up at her with pleading eyes. That did it. Gugu dropped the uneaten strawberry on her dinner plate and left her not-a-date to find friends and enjoy the rest of the dance.

With an outsize physicality that belied her small self, Gugu knew how to tell a good story. To mime the drama, she imitated the boy's posture, puckering and opening her mouth while one hand curved overhead to dangle a nonexistent strawberry, all while bending sideways to lean into Mandlakazi's lap, forced to serve as the imaginary dinner table even as the girl gasped in fits of laughter. Like Sharon and Ntombi, these two were becoming close friends. Mandlakazi was sixteen and had, so far, been one of the quieter girls. Increasingly she revealed a gift for cartoonish facial expressions. She had a widow's peak in the middle of her forehead that seemed to point an observer to whatever facial feature gave away what she was thinking—be it surreptitiously darting eyes, a scrunched nose, or puckered lips. By the way she sometimes tried, and failed, to hold her grin in check, I imagined the faces she pulled had gotten her into trouble before at school. Here, I could count on them to amplify our fits of hysterics, especially during a tale like this. These two girls always made me laugh harder.

The girls concluded that Gugu had handled this boy well, though possibly she had been a little too nice for too long. Once we had settled down from her story, Sharon took over. She had come well prepared to lead and distributed a handout of freewrite prompts she had created. Words and visuals filled both sides of the photocopied page. The girls could choose which prompt to use for their writing. The range included such phrases as "If walls could talk," "What I can't live without," and "Heh, can you believe it?" Four photographs cut from magazines were also printed on the prompt page: an AIDS ribbon; a stiletto shoe; the face of a Fendi watch encrusted with diamonds; and a beautiful woman in a glamorous evening gown, her neck draped with gold jewelry.

After her dogged reluctance to read aloud, Ntombi discovered that once she started, she actually enjoyed it. Now her hand shot up quickly to volunteer, sometimes before she had even finished writing. For Sharon's session, Ntombi chose this prompt: "We girls have a terrible tendency of looking at other girls and almost immediately our radar goes haywire (beep beep beep beep)." She still took a deep breath each time to steady herself before she read, but her voice had grown progressively stronger and louder.

We love to stress about what other girls might say about how we look. Firstly, we start from the hair down to the painted toe nails. Then we look at ourselves and that's where all the problem starts. I think it is a lack of self confidence and self esteem. We cannot all look the same. I've been told I talk a lot and this is one topic that I mostly talk about when I'm with my girlfriends. They've come to understand that fashion will come and go, but if it does not look good on, then it doesn't. I've told them this over and over. You just have to love yourself and stop comparing yourself with other girls. You can wear your Gucci or your Prada, but I don't have to feel insecure just because I'm wearing my Mr. Price. I can feel ecstatic and happy wearing my Mr. P while you feel awful with your brand. This gets tiring, for all the better things we can think about than comparing ourselves with each other. Instead, we can tell each other how good we are. Because let's face it, girls, we love to be told how good we look and to be desired by others.

"I love Mr. Price!" Gugu blurted out, as if in confession, as soon as Ntombi had finished reading.

"I love Mr. Price, too," I agreed. Before I'd discovered the discount store, I found clothing surprisingly pricey in South Africa, given the relatively low cost of living. Books, too, were exorbitant, even paperbacks. I had seen very few books, beside a copy of the Bible, in the Gugulethu homes I'd visited and began to understand why, when I found titles published only in South Africa that I wanted to take back home with me and saw what they cost. "What do the rest of you think about what Ntombi wrote? Do you feel like others judge you on how you look?"

"All the time," Ayanda said, leaning back against her chair and crossing her arms. She was currently attending Camps Bay High School, where Sharon went.

"But since you all wear uniforms," I asked, "you don't have to deal with that at school, right? What people think of your clothes?"

"*Sjoe*, it's worse back in the township," said Ayanda. "People will look you up and down if you're just out walking on the street. You can't even run to the shop without feeling like you have to dress up to do it."

"But you don't *have* to dress up. Nobody can make you do that except yourself," Sharon countered. Ayanda simply shrugged.

"If someone's going to judge you, they'll find any reason to do it," Mandlakazi said, then clamped her mouth shut when she realized we all were looking over at her.

"You know you can keep on talking," I said, and she tittered.

"Okay, like, when I came to Cape Town from Eastern Cape and started Grade 10 at Plumstead [a high school in a middle-class Cape Town suburb], I got called *amaqaba*, because I sounded different from them."

"What does that mean?"

"It means, like, uneducated people. They think if you're from Eastern Cape, from a rural area, you're ignorant and you're going to know less than they do already. And that you'll learn slower. They didn't know anything about me and they thought I was stupid already."

Mandlakazi was anything but stupid. She had chosen to come to Cape Town, to live with her Aunt Lisiwe in Gugulethu, because the schools were better in the city than in Butterworth, her Eastern Cape hometown. In Butterworth, her mother worked as a nurse, and her father was an English and social studies teacher before he was promoted to school inspector. She was a daddy's girl and always sat in their lounge at night doing her homework while her father sat nearby reading the newspaper. Whenever she ran up against difficulties or things she didn't know, she could interrupt him and ask, though he would not give her easy answers. Instead, he would rework her questions into different scenarios that made his daughter approach a problem in a new way. "Think it through," he told her. "Just think." He had died in a car accident in Eastern Cape the year before Mandlakazi came to Cape Town. In her grief, she nearly changed her mind and chose to remain with her family. But she wanted a good education, wanted to attend varsity (university), and knew her father wanted that for her as well, so she pressed on with the move.

I told the girls I had faced these same sorts of judgments when, in Grade 6, I moved from Arkansas to Ohio with a thick Southern drawl that I promptly abandoned after my classmates teased me. "On a visit back to Arkansas, my grandfather said I sounded like a damn Yankee, which was the worst thing a Southern man could say about his granddaughter. So, either way, I couldn't win.

"My parents had moved our family to a suburb we couldn't really afford, because it had one of the best schools," I told them, "It also had the preppiest, best-dressed students. And we didn't wear uniforms. My grandfather was a big shopper who lived to snag a bargain. He gave me three Izod shirts, the ones with the crocodiles, do you know them?" Most of the girls nodded. "He was very proud of himself for finding these on sale. But I wouldn't wear them to school because everyone had moved on to Ralph Lauren Polos, which cost even more. I wish I could have just not cared what other girls thought and found a funky style all my own. I'm *still* trying to find that."

"But it's hard not to care what other people think," Gugu insisted, "even if that's really what you want to do."

"It *is* hard, but you have to stay true to yourself." Sharon would not relent. She switched to Xhosa then and gave an impassioned speech to the girls that I comprehended not a word of, but they did, as their nods and audible exclamations indicated. She waved the index finger of her right hand in the air, looked from side to side around the circle of chairs to make eye contact with each girl, and flipped back to speaking English, seemingly without thought. "Who else are you going to be, besides yourself? If people don't like that, *eish*! Enough with them!" She batted away those who would judge her and finished her speech in a flourish, then leaned back against her seat.

Even beyond the scorn of fashion-conscious adolescents, the Born Frees live in a material world. There is a growing black middle class in urban South Africa, but it is growing far more slowly than the rise of a much smaller number of elite, wealthy people perched at the top of business and politics. With those examples of success, and after so many years of deprivation, comes a materialism that some feel is running rampant. Julius Malema, the thirty-year-old rabble-rousing former leader of the African National Congress Youth League, wore a Breitling watch worth R250,000 as he rallied this generation to stand up for their rights by singing, "Shoot the Boer!" (He was found guilty of hate speech, as the historical reference to Afrikaner farmers is seen as directed toward all white South Africans. For this and other antics, the ANC removed him from leadership and membership through an internal disciplinary process, and it has now officially banned the song from ANC gatherings.) Malema was trying to cajole young people by tapping in to the dissatisfaction of fifteen-to-twenty-four-year-olds, who have the country's highest unemployment rate: 48 percent, third highest in the world for this age group.

Malema's friend and financial backer, Kenny Kunene, described as a gangster-turned-businessman, is also renowned for his extravagant spending—$2,000 Billionaire jeans, "the most expensive in the world"—and lavish parties. Growing up in a Free State Province township, he came from a family that could never afford to throw him a birthday party, according to an article in the *New York Times*. In 2010, he made up for that deprivation when he threw himself the "mother of all parties" for his fortieth birthday in Sandton, Johannesburg's wealthiest suburb. The most memorable moment during the celebration came when he ate sushi off the belly of a woman who wore only lingerie and high heels, in front of hundreds of party guests. When the party set off a media firestorm, he threw another one in Cape Town and repeated the stunt, earning him the nickname "Sushi King" in the press. He called both parties "honest money spent on honest fun."

Some called them other things. Zwelinzima Vavi, the head of COSATU, South Africa's powerful and political federation of trade unions, said Kunene's antics amounted to "spitting in the face of the poor." Countering that his success showcased South Africa's embrace of democracy, Kunene fired back at Vavi, who is also black: "You remind me of what it felt like to live under apartheid. You are telling me, a black man, what I can and cannot do with my life." Kunene's affiliation with Julius Malema and the Youth League led the ANC's general secretary to insist that the political party was not into nightclubs or partying but was, rather, a revolutionary movement, adding, "We furthermore reiterate our condemnation to the act of serving sushi on a woman's body."

Kunene swore off any further sushi parties but could not resist noting the multiracial aspect of his actions: "I ate sushi off a black girl in Johannesburg. In Cape Town, I ate it off a white girl. I was intending to eat it off an Indian girl in Durban." He also insisted that he was not sexist, that he respects women and was only trying to create jobs for these particular women, who worked as models.

Sushi parties with women as serving tables are an extreme example, but the spirit of that excess spreads beyond wealthy enclaves such as Sandton and Camps Bay. Now BMWs and Mercedes-Benzes make their way into townships such as Soweto and even Gugulethu, where parties at Mzoli's run late into the weekend nights. In the City Bowl, Long Street lies at the center of Cape Town's nightlife, where restaurants, bars, and nightclubs attract a multiracial clientele. "It raises in such wonderfully stark terms what freedom is and what one does with it," South African author Jonny Steinberg said in the *New York Times*. "The idea that one uses it to get rich, and ostentatiously so, and that this is the most important dividend of freedom, is very powerful."

Democracy earned every South African the right to pursue happiness and prosperity equally, in theory. In reality, the extremes are more sharply defined now. The country is the third most unequal place on earth, after Comoros and Namibia, in the Gini Index ranking of distribution of family income. (For comparison's sake, the United States ranks fortieth most unequal, out of 140 countries worldwide.) Forty-seven percent of South Africans are impoverished, earning less than $43 a month. The number of people living on less than a dollar a day doubled from two million in 1994 to four million in 2006.

With liberation came a pressure not only to succeed but also to flaunt that success. Even J. L. Zwane Presbyterian Church is not immune to these material expectations. A few weeks after I arrived, the church held its annual fundraising Sunday. Most members of the congregation dressed in traditional Xhosa clothing for this five-hour service. Women wore cotton wrap dresses printed with geometric patterns in earth tones of brown and orange and cream, or they wore the primary colors of the South African flag. Girls mixed their clothing, wearing a modern cap-sleeved top paired with a traditional skirt that fell, uncharacteristically, below their knees. There was beautiful beaded jewelry around necks and arms and waists and heads. Most of the girls, and some of the women, had their faces painted in delicate patterns with white, green, and black colored clay. Small dots in an S-shaped swirl around their eyes and down along cheekbones looked like the tracks of a small bird.

Besides being a celebration of their Xhosa heritage, this day was intended for every member of the church to contribute financially to its building upkeep and ministries, as well as the work of the community center. Church members belong to different geographic zones within Gugulethu, and there is an

annual competition among zones to see who contributes the
most. Residents from each zone paraded in turn from the back
of the sanctuary forward, singing and dancing and waving ban-
ners in the air, to lay their offering on the altar. There was a
World Cup theme in 2010, so the incessant buzzing of vuvuzelas added to the commotion. In lieu of a sermon, Reverend
Xapile periodically interrupted the proceedings to give exhor-
tations in Xhosa and English. "If you cannot see far, you cannot go far," he told his parishioners. "We can't let the fact that
we were born in informal settlements bring us down." Church
elders tallied the offerings and announced the winning zone,
whose members got the right to claim a three-foot-high gold
cup trophy for the year. All told, the church raised R400,000
(about $34,000) that day.

J. L. Zwane has some church members who live comfortable
lives relative to those of Gugulethu's poorer residents. Reverend Xapile himself owns multiple homes—in Cape Town and
in Eastern Cape—and drives a late-model Volvo. The church
also has members who live on less than a dollar a day. I realize that giving back fosters a sense of community and brings
dignity to everyone, perhaps especially to those who can only
summon a few rands to drop into the offering plate. But something about the production of it all that day—the expectation
of coughing up as much as possible, and the competitive nature
of sacrificial giving to a church—made me squirm. It was hard
not to think of the Scripture passage where Jesus overturns the
moneychangers' tables outside the temple.

With the opportunities now before them, the girls of
Amazw'Entombi face the dilemma of how to define success for
themselves and their generation. Is success earning the right to
throw lavish parties and wear designer clothing? Is it a grand-

child able to build onto the family house, where a dozen or more people might be living, even if that means curtailing her education to get a job and bring in the money? Is it winning the giving trophy at church? Sharon, Gugu, Ntombi, and all the other girls are keenly aware that they are expected to have something to show—and to give—for being one of the Born Frees.

8

Do You Even Ask Yourself Who Is She?

Mother's Day in South Africa falls on the same Sunday in May as the American holiday and brings the same level of praise, attention, and honoring of mothers. While the season outside is busy turning autumnal, pastels bloom in the shopping malls in a meadow of maternal appreciation. Stores run specials on greeting cards, bouquets of flowers, balloons, perfume, chocolates. At Amazw'Entombi, in keeping with our devotion to writing and our enjoyment of snacking, we decided to celebrate the women at J. L. Zwane Presbyterian Church with words and sweets.

We spent the Saturday session before Mother's Day writing out slips of colored paper with a few lines of verse or a quote—one of the girls' own, or drawn from something I'd brought along. "A mother is strong as a diamond." "Our teachers, our leaders, our feeders, our mothers." "Mothers sometimes leave us too soon, but they remain with us forever."

We used words from Sindiwe Magona, a renowned and elegant writer who once lived in Gugulethu, from her poem "Motherhood":

> In calm and in storm—unbowed,
> Tall she stands. Afrika's Beacon
> Motherhood is her name.

I bought packages of chocolates and hard candies for the girls to hand out with the slips of paper as women arrived at church on Sunday. I made a point to tell the girls to distribute the tokens to all women, whether or not they were mothers. This would be Amazw'Entombi's debut at J. L. Zwane.

Mother's Day arrived in a cold, steady rain, a preview of the wet Cape Town winter to come. The congregation size shrank noticeably whenever it rained on a Sunday, as so many traveled on foot through Gugulethu to church. Parishioners who braved the elements this day came layered in anything warm, keeping on their coats, scarves, and woolen hats. Reverend Xapile was away in Eastern Cape and Mel preached, one of her last Sundays before she was to return home to the States.

When I arrived, I saw Johanna, hugged her, and wished her a happy Mother's Day. "So people stayed home even though it's Mother's Day?" I asked.

"Oh, lovey," she said, "we're like sugar when it rains."

During the service, Ayanda and Gugu stood up at the podium and shared the task of introducing the writing club. Switching between Xhosa and English, they told the congregation how the club worked, about the freewriting we did each week, why we had handed out words along with candy this day. "Amazw'Entombi gives us a chance to get together and talk about our feelings, too," Gugu added. "I didn't know most of these girls when we started. Now I feel like I have many sisters."

After the girls finished speaking, a woman I did not know stood up in the sanctuary, went forward to the microphone, and spoke in English. "I want to say how much this means to me. I come to this church every week, for years. To walk in here and be handed a sweet and these words today. . . ." She pressed one flattened palm below her throat as she spoke. "I have no children. No one has ever done anything for me on this day. Thank you, girls."

A stab of recognition pierced me then, a moment before I heard another woman call my name and ask me to join her at the altar. On behalf of the women's guild, she said she wanted to thank me for my work with the girls. Then she presented me with a small paperback book of Bible reflections for women. It was nothing I expected. I imagined this was a gesture prepared in haste that morning when women of the church saw what the girls were doing, since they had not known of our plans in advance. After saying my thanks for the gift, I swallowed hard and prayed my voice wouldn't catch. I don't have children either, I told the congregation. But this day I felt like I had been blessed with many daughters. I thanked this community for sharing them with me.

As with Amazw'Entombi, Annasuena's attendance at orphans' group fluctuated. When I saw her there one week, she mentioned that the following evening was school night at her high school. Parents, guardians, and other family members were invited to visit the school.

"Is your aunt going with you to it?"

She scoffed loudly. "I told her about it and she said nothing. There's no way she'd come to it for free."

"So what happens at school night?"

"You go round to each of your classes and meet with the teacher. You're supposed to show up there to get your marks."

"Yeah, we have those back home. Parent–teacher conferences. I assume schools still have them. I've actually never been to one." I hesitated for a moment, then asked, "Could I go with you to school night?"

She grinned and gave me a look I'd come to know from Anna-suena, pleased but trying to be cool about it. *"Ja,* that's fine."

As with the places she lived, Annasuena's primary school-ing had been peripatetic. She began Grade 1 while staying with her mother in Johannesburg, at a good suburban school whose name she could not recall. By Grade 2, she was in Gugulethu with her uncle and aunt, attending Norma Road Primary School in Athlone, until her uncle withdrew her. With her mother's money after her death, her aunts who were her guardians enrolled her in semiprivate schools, Holy Cross and Sans Souci, until the money ran out. Then she had to return to the township schools.

The weather had warmed again and the evening air felt enjoy-ably balmy when I met up with Annasuena for school night. At Cathkin High School in Heideveld, the township adjacent to Gugulethu, graffiti marked up the backs of chairs and walls inside and outside the classrooms. We gathered first in a large room that served as an auditorium to hear from the principal. Annasuena and I took seats in the middle of the rows of chairs, most of them empty. By the time the principal began to speak, there were maybe forty or fifty parents or other adults pres-ent, a sparse assembly for a school attended by several hundred children.

The principal said classes at Cathkin were large, with forty to forty-five students in each. Matric classes were an exception. These had smaller numbers of students because so many had dropped out of school by Grade 12. He spoke of some of the challenges the school's students faced. Most read at a level two to three years behind their grade, so the school had instituted a peer-to-peer reading program. He also encouraged parents to make reading a priority in the home, sharing the activity with their children. "Because language is the foundation of learning," he said.

Given that this was high school, I had trouble imagining teenage students staying home to read aloud with their parents. Maybe these parents would absorb his words for their younger children. Maybe the students present, like Annasuena, would take his words to heart and read more on their own. But the learners present didn't look like they were paying much attention to the principal's talk, only waiting to be released so they could collect their grades.

Several organizations worked with Cathkin to provide AIDS testing, psychological counseling, social-work services, and parenting classes for learners who were already mothers and fathers. "Have you ever checked out any of the counseling sessions?" I whispered to Annasuena. She wrinkled her nose and shook her head. "Why not?" I asked.

A shrug and another shake, this one disgusted. "I don't want these people knowing my business. Too many people know already."

The principal also made a plea for students to wear proper uniforms. "Some learners are coming to class in the wrong clothes. I know these might not be your children. In one class of forty-two, we have only four who have their own mommy or their own daddy at home. But please make sure the child you are responsible for is dressed properly for school."

After the principal's presentation, we stood in a queue to pick up Annasuena's report card before visiting her teachers. She tapped her fingers nervously against her thigh as we waited. When it was our turn, she inhaled sharply and puffed her cheeks out before she opened the folded paper and took a look.

I needed her explanation to see that her grades, overall, were quite good. She received her highest grade in English, 77 percent (Code 6, Meritorious Achievement, equivalent to a B+). She had similar grades in Business, Technology, Arts and Culture, and Life Orientation. For Social Science and Natural Science, she received Codes of 4 (50–59 percent, Adequate Achievement), and she struggled with Afrikaans and Mathematics (Codes 3 and 2, the latter a failing grade).

Two of her teachers were not present for the school night, but the teachers who were there complimented her abilities and hard work. Her English teacher in particular, Mr. Makonda, said she was quite clever and had caught up with the work quickly, despite starting school more than a month behind the other students. I told him I was not surprised by her success in English.

"She's a poet, a really good one." I glanced over in time to see Annasuena roll her eyes and smile, pride and embarrassment once again sharing space in her expression. "Well, you *are*," I said.

After we'd walked out of the classroom, I turned to her. "I just became my mother and bragged about you while you were standing right there. I'm sorry!" She laughed and threw an arm over my shoulder. I gave her a hug and told her I was proud of her.

"So, speaking of poetry . . . ," I began.

"*Ja?*"

"I think you need to lead Amazw'Entombi in a poetry writing session."

"Really?" She seemed shocked at the suggestion. "Why?"

"Because I don't know how to write poetry, and you do. And now some of you girls are going to lead the group sessions. Sharon's already started. You don't want to hear only from me every week."

She said nothing but raised her eyebrows and glanced sideways at me.

"So will you do it?"

Now she answered without hesitation. "Yes. I will. "

Walking back out to my car, we danced a little, to celebrate her marks. Annasuena held her hand against her mouth to stifle a laugh as I tried to make my rhythmless arms and feet move fluidly, to mimic motions that came to her so effortlessly.

"*Yhuu*, you need some new moves."

"Girl, I need a *lot* of new moves."

We ended the day, and my first-ever parent–teacher conference, bopping to music in the car and sipping cooldrinks.

Poetry suited Annasuena's talents and temperament. From her mother she possessed an inherent musicality, a feel for the rhythm of words and the dance they can create together within a sentence. She also felt emotions on a grand scale that prose, for her, could rarely capture. When the Saturday arrived for her to lead Amazw'Entombi, she surprised me by preparing as well as Sharon had for her day of leadership. She unfolded a piece of paper, shuffled back and forth on her feet a few times, then cleared her throat with an uncharacteristic nervousness before she spoke.

"I wrote down some notes about what poetry is, so I'll start there. Poetry is expressing yourself, using feelings you can imagine and feelings you have experienced yourself. Poetry is a form of art. When you're holding the stick with ink and the piece of paper, the impossible can simply become possible. Poetry has a freedom of speech. It has no rules and regulations. It's a form of exaggeration, inspiration, realization. It's a form of humanity, equality, prophecy. That's what poetry means to me."

"Was that a poem?" Mandlakazi asked. "What you just read? It rhymed like a poem."

"It wasn't supposed to be," said Annasuena, "but it *could* be a poem. But poetry doesn't have to rhyme. Everyone thinks that. That's what stops people from writing it. They get nervous about how it should sound."

"I think that's true," I said. "I love to read poetry, but the thought of writing it has always intimidated me."

"It does intimidate people, and it shouldn't!" Annasuena grew animated now, all signs of nerves evaporated. "Poetry is beautiful and it should be easy. Just write from your heart and you can write something that another person might read and say, 'I know how that feels.'" She shuffled her papers around and continued. "Now I'm going to read a poem I wrote a while ago. This one doesn't have a title, but I think you'll be able to tell what this is about."

Thulisa closed her eyes to take in the words. The room stilled and no one shifted in her seat as Annasuena read.

> *If only he were a breeze*
> *That passed me by every single day.*
> *A smile nurtured upon a face of a*
> *Newborn, always uncertain, but never cold.*
> *If only magic had a life in the night*
> *So that his existence would penetrate my blankets*

And sigh of pure breath would thrill against my skinned neck.
Only dreaming.
If only he were here.

His voice in song
A tune of a mimic bird. His gaze so strong,
A kiss of summer sun that cracks every dawn
To life each day.
His presence an epiphany worth repeating.
His unique mentality
A void that's reaping
Life so beautiful that nothing impossible exists.

For now I wish to hold him close
Tell him how he's a reflection of a rose.
See, fortune and fame may be a pillar in the day,
Yet I need a pillow every now and then.

Someone to love me more than I myself can.
Exhilarate the blues that have me webbed
Every Monday noon.
Not only take a dip with him in the sand
But also feel him between my hands.
Yet he's far away, across my physical borders
Of pure pleasure outside my temple of ecstasy.
His memory is still captivated in my mind.
His scent still penetrates my nostrils in my dreams.
His lips on mine like a good refined wine. A beautiful blend.
Love him more than my daily dose of soapies,
More than words connected with melodies put into strings
    of song.

*For he is the beginning of my dimension, the soul that captures
my attention,
A few things that I'd like to mention, like the tilt of his head,
the plumpness
Of his nipples, the taste of his lips beyond the kiss of his
breathtaking breath.
I never knew a love like this existed, never knew that absence
does make the heart
Grow fonder.
If only he were here
To keep me under his wings of love,
To only dream.*

"*Yhuu*, I guess we do know what that's about," Sharon said
to a mixture of applause and appreciative whoops. Annasuena
covered her face with the paper for a brief moment. I didn't
realize she could be embarrassed.

"*Ja*, okay, so this is about being in love and missing someone
you can't be with any longer. But do you see? It's just words and
feelings put together."

"There were some beautiful images in there, too," I said. "It's
a well-written poem."

"Thank you. So now you all write. Don't worry about rules.
We have enough rules everywhere. Just write." She offered four
prompts the girls could use to spur their own poetry.

"Who am I?"

"Proudly South African."

"Missing someone."

And "State of Mind," the title from another earlier poem
Annasuena had written.

"Or if you have another idea, go with it," she said. We gave

ourselves half an hour to write. Usually we all stayed sitting
in the circle as we wrote. This time, Ntombi moved away to a
corner of the room to sit alone. Sharon sat sideways in a chair
with her short legs stretched out across another one. Thulisa
sprawled on the floor, stomach down, and perched on her
elbows, pencil hovering above her notebook.

When we came back together to read, pairs of eyes reflex-
ively turned toward Sharon. She sighed loudly and said, "Fine.
But next week, I'm not going to be the one who starts." She
began to read and Annasuena interrupted her.

"Come stand up in front of the circle. That's how poetry
should be read out to an audience."

"What? We're all going to have to stand up?" Mandlakazi's
jaw went slack.

"You need to be able to move and gesture when you read
poetry," said Annasuena, extending one arm in demonstration.

Sharon said, "I'm not gesturing now. I'm just reading." She
began again. "This is called 'Proudly South African.'"

It's a long story, a very long one.
It's a truly great story
One which speaks of pain, suffering, hope, joy, freedom, growth,
New beginnings, a new dawn, a new day, democracy.
It is my history, my present, my future, my dreams and the
Legacy which will live on.
It is the story of South Africa.

Proudly South African.
What a statement!
True and real in every essence of the word.
The motherland where ancestral roots are buried,

Where history was made as a legend once again roamed free
To right what had been wronged.
Where heroes are made
Where green pastures lay, vast lands lie,
Blue seas and blue skies, skyscrapers, wildlife, the list is
    endless.
Where diversity is celebrated
And unique is embraced.
Where love can be seen with the naked eye.

We have come very far from the days of oppression
To hosting a World Cup.
I can officially stand up and scream
Proudly South African!
A place where the mistakes and errors of yesterday
Are not forgotten but corrected.
South Africa is the place where everyone wants to be.

Africa is the heart and soul of the world.
We have culture, history, diversity,
Ubuntu, wisdom, and, most importantly, freedom.

South Africa is the place where my grandmother came from,
My mom grew up, and where I will rest.
It is the place of many things and many things will come
    from it.
I believe South Africa has a great future
And will go places with its people.
We define what South Africa is and what it will become,
It is our home, our place of dwelling and being.
So let's stand up and proudly be South African,

Actually scream it,
PROUDLY SOUTH AFRICAN!

She might not have gestured, but her voice swelled as she read, and she whipped up a patriotic response in her audience. Sharon's reading set the right tone for a day of poetry.

Thulisa volunteered to go next. She was sixteen and serious. Like Annasuena, she'd told me the first time I met her that she was a writer and happy to discover Amazw'Entombi. She stood before us and read in a sure voice, "This is called, 'Who Am I?'"

> *This is who I am.*
> *I don't need to introduce myself,*
> *Cause it's clear who I am.*
> *Question is,*
> *Who do you see when you look at me?*
> *Do you see just a petite girl living*
> *In a township called Gugulethu?*
> *Do you even ask yourself who is she?*
> *Or do you then reply to yourself and say,*
> *She is just an ordinary person?*
> *What do you see?*
> *I am a fighter, a leader,*
> *A born achiever.*
> *I walk and wave*
> *With pride and confidence of knowing*
> *Where I come from and where I am going.*
> *Take a look at me.*
> *This is who I am.*
> *And I am proud to be who I am.*
> *Don't come and change me.*

"I think everyone's going to be very good at this exercise," I said.

"That's what I mean!" Annasuena exclaimed. "Everyone can be a poet. We're all poets!" She swept around the circle with a wave of one arm.

Ntombi was not as eager to read as she had been the previous couple of weeks. She seemed more subdued this day than she had since the beginning of the club. But she too stood up before the circle, holding her notebook so high that it obscured half of her face. "My poem is called 'State of Mind.'"

> *I took a tour of*
> *The mind as I*
> *Was suppressed by*
> *The emotions of grief,*
> *But I found only myself*
> *There.*
>
> *The pain and the loneliness*
> *Were much too much to ignore*
> *And I was held hostage*
> *By this part of my adventure.*
> *I cried and I screamed to*
> *Be released, but I was*
> *The only one who could*
> *Set myself free.*
>
> *But if only I was prepared*
> *By those who gave birth to me,*
> *The end would have been*
> *Much easier*
> *For me to accept.*

I seeked refuge in
The tales of this world
Written by those
With free spirits, but
Every time I held my
Crown to rest
This mind from desire
Of death, it was another
Battlefield between
Me, myself, and I.

Today I'm screaming
Because I am free
From the control of my mind.
I realized that the whole of me,
Which is the heart and soul and spirit,
And also my mind, can reach
That which is me.

She sat down quickly when she had finished and looked toward the floor, trying to ignore the recognition and respect coming back to her from everyone else. Something was going on with Ntombi, and I hoped for a chance to speak with her after the club session was over.

Mandlakazi shrank down into her seat a little more after each girl read. Finally, Annasuena called her out. Convinced she might have been overlooked, she thumped her notebook against her thighs before standing up slowly and moving forward. In a soft voice, she read her poem, "Missing."

I miss you.
I miss the talks we had,
The walks we had,
The laughter that we shared,
The bad and the good times we had.
Sometimes I worked on your nerves
And you worked on mine too.
I miss the goals that we worked towards.
The day you said you want to see me
Driving my own car.
I miss the fact that I never understood you
And you never understood me,
But we had a good relationship.
I miss every moment that we shared together
Because I didn't know that life would be so short.
I miss you, Daddy.

Like Ntombi, Mandlakazi sat down quickly once she had finished, but she also allowed herself a small smile of satisfaction at her courage.

Annasuena praised all the newfound poets and told them she hoped they would continue to write poetry, in Amazw'Entombi and on their own. "When I can write, it really helps to clear my head to all the thoughts running through it. Sometimes it even helps me to understand what I'm thinking and how I'm feeling, when I couldn't really know that before."

When we'd finished and were collecting notebooks and pencils, I congratulated Annasuena and told her she made a good teacher. Then I looked around to find Ntombi so I could speak with her, but she had already left the room without saying good-bye.

As some of the girls had a natural affinity for poetry, many young South Africans I met loved drama and skits as both entertainment and education, a reflection of African cultures steeped in oral storytelling. Some of the younger girls from Amazw'Entombi attended a drama and music event at J. L. Zwane produced by YouthAIDS, an HIV-prevention program through the Society for Family Health, which conducts peer-to-peer education to encourage behavior change among young people. YouthAIDS brought along a DJ and a robust sound system to throw a small dance party. I watched one of Portia's cousins, Nompumelelo, dance alone into the center of a large circle. She was a quiet girl, maybe sixteen, not a talker at all, and she struggled to write as well. Several of the girls in Amazw'Entombi had deficient literacy skills in their written English, but the club wasn't meant to focus on that. I tried to praise anyone who kept coming back. For months I had only been able to exchange a few words with Nompumelelo one-on-one, and I assumed she was quite shy. She surprised me now when she reveled in the attention of a crowd, shook her narrow hips, and dipped low to the ground while the DJ and her peers urged her on.

For the drama staged in the sanctuary, I took a seat in the audience with the kids, next to a girl I didn't know, who was probably around thirteen years old. The "actors," YouthAIDS staff and volunteers, spoke a mixture of English and Xhosa. I asked the girl to explain the story setup for me at the beginning, and then I periodically asked her questions as it went along.

When "Desi," a teenage girl, told her aunt that she was a lesbian, the aunt kicked her out of the house. As word spread through the community about Desi, others began to shun her as well. She dropped out of school and lived on the street. The actress played the girl with shoulders slumped in defeat and feet that shuffled across the stage.

A boy came up behind her, shouting and waving one arm as she crouched low to the ground. Then he drew the other arm from behind his back, hand shaped into a gun, and pulled her behind a screen at the back of the stage. He came out alone a moment later, grinning and pretending to zip up his pants.

The audience laughed.

Desi crawled out from behind the screen, drew her legs up under her, and huddled on the floor until she lay down and fell asleep. Then a drunken man staggered onstage, his wife chasing after him, complaining loudly that she wanted him back at home. When the wife gave up and exited, the drunk saw Desi. He wiggled his eyebrows at the audience, a gesture that elicited more and louder laughter. He dragged Desi back behind the screen and then emerged, smiling and zipping, to further audience laughter.

Desi walked back out onstage again, running her hands over her arms as if to warm herself. The drunk was still there. "*Eish*, girl, what are you worried about? Lesbians can't get pregnant!"

Desi walked behind the screen and emerged on the other side, to denote the passage of time. She carried a bundle in her arms, a doll wrapped in a blanket. The drunk's eyes grew wide and his jaw dropped. By now the audience was howling. His wife returned to fetch him, saw the baby, and said to Desi, "He did you a favor! Now you're a real woman."

Now Desi was HIV positive, homeless, with a child, yet somehow this girl found the determination to stand up for herself when no one else would. She reported the rapes to the police. An officer rushed onto the stage and arrested the drunk;

another appeared with the first rapist. Both were carted off
as they protested their innocence. Desi straightened her back,
stood taller, and returned to school. She finished Matric, graduated, and announced to the audience that she was proud of who
she was. People would not change her, and she would accept her
child no matter what, just as she herself longed to be accepted.
During this final speech, the kids had finally grown quiet. No
more laughter.

When the show ended, the audience applauded and I sat
there feeling ill. I thought I must have missed some vital piece
of information. I turned to the girl next to me, my young inter-
preter, to make sure I understood.

"Tell me again what happened."

"She's a lesbian and she was raped and now she has a baby."
She summarized in one breath, grinning as she spoke.

"But why would everyone laugh at that?"

"I don't know," she said, shaking her head. Now her grin
turned to uncomfortable giggles.

I didn't know either. Talking about sex evokes embarrassment and discomfort in many, if not most, people. That youth
might respond to such talk with giggles and raucous laughter
would not be surprising, except for the implied violence in the
scenario they had witnessed. It felt as though this educational
drama was presented with a wink and a nod, a perfunctory
acknowledgment of the dangers women and girls faced every
day in Gugulethu and across South Africa. Maybe the aim
was simply to bring the subject up at all, to begin to help
young people grow comfortable hearing rape discussed publicly. That has not seemed to be a priority for the country up
to this point.

Of all the complexities and contradictions I have encountered about South Africa, the one that has perplexed me most is what the country's Medical Research Council (MRC) calls "a globally unprecedented problem of violence against women and girls," one that is "undermining [the] nation's health and economic and social development." It is also multiplying HIV and sexually transmitted infections, as well as creating or exacerbating post-traumatic stress disorder, depression, and suicide.

Reliable rape statistics are difficult to acquire. Doctors Without Borders has estimated a woman is raped every twenty-six seconds in South Africa, likely accounting for the vast number of unreported cases. A more conservative estimate is one rape every eleven minutes—48,060 rapes a year. More than half of women who are murdered are killed by their intimate partners, one every six hours. That is the highest rate in the world, the MRC found. In an anonymous MRC survey in 2009, one in four men admitted to having raped a woman; 46 percent of them said they had raped repeatedly. Nearly three-quarters—73 percent—of the admitted perpetrators said they carried out their first assault before the age of twenty.

Ignorance breeds violence. As shown with "Desi" in the YouthAIDS skit, lesbians are subjected to "corrective" rape in an attempt to change their sexual orientation. A myth perpetuates even today that sex with a virgin will cure AIDS. Girls, toddlers, even infants have been raped in pursuit of this "cure." But that's not the only driving force behind the sexual abuse of girls. The crime is hidden even further by girls' historically low social status in a hierarchical, patriarchal society. As, by tradition, men dominated women, likewise elders dominated children, leaving girls to occupy the lowest rung and wield the least power. An attitude persists that child sexual abuse is best dealt with, if at all, privately, especially within families. The police force and justice system often provide more obstacles than redress. According to Dr. Rachel Jewkes, an MRC specialist on sexual violence, "The prevalence of child rape in South Africa goes from really, really high to astronomically high."

There are various opinions on why South Africa has such a high level of violence in general, and against women and girls in particular. Poverty undoubtedly contributes. Again, from the MRC: "Poverty and unemployment are barriers to men and women accessing traditional sources of well being, status, and respect. Inequality in access to wealth and opportunity results in feelings of low self-esteem, which are channeled into anger and frustration, and violence is often used to gain the sought after respect and power, whether through robbery, rape, fighting between men, severe punishment of children, or violence against partners."

Certainly not only in South Africa but worldwide, gender-based violence has been seen for too many years as only a gender issue. I was speaking with a South African pastor who had been involved in the anti-apartheid movement and remains an ardent activist on a wide range of social-justice issues. This is someone who would, I think, comfortably call himself a feminist. I asked him what was being done in the churches about violence against women and girls. How were pastors addressing this scourge? He suggested I speak with women theologians in the seminary about that. When I countered that this was not a matter solely for the women to address, I received a testy response that there were *many* injustices remaining in the country. Pastors had to pick and choose. Well, I thought, they might want to pick one that threatens half of the country's population and harms fully everyone, victim and perpetrator alike. Especially since many women also use their personal faith as a coping mechanism for issues of violence in the home.

Thankfully, some are beginning to make those connections. The South African Faith and Family Institute (SAFFI) is a relatively new organization working on issues of gender-based violence from an interfaith perspective. SAFFI "recognizes that religion plays an integral part both in the continuation of violence against women and in its eradication. Thus SAFFI's main objective is to build the capacity of religious leaders and faith communities in addressing issues of gender-based violence in our communities and becoming a positive catalyst for change." The organization provides training for pastors and religious leaders to help ensure the safety and empowerment of survivors, to hold offenders accountable, and to challenge from a theological perspective patriarchal traditions and "other root causes of intimate partner abuse, which destroys the dignity of women, children, and men."

Patriarchy inflames gender-based violence. Although he was found not guilty of rape, South African President Jacob Zuma claimed at his 2006 trial that he had no choice, as a proud Zulu man, but to have sex with a woman because of the skirt she wore. Again, as in places around the world, South African men of every race are expected and socialized to see themselves as superior to women, and taught that to be a man is to be "tough, brave, strong, and respected" (MRC).

But even among South Africa's dismally tepid response to violence against women, I found a sign of hope in Sonke Gender Justice. This organization has become a leader in the burgeoning movement to tackle the violence where it generally originates—with men—working with them and with boys to challenge traditional concepts of masculinity and to prevent gender-based violence.

In Gugulethu, Sonke (pronounced SOHN-kay) brings together young men in a Youth Indaba, a Xhosa and Zulu word for a meeting to raise important issues. The boys gather at the biweekly *indaba* to discuss challenges they face living in Gugulethu. As with the girls in Amazw'Entombi, these male youth long to be heard, to have their opinions sought. Leaders in the *indaba* also want to see them modeling new behaviors, find ways to step away from violence in their community, and change their own attitudes toward the girls and women in their lives.

Sonke also focuses on the issue of male health through the One Man Can Men's Wellness Center, also based in Gugulethu. At this clinic, the work begins with creating a safe and judgment-free space where men and boys can discuss their health and emotional issues with male nurses and doctors. "[We] focus mainly on HIV and AIDS prevention and gender-based violence, with the initiative of being able to change men's behaviors so that they care more about their health and their partners," Nelisiwe Ohajunwa, a One Man Can trainer working in Gugulethu, told me. "In most cases, men are more open to talking about issues of violence [than of health]. The HIV follows into the conversation and that's where we come in with the link to gender-based violence and HIV. Because they are linked."

They certainly are. I saw that with Annasuena.

Like her mother, Annasuena had contracted HIV when she was raped. I had assumed this occurred when she was a teenager. But once, when we were alone together talking, she told me what had happened.

When Annasuena was seven or eight, she was living happily in Johannesburg with Anneline, Vuyisile, the man she called her stepfather, her elder brother Linden, and younger sister, Naledi. Then things changed, for no reason Annasuena could understand. Vuyisile took Naledi to Port Elizabeth, while Anneline sent Linden and Annasuena to Cape Town to live with her eldest brother and his wife in Gugulethu. Anneline never told her children why they were going away. Their aunt worked as a domestic for a family in the Southern Suburbs. As the eldest of Anneline's siblings, her uncle was considered head of the extended family. He did not work. Linden was in high school, Annasuena in Grade 2.

The aunt spent most nights sleeping at her employers' home. When she stayed the night in Gugs, she slept in a chair in the lounge. The children shared the home's only bed with their uncle, with Annasuena sleeping in the middle, between the older man and her brother. She was not used to an arrangement like this one. In Johannesburg, she had slept in her own bed, all alone.

It began the very first night, in the bed, after Linden fell asleep. Her uncle began to touch her. Annasuena was confused and frightened, as any little girl would be, especially in a new and strange home. She knew Vuyisile's hands as he washed her in the bath or tickled her when trying to make her laugh. That was a loving touch that made her feel safe. Now an old man's wrinkled hand roamed over her body in a way that forced her to hold her breath inside, to stop her flat chest from moving, to separate her mind from what was happening to her body. This occurred night after night.

She wondered whether Linden knew. Surely he felt the bed move and awoke during the night sometimes. Later, looking back, Annasuena thought he did know what their uncle was doing but felt too embarrassed to bring it up with her, and too powerless to confront their uncle, his elder. Her brother began to stay away from home many nights, leaving Annasuena alone with the man.

It didn't take long until he raped her. Maybe he knew he had the virus. Maybe he'd heard stories that sex with a virgin offered a cure. Maybe he violated this girl-child simply because he could. Annasuena told no one.

Her uncle began to keep her home from school many days. He locked her outside the house while he visited a *shebeen* to drink for a few hours. She played with any children she could find in the street, though most kids her age were in school. Then the uncle would come home, drunk, to take her inside. If she was not home then, she got a beating later when she returned. She thought her aunt knew what was going on. But her aunt disliked Anneline fiercely, and didn't like her children any better. She hit Annasuena sometimes, or pinched her hard enough to leave behind a bruise that yellowed her arm.

Annasuena couldn't remember whether there was any one particular incident that told her, *Enough*. But when she spoke on the phone to her mother, she told her she *must* live in Johannesburg—she would not live with her uncle any longer. She would live on the street instead, if she had to. So Anneline sent for her daughter, never asking why the child was so insistent.

Her uncle died when Annasuena was seventeen. She enraged her family by refusing to attend his funeral.

9

All These Thoughts in My Head and Heart

To me, writing is . . .

To me, writing is peaceful and allows the mind to venture into creation developed in the brain. I find calmness and a sense of myself when I write. I can put any word that fits my sentence. I can be free. I can feel any kind of emotion I want to go through. And I find that I am able to heal myself with my own words. There is energy transferred within the environment of my writing, which brings my inner being to the paper in front of me. I guess you can find me in my writing, especially those who think they know me.

—Ntombi

Ntombi grew up in a home filled with women. Her immediate family—mother Ncikazi, an older sister and brother, and younger brother—shared a house in Gugulethu with her grandmother, Ncikazi's twin sister, another sister, and their children, a dozen people in total in the family home. Ntombi and her sister had the same father; her brothers had different ones. Her father came from Ndevana, near East London in Eastern Cape. She met him a few times as a child but could only recall vague memories of him as she grew older. When Ntombi was around ten years old, the family heard that he had died, and several months later his wife also died.

A few years later, in 2005, Ncikazi called her four children together. She said she wanted to be the one to tell them, before they heard it from anyone else, that she was ill. She was HIV positive. As she told them this news, she began to cry. Ntombi and her siblings sat quietly, uncomfortably, unsure how to respond. They knew a little about AIDS, mostly that the disease almost always killed the people it struck. Family members suspected Ntombi's father and his wife had died as a result of AIDS as well. Now the children had no idea what to say to their mother, who had never before cried in front of them.

After Ncikazi's sisters learned her status, they isolated her and her children into one room of the house. They would not share the kitchen or the lounge, and the toilet only reluctantly. They brought in separate dishes for her and her family to use, forbidding her or her children to lay a hand on anything else used by other members of the family. The children were treated as though they were infected with HIV as well. As her illness progressed, Ntombi and her sister were their mother's primary caretakers. She rubbed her mother's feet to warm them and applied ointment to her sores each day after she came home from school, where she was finishing Grade 7.

Ncikazi died when Ntombi had just turned fourteen. After the way her aunts treated her mother while she was ill, she did not want to continue living with them, but she had no alternatives. Her closest sibling, her sister, was only three years older and still at school herself. Without a living parent or another place to go, the children had no choice but to remain living with their aunts. Like Annasuena, Olwethu, and Sive, like hundreds of thousands of orphans in South Africa, Ntombi was taken in by family members who saw to her physical needs, for the most part, yet offered her little in the way of parenting.

This was another, less-discussed casualty of the AIDS crisis. Mamphela Ramphele, former vice-chancellor at the University of Cape Town and a longtime social and political activist, wrote about this family dynamic in a 2002 book, *Steering by the Stars: Being Young in South Africa*, a study of children's lives in Nyanga, a township near Gugulethu. "Children were often partially adopted into an extended family, but not afforded the same level of resources offered to the 'real' family members. Although the adopting family accepted the presence of the child, it became hard pressed by the scarcity of resources, both emotional and financial. It was only natural that when it came to allocating scarce resources your own offspring would get priority. Doing the right thing was not easy."

It rarely is. Ntombi's aunts had their own children to raise, and now four more under their responsibility. They did get some assistance in terms of financial resources; for each of Ncikazi's children, they received a foster-child grant from the South African government, an amount currently at R830 (about $71) a month.

But Ntombi, a sensitive, intuitive girl, understood completely that her aunts resented her and her siblings' intrusion into their lives. She vowed to herself that she would be as inconspicuous as she could possibly be, needing or requesting nothing from her aunts beyond a roof over her head and food in her stomach. She spent her teenage years raising herself, and when she began to encounter difficulties at school, she told no one. Ntombi was extremely bright, articulate and opinionated in her writing and whenever she chose to speak. But she struggled through her years at Heideveld High School, an Afrikaans-speaking government school not far from Gugulethu. When she took her Matric exams, she failed to pass two difficult subjects, Mathematics and Physical Science.

As an outsider schooled in a different country, I've struggled to understand the complexities of the South African educational system, especially high school, the Matric certificate, and what these results mean for students' future study and work prospects. It is a situation plenty of learners and parents inside the country grapple with as well. Under the South African Schools Act of 1996, education is compulsory for all from the age of seven (Grade 1) to age fifteen, or the completion of Grade 9. Further Education and Training (FET) takes place from Grades 10 to 12 and can include vocational, career-oriented education offered at separate FET technical, community, and private colleges, leading to diploma and certificate qualifications for certain forms of employment. If a student is pursuing Matric, formally known as the National Senior Certificate (equivalent to a high school diploma and required for higher levels of postsecondary study), Grades 10 through 12 are considered senior secondary school.

In Grade 10, learners choose seven subjects to study over the next two years, leading to the nationally moderated Matriculation examinations at the end of Grade 12. Four subjects are compulsory: English; a secondary South African language (such as Xhosa or Afrikaans); Life Orientation, which encompasses nonacademic skills including career choices and work matters, health and physical education, religious education, social responsibility and citizenship; and either Mathematics or the less rigorous Mathematical Literacy. The remaining three courses are electives, chosen from a long list that includes Physical or Life

Science (Physics and Biology), Social Science (History, Economics, Geography), Business Studies, Arts, Hospitality, and Information Technology. High school culminates when learners "write Matric," taking exams at the end of Grade 12.

There are three possible results for passing Matric, with the minimum bar set staggeringly low. For a Higher Certificate Pass, students must receive a minimum of just 40 percent for three subjects, a minimum of 30 percent for three subjects, and can fail a seventh subject. With this result, a student can say she has passed Matric, but she does not qualify to pursue higher education at a university (or varsity, as South Africans call it) such as the University of Cape Town (UCT) or University of the Western Cape (UWC), or at a technical institution such as Cape Peninsula University of Technology (CPUT). Simply having a Matric certificate, however, is a requirement for many service jobs and on-the-job training programs. If a learner fails two or more subjects, a Matric certificate is not awarded. For a Diploma Pass, the required pass rates are 40 percent for four subjects and 30 percent for the other three, with no failing marks (anything less than 30 percent). This level allows for study at a technical university like CPUT, but not at UCT or UWC. The highest level, known as the Bachelor's Pass, requires a pass rate of at least 50 percent in four subjects and 30 percent in three; this can also be given with distinction for higher pass rates. Learners must receive a Bachelor's Pass in order to be considered for study at any tertiary institution in South Africa, along with meeting any additional prerequisites of the particular degree program, such as specific subjects studied.

Jonathan Jansen, a prominent education advocate, vice-chancellor of the University of the Free State, and newspaper columnist, calls the current system a "sinkhole of mediocrity" and argues that the minimum pass mark for all school subjects should be raised to 50 percent, "the (still admittedly low) standard set for academic work in most contexts." In one of his columns, he relates a story of a student who "demands" to study at his university. Her Statement of Results concludes with a phrase that Jansen says she, understandably, takes literally: "The candidate qualifies for the National Senior Certificate and fulfills the minimum requirements for admission to higher education." Her Matric results? Afrikaans 43, English 39, Mathematical Literacy 38, Life Orientation 78, Business Studies 41, Computer Applications Technology 31, Life Sciences 28. Jansen goes on: "With the young woman's claim to study I have no problem. With society that sets the bar for performance so low, I have serious problems. . . . Our society, schools, and universities have adjusted expectations downwards, especially in relation to black students, and that is dangerous in a country that holds so much promise for excellence."

President Zuma and Minister of Basic Education Angie Motshekga have boasted of the improving Matric pass rate in recent years. Results went from 62.6 percent passing Matric in 2008 to 73.9 percent in 2012. What this upward trend ignores, however, is the dropout rate that hovers above 50 percent for students who leave school long before they even make it to Grade 12. Jansen calls this a "culling process," in which 500,000 people a year are left behind with little or no proper education. He goes so far as to call the South African education system a "massive fraud."

In the rest of her Matric subjects, Ntombi's results were comparatively quite good: English, 57; Xhosa, 72; Life Orientation, 60; Geography, 55; Life Science, 47. Then the two that held her back: Mathematics, 26; Physical Science, 23. She was not alone in receiving these unsatisfactory results. In the 2014 World Economic Forum (WEF) country rankings for the Global Competitive Index, South Africa's mathematics and science education came in dead last, 148 out of 148 countries. For overall quality of the education system, progress was minuscule: 146 out of 148. Not surprisingly, an "inadequately educated workforce" topped the list of most problematic factors for doing business in South Africa in the WEF index.

Education spending receives the largest share of South Africa's annual budget, at 20 percent. Yet there remain deeply rooted inequalities between black township schools, which still fail the majority of South Africa's children, and suburban, formerly all-white schools, where students are far more likely to succeed. Most teachers today received their training under the inferior educational system during apartheid, and their own knowledge of the subjects they teach is strikingly lacking. Yet not all shortcomings can be blamed on apartheid. Absenteeism is high among students but also among teachers, school administrators, and principals. Sometimes teachers can be in the school building and simply not report for class. Learners complain of having to teach themselves or choosing one among them to lead the class when a teacher fails to show up. Some teachers fear the violence that occasionally erupts in township schools and stay away because of that. A powerful trade union, SA Democratic Teachers Union (SADTU), protects teachers' interests—at the expense of the students, according to some critics. Strikes are common, for wage increases but also for political reasons. In late 2010, just weeks before Matric and end-of-year exams, schools closed for twenty days when teachers, nurses, and other state workers went on strike to demand higher wages and housing allowances. There are infrastructure and administrative failures, too. Textbooks are sometimes not delivered to schools until halfway through the year.

Sharon, Mandlakazi, and Gugu all had a parent willing to seek out the best school environment for their girls and to struggle financially to send them there. As an orphan being raised by aunts who were, at best, indifferent to her education, Ntombi lacked guidance and resources in pursuing her education. Still, she was not in the majority of township learners; she did not drop out of school before Matric. Her drive and determination served her when her guardians did not. She hoped to study communications at nearby UWC, a dream that would elude her until she passed her two most challenging subjects. With no school or job to attend, she was left to her own devices, using old textbooks and library books to try to teach herself everything about mathematics and science that she didn't learn the first time round, so she could retake those Matric exams.

One Saturday, Ntombi missed Amazw'Entombi, a rare occurrence for her. When she returned the following week, we all knew something was wrong. She appeared to have aged twenty years in two weeks. Shadows darkened her eyes, which looked hollow and dull. Where large, colorful earrings normally dangled and spun, her earlobes were now bare. Even the girly turquoise T-shirt she wore, printed with a grinning Minnie Mouse playing a pink guitar and wearing a pink flower behind one ear, seemed designed to mock her mood. This day's gathering was the smallest one yet, with only Sharon, Mandlakazi, Ntombi, and Annasuena. Once we had shrunk the circle down and taken our seats, Ntombi told us her news. She had received the results of her Matric exam retakes, and she did not pass. She had no idea what she would, or could, do next with her life.

She couldn't face anyone. Instead, during the week, she had taken a taxi into town and visited the Cape Town Public Library. She checked out seven books, the maximum number allowed—all novels, romances and mysteries. Then she returned home, crawled into bed, began to read, and stayed there for two weeks. Ntombi was eighteen years old, with no school to attend, no job prospects, and nowhere to go each day. Her only responsibility was a house her aunts expected her to clean, duties that always fell to the family's girl-child. Reading helped her disappear from her own life.

Her sister came home and saw the pile of books beside the bed they shared. "What's wrong with you?" she asked. "You're in a relationship with books! Go make friends. Get out of the house." Ntombi could not bear to tell her about the Matric results.

"I don't want to make friends!" she declared to the four of us sitting in the circle. "It was hard enough coming here today, and you're already my friends."

"Can you retake the exams again?" I asked. "Or was this it?"

"I can, but not until next year. But why bother? I can't pass. Why put myself through that again?"

"You don't know you won't pass," Sharon insisted. "Wait and see how you feel later. Don't decide anything now."

"You can't always know what you're capable of doing. I come through the best when life treats me like shit." Annasuena looked over toward me as though she suddenly remembered my presence in the room. "Sorry for the curse."

"Hey, that's when you need to be your strongest, when life treats you like shit. But don't repeat those words of wisdom to *umfundisi*," I said, drawing snickers from Annasuena, Mandlakazi, and Sharon. Ntombi did not crack a smile. "Did you try writing about how you were feeling?"

"I couldn't even do that. I didn't want to do anything," she said. "I didn't want to think. I still don't. If I can get the taxi fare, I'm going back to the library and getting more books and going back to bed and staying there."

"What you're describing," I ventured gently, "staying in bed and hiding out, that sounds like depression." Sharon and Anna-suena both nodded.

"I know it is!" Ntombi said with exasperation. "I know what depression is. I know it, but . . ."

She clamped her mouth shut and shook her head. Her dark eyes glinted with pooled tears. Ntombi had told me once how much she hated to cry in front of anyone. We sat in silence, waiting for her cue, if she wanted to continue this conversation. After a moment, she simply shrugged her shoulders and set her mouth in the way she did when she was finished with talking.

"Well, I'm glad you came here today," I said. She stared down at her hands clasped together in her lap and dipped her chin to her chest in the smallest of nods.

For the writing session, I offered the girls two options and let them choose the one they wanted to use as a prompt. Given the tone of the day, the first choice was a single word: frustration. What frustrates you, and how do you cope with feeling frustrated? I had brought along a paperback thesaurus that I'd picked up in the charity secondhand bookstore attached to St. George's Cathedral in the City Bowl. Its pages were yellowed and smelled like a musty cellar. I passed it to Mandlakazi and asked her to read aloud the synonyms for frustration. She thumbed through the pages a moment before reading in a low voice.

"Irritation. Agitated. Depressed. Angry. Vexation. Disappointment. Dissatisfaction. Stressed. Aggravation."

When she finished, she immediately closed the book and handed it back to me, as though she didn't want to be in possession of such forceful words any longer. Or, if they'd rather not focus on their frustration, I told the girls they could finish this sentence: "I wish I could . . ." We wrote for twenty minutes, and then Annasuena volunteered to read aloud first.

A big disappointment that I have experienced lately, my best friend has relapsed on drugs and another friend has betrayed my trust in her. It's something I never expected to happen. The moment has filled me with anger, resentment, and also feeling confused. I don't know what to do with all these thoughts in my head and heart. I was hoping this month could be a great month where I would just be focusing on school and these exams so I could get an achieving mark at the end of this term. I also felt very lonely and depressed in this week. It's like I'm suffocating in all the mixed up feelings I have. My boyfriend is another person who is also pressuring me to be with him. He irritates me!

"Sounds like you're dealing with some stuff as well," I said.

"*Ja*, I am." She shook her head, rolled her eyes, and shrugged one shoulder in something between disgust and resignation.

"Anything we could do to help?"

"No, I just need to figure things out for myself right now."

Sharon read next.

I was told to write anything on frustration or a time in my life where I felt that feeling. But I just couldn't bring myself to do it. It's not that I haven't felt frustrated, angry, disappointed, or vexed. It's just that the one time I felt all those feelings I felt more than frustration. And it's not easy going back to a place where you fought so long to get out of. My fear is that after moving out of that hate space I had for those people and forgiving them, I just might end up back there. That time in my life was my lowest point thus far, in my whole life, and it took—actually it still is taking—a while to heal. Wow, now I'm getting frustrated cause the time [to write] hasn't ended but my words seem to have disappeared. It's ironic. I started writing about how I can't bring myself to write about frustration yet here I am, pen in hand, and STILL writing, now about the frustration of running out of words. Yep. Ironic.

"So you didn't want to write about frustration, yet you still chose that prompt. Interesting." I stretched the word out in an exaggeratedly intrigued voice and she chuckled.

"*Ja.* I didn't think I would. I just started writing and it came out. It's hard. To think about these things takes you back to a place you don't want to be."

"Do you think you're the same person you were when you were in that hate space? I like that phrase, by the way."

"No, I'm not the same. I know I'm not. But it feels like you can lose the progress you've made so easily, hey?"

"Do you think you have any choice in that? Whether or not you regress to be in that space again?"

"I think you have some," Sharon said. "A lot, probably."

"But," Annasuena broke in, "it depends on what people are putting you through at the moment too, yeah?"

"What can you do about those people putting you through stuff?" I asked.

"*Yhuu!* Stay far, far away from them," Sharon said.

"But you can't always." Annasuena moved forward to perch on the edge of her seat as she pressed her point. "Not if you care about them."

"Don't you have to balance caring about other people with caring about yourself?" I asked.

"Of course you do. But if these are the people you have in your life, and everyone needs someone in their life to be there for them, at least most of the time . . ." She trailed off then. It would be difficult to advise Annasuena to ditch her best friend and her boyfriend and other people who have disappointed her and who hold her back, when so many people in her life have been lost without her consent. This girl knows she has it within herself to be independent and self-sufficient, and still, like almost every one of us, she craves relationships, even an unsound and ill-advised one.

"Ntombi? Don't tell Sharon, but I'm giving you a choice to read or not today."

"I'll read," she murmured. "But I didn't write much this time." I leaned toward her, thinking she would revert to her quietest tone, but her voice intensified as she spoke.

Last week would have started like any other week for somebody else, but mine was totally frustrating. A person might wonder if something happened to make me that frustrated. But the issue is that nothing happened. It isn't about my Matric results. I guess all the feelings and disappointments, of not being at school and not having anything to do for the past months, decided to come back and hit me really hard in my emotions. It's hard for some people to understand when I'm trying to explain to them how I feel emotionally worn out.

She puffed her cheeks with air and blew it out when she was through. Usually we all clapped when one girl finished reading, but this day instead brought exchanges of empathetic smiles and quiet expressions of solidarity.

"Mandlakazi, it's come down to you," I said to the youngest girl. "Tell us your frustrations."

"I chose the other prompt, actually."

"Good for you! Let's hear it."

Like Ntombi, she was growing increasingly confident in reading her words aloud. Today, in particular, she seemed to reach for the rhythm in her sentences.

I wish I could get out of my comfort zone. I wish I could be as adventurous as George of the Jungle. I wish I could turn my weaknesses into strengths. I wish I could conquer my fears. I wish I could be more focused in whatever I do. I wish I could fly like a bird and be as bright as a jackal. I wish I could be as tall as a giraffe. I wish I could dance like Beyoncé. I wish I could be as courageous as Kimberly. And most of all I wish I could be as loving, kind, and caring as God.

"I wish I could dance like Beyoncé, too," I said. "Annasuena will tell you I can't dance."

Annasuena laughed her guttural *kee-hee-hee* and said, "It's true! She really can't."

"Mandlakazi, you used some beautiful images in there," I told her. "Birds and jackals and giraffes. I love it."

"Thank you." I really loved to watch these girls grow more comfortable receiving praise.

After our writing session, Mandlakazi and Sharon both had to leave straightaway, but Annasuena and Ntombi lingered, talking and stacking away the chairs to clean up the classroom. Annasuena seemed to be trying to offer encouragement to Ntombi. I asked the girls whether they'd like a ride home, with maybe a side trip to KFC to grab an early dinner. Annasuena agreed at once, with the girlish grin she always gave at the prospect of an unexpected outing. I thought Ntombi might decline, but she said okay in her quiet, raspy voice, with the first glimpse of a smile I had seen from her all day.

Months into my time in South Africa, seeing Colonel Sanders's face hovering alongside NY 1 at the Gugulethu Square Shopping Center still jolted me, a strange cameo appearance from America. KFC was the kind of treat for the girls that I could afford on my Fulbright stipend. When it came to our turn to order, they grew reticent and insisted I choose for all three of us. So we ate chicken twister sandwich wraps and chips, washed down with Fanta Orange sodas for them and a Coke Light for me. Annasuena and Ntombi had attended different schools and had not known one another before Amazw'Entombi. Sitting across from the two of them now, I realized the parallels in the lives they both had led. Each girl had lost her mother to AIDS. Each had been taken in by aunts who seemed lukewarm, at best, at the prospect of raising them to adulthood. These two had firm notions about why they had been welcomed into the homes where they now lived.

"It's only for the grant!" Ntombi railed, referring to the monthly foster-child grant. "My aunt gets our grant money every month, and my father's pension as well. But we never see the money. I still have to go to her to ask for money, if I need anything at all. She looks at me like I'm trying to rob her! This was money from my father. Why can't it come directly to me and to my sister?"

As she ate, Annasuena nodded continually at everything Ntombi said. "That's what they do. Do they tell you you're just like your mother as well?"

"Yes!" Ntombi nearly rose up out of her seat with the explosion of that one-word response. It was good to see her animated rather than numb, even if it took indignation at her family. The two girls heard similar complaints from their aunts. You speak out. You talk back. You mope about and work on everyone's nerves. You run around too much. You have too many friends. You're just like your mother. And—implied always, sometimes spoken out loud—you'll end up just like your mother as well.

"I tell them it's a good inheritance she left me then, to speak up for myself." Annasuena shoved another chip into her mouth. She always had a retort at the ready.

Soon the girls grew quieter, less outraged. Annasuena said she tries to forgive her family and people who have done wrong by her. "Because if you don't, it just hurts you. You keep reliving it."

Ntombi sat for a moment, absently running one finger along the side of the tray that held her food. Then she furrowed her smooth brow and said in a soft voice, "But do you know the phrase, 'I can forgive, but I can't forget?' That's how I feel some days. *Most* days. I can't forget. I won't. Not the way they treated my mother, or the way they've treated me." She narrowed her eyes and pressed her lips together, mouth set once again in the same resolute line.

I dropped Annasuena off at Phelo's house, then drove Ntombi to her home. When we pulled up in front of the house, she sat with her eyes fixed on the passenger-side window, staring into the growing twilight. She seemed reluctant to leave the car, and I turned off the engine and sat quietly with her. Then she told me about the aspirin and sleeping pills she swallowed, more than once, when she was fifteen, after her mother's death. She had always been found by a family member and made to vomit them up. She was never taken to hospital, never met with a counselor. No one spoke about her suicide attempts and she didn't either.

"Does depression ever go away?"

Ntombi finally looked at me when she asked this question, her large, lovely eyes shining. I hesitated for a moment that stretched out too long, wishing desperately I had had training as a counselor. With my expertise, I could only rattle off to her facts I knew from the few studies conducted about mental health and South Africa's orphans. That young people living without their mother are more likely to be depressed. That witnessing a parent's lingering illness and death firsthand, coupled with the associated stigma of AIDS, the insecurity of a child's living situation, and pervasive poverty can all contribute to experiences of post-traumatic stress disorder. That girls are more likely to internalize their problems with feelings of anxiety, stress, and depression. That she was not alone in her struggles. None of that addressed what she was asking me now, though, and I knew better than to offer any false hopes to this perceptive girl.

Depression has plagued me, too, and people I love, and I know the stranglehold it can wield over a life. I know depression lies—about the present and the future, about joy, about what a person is capable of coping with and surviving. I know that it is nearly impossible to see through those lies when you are in the abyss. How in the world could I walk with this young woman through that darkness? The only wisdom I could offer was what I was still trying to learn myself.

"I think, if you're prone to depression, then it's something you'll have at different times throughout your life. But I think you get stronger and you learn what you need to do to take care of yourself." I offered that up with a small shrug and a sigh, know-

ing how completely insufficient the words felt to me, how hollow
they must ring to her. Ntombi nodded and even braved a smile.
She leaned over to kiss my cheek before getting out of the car.

"Be careful leaving Gugs," she said as she closed the door.

Nightfall approached quickly as I drove out of the township.
People walked along the sidewalks headed to the relative safety
of their homes. Ramshackle cars hooted and swerved around
me. Several pulled up and stopped abruptly alongside the pave-
ment to collect passengers. These were unlicensed taxis, with
loose bumpers, banged-in doors, and drivers who maneuvered
as though they had nothing to lose. They might not be safe, but
they saved tired feet and arms from a long walk carrying bags of
groceries from the Spar supermarket at the mall. *Iphela*, people
called these taxis. Cockroaches. They lurched away from the
curb and drove deeper into the darkness.

To me, writing is . . .

*To me, writing is about finding my inner self and expressing my
views and opinions on how I see and react to things. Writing is a
therapy for me, because of acknowledging my visions and dreams I
have about being positive and accepting my mistakes I have made.
By improving my self-esteem in terms of having confidence in everything I do. And also not forgetting about believing in myself.*

—Olwethu

I only saw Olwethu at orphans' group now, when she showed
up there. I knew she was not in a good place. Her Aunt Pinky
approached me after church one Sunday morning and asked

whether Olwethu had been attending writing club lately. I had to tell her no, that she had not been there in a long time.

"*Eish*! I knew she was telling lies about that." Pinky shook her head in frustration. She was an ample woman in her fifties, with generous hips and breasts and a smattering of tiny ebony freckles around her eyes and across the bridge of her nose, rather like an inky constellation. This morning, she wore the black skirt, white blouse, and black-brimmed hat that was the Presbyterian Women's Guild uniform. She told me that Olwethu had been staying away nights, presumably with her boyfriend. She had stopped attending school and, alarmingly, even while she was still at home, had stopped taking her ARVs.

"She must take those tablets every day at half-five in the morning and again in the evening. I wake up with her when she's here and watch her take them. But when she's not at home . . ." She held out both hands, palms up. "She will get TB again, and it will kill her this time."

I asked Pinky whether she had spoken with anyone at the school. Olwethu was repeating Grade 11, because she had missed too many days the year before when she was in and out of hospital with TB. She couldn't afford to fail again this year if she wanted to earn her Matric.

"I did, I went down to the school and spoke to the counselor. She told me all we could do is pray for her, until she decides for herself what she wants. Until she sees what she's doing to herself and to her family. And so I pray. I give it over to God. What else to do for her, Kim? We just must pray."

I couldn't ask Annasuena what she knew about Olwethu, whether what Pinky said was true. The two friends had fallen out. A friend of Mel's from America had donated a used laptop for a high school student's use. Mel decided that it would best be put to use if shared among Olwethu, Sive (when she was home from boarding school), and Annasuena. The laptop was to remain with Olwethu, because Pinky's house was more secure than either of the shacks where Annasuena stayed with her Aunt Lillian or with Phelo. Annasuena agreed with this. Within a week of taking possession of the laptop, however, Olwethu told Mel there was a problem. It had been stolen. She'd taken it into Cape Town to do schoolwork, she said, and some boys saw her with it. When she was alone, they accosted and robbed her.

Annasuena did not buy any of this story. She knew, before Mel did, that Olwethu was skipping out of school. On the day she claimed the laptop was taken, Annasuena had spotted her in Gugulethu. She believed Olwethu's boyfriend had taken the laptop, maybe even sold it. Olwethu would cover for him, if that had happened, Annasuena was sure. She felt robbed of personal property she had never actually possessed, though she had already grown keen on the idea of a laptop she could partially own, to use at home. More than that, she felt affronted by what she saw as her friend's deception. But Olwethu had stood by her story, and now the two girls no longer spoke.

The Tuesday after I'd talked with Pinky, Olwethu arrived at orphans' group looking—there was no other word for it—haggard. Her face was sallow and a little bloated. She dragged herself over to a seat, sat down, and spoke to no one. Annasuena sat across the room and ignored her. Milly was away this week and Mel was leading the group. She read a passage from Old Testament scripture, when Solomon asks God for wisdom to lead God's people. Over the chatter from the younger children, Mel said, "If you could ask God for anything, what would you ask for?"

"Money!" Lifa, a rambunctious boy of ten, shouted out.

"Okay. But God praised Solomon because he did not ask for wealth and money, and then God gave it to him anyway. Just something to think about. Anyone else?"

Annasuena raised her hand. "I would ask for peace of mind. Because when you have that, you can cope with other things."

"True," Mel said. "Olwethu, what would you ask for?"

Olwethu often spoke in a low mumble that could be difficult to understand even when standing close to her. I was not sure whether this was due to diffidence or to her missing teeth. I strained to hear her response.

"I would ask for a positive attitude," she responded. "Right now I feel very negative about my life. I wish I could see things another way."

I caught sight of Annasuena rolling her eyes. She saw me too and looked away, chastened.

"That's a good one," Mel said. "Everyone needs a new perspective sometimes."

After the group ended, as each child waited for his or her name to be called to collect the week's bag of groceries, I sat down next to Olwethu. She had been sitting hunched over, hugging her knees, nearly bent double. Now she sat up in her chair and offered a tight smile.

"How are you?" I asked.

"Not so good."

"Yeah. Doesn't sound like it. I spoke to Pinky at church. She's worried about you."

"I know. What did she say?"

"That you've been sleeping away from home and stopped going to school."

"She's exaggerating. I only stayed away a couple of times."

"Did you have her permission to stay away, or let her know?"

Olwethu did not answer, only balled her hands into fists and shoved them roughly over her eyes.

"I'm sorry. I didn't mean to upset you. I think people who care about you want to help, but we don't know what to do." She pulled one sleeve of her shirt down over her hand and rubbed her eyes dry. I didn't know any more about how to help her than I knew how to help Ntombi. I did know, though, that because Olwethu had started on ARVs, she really needed to continue taking them on schedule or they could lose their effectiveness in keeping her from developing full-blown AIDS. I told her what Pinky had told me and asked whether it was true she wasn't taking her tablets.

"Yes, that's true. I ran out a while ago and haven't been back to the clinic to get more. I haven't felt like walking there and I didn't have taxi money. It's a long way." The clinic was in Gugs, maybe a forty-five-minute walk from her house. Then she might need to wait for hours before being seen. I asked whether she would go if I drove her there and waited with her; she agreed. I had meetings the next two days, but we made plans to meet Friday morning at J. L. Zwane.

The day arrived cold, windy, and rainy, as winter officially moved into the Cape. Few people were out on the streets in Gugs. The ones who had to walk anywhere bundled up in coats and scarves, sometimes holding a flattened-out plastic bag over their heads. Umbrellas were useless when the wind lashed the rain almost horizontally. I fully expected Olwethu not to show up. But she was there, waiting under the roof outside J. L. Zwane's front door. When she got into my car, I leaned over to give her a hug.

"Ahh," she winced sharply and grabbed her elbow. I pulled

back and saw that the side of her face was bruised, her cheek-bone streaked in shades of black and yellow, swollen and puffed out as though her face had been inflated.

"What happened to you?"

"I was in a car wreck."

"When?

"Two nights ago."

She said she was coming home from a party with a friend and another person, someone she did not know, who was driving. The driver was drunk, she said, and they ran off the road and hit something, she wasn't sure what. She had been thrown forward. Her face hit the back of the front seat and her arm banged against the door handle.

"*What* . . . ," I started, and then realized I had to soften my tone. "What were you doing getting in a car with someone you knew was drunk?"

"It was the only way we could get home and it was late."

"Was anyone else hurt?"

"Just bruised. Nothing else. I guess we were lucky." She faced forward and looked out the front window as she spoke, cradling her elbow with her other hand. I didn't know how to respond, because I didn't know whether I believed her. I didn't know whether I believed anything she said.

We drove in silence to Hannan Crusaid Adolescent AIDS Clinic and took seats in the waiting room of a mobile trailer converted into the clinic. It had been more than a month since Olwethu had last taken her medication, so she had to see a doctor. That meant a longer wait, and then more waiting for the pills themselves from the pharmacy. When they come to a clinic, people must plan for the possibility that they could be waiting all day, and they still might not be seen by a doctor or nurse if too many visits run too long. In the waiting room, older women waited with young children. There were more grannies than there were mothers. Teens came and went, picking up their own medications, I guessed; each of them came alone.

Olwethu got in to see the doctor relatively quickly and returned to the waiting room ten minutes later.

"We have to wait now for my tablets."

"Is everything all right?"

"*Ja*, it's fine."

I wasn't sure what to ask, what questions would be intrusive, what she would be willing or able to tell me. Conversations with the others girls came far more naturally. Annasuena in particular could prattle at length, just knowing someone was listening to her. She had also been comfortable, almost from the time we met, discussing her HIV status with me. Olwethu did not seem comfortable discussing anything with anyone.

"Did the doctor say you'd have any problems since you've been off the tablets?"

"She said I might have side effects again. And she told me it made her sad that I waited so long to come here." Olwethu grimaced in pain and again rubbed her elbow and the side of her arm.

"Did the doctor say anything about the bruising on your face?"

"No."

We sat there for more than two hours, waiting for her pills to arrive from the pharmacy next door. She only spoke when I spoke to her, with the briefest responses she could give. A steady rain thrummed on the trailer's tin roof. A poster shaped like a stop sign hung on the waiting-room wall and begged, "Stop TB! Open the window." No windows were opened in this cramped space.

I gave up trying to make conversation and instead watched her in silence. She sat almost completely still, not antsy or impatient to get her medicine and leave. I stared at the side of her face. It didn't look like it had slammed into the back of a car seat. It looked like it had been hit. Like fist-pounded flesh. I finally had to ask.

"Did your boyfriend do this to you?" She laughed and immediately looked to the floor.

"No. It was a wreck."

I stared hard at her. She would not meet my eyes. Olwethu's sullenness had made sense to me as a reaction to an unhappy adolescence, to the losses life had dealt her by the age of ten. Now her speechlessness seemed nothing so much as resigned.

Fifteen minutes later, the TB sign had done its job. I could not breathe any more of this stale air, nor sit with the oppressive silence coming from the girl next to me. I told Olwethu I was going to find a toilet, then I stepped outside into a cold downpour. With my back pressed against the trailer, I inhaled great gulps of air and let raindrops run down my face until my body shivered.

From the beginning, I knew why I had come to South Africa. I had come to start a writing club in Gugulethu, to help girls write about their lives, hear their own voices. That was my role. Now I was sitting in a clinic with a terribly sick, abused, and orphaned girl who rarely used her voice. I remembered what Pinky had said, that we must pray for Olwethu. I wanted to believe that prayer changes situations, changes people. With this fragile girl who seemed hellbent on destroying herself, prayer felt essential, yet wholly inadequate.

10

Be You to the Full

Colour Painting

You see me across continents and wonder
About my smile that continues to uphold a soul
And reaches for the liquid
Within sores.

You hear me throughout the
Golden trees and ponder about my integrity,
The integrity transcending from stricken
Bullets deep inside their young hearts
And opening the dirt inside pores.
But I say listen to what I say.

I have walked under your skin
But you couldn't notice me.
Left me painted as blue which reflects the
Tears that had flooded for me and for you.
I stepped on your heart but you couldn't feel
Me, deserted me, painted as red which reflects
The blood that they have spilt for me and you.

I tried blocking your sight with my existence
But you couldn't see me.

Displayed me painted as yellow which reflects
The sun that has shone for me and you.
I wrote a name but you couldn't spell it.
Abandoning me painted as green which
Reflects the veins that have run for me and you.
I left a footprint but you couldn't trace me, chased me,
Painted as black which reflects the shadow that has shaded
For me and you.

I lastly divided myself into multiple
Different stars but you still couldn't count me.
Threw me painted as white which reflects the wings
As they have flown for me and you.
But these colours—blue, red, yellow, green, black, and white—
Are the colours that made me who I am today.
The South African flag.
For because of them, I am proudly South African.

—Annasuena

June brought an extended winter school break for the girls and the drone of vuvuzelas for everyone. The horns buzzed at any hour of the day or night, from the City Bowl to the Southern Suburbs to the Cape Flats, like an infestation of locusts. World Cup had arrived, the first time the monthlong tournament would be held on the African continent. South Africa eagerly awaited the opportunity to bask in the international spotlight and prove to the world that it could host a global sporting event without calamity. Naysayers, British soc-cer fans in particular, had already proclaimed the likelihood that any trip to the World Cup in 2010 would end in a carjack-ing, or worse. Many white South Africans also took some con-vincing that their country could pull off the feat.

As with so many areas of life in this country, sport has tra-ditionally split along racial lines. White South Africans follow rugby and the national team, the Springboks, named after the leaping antelope. Early in his presidency, Nelson Mandela stra-tegically used the 1995 Rugby World Cup, hosted by South Africa, to rally people across races to support the home team. His efforts succeeded: Whites and blacks united to cheer the Springboks on to victory (later depicted in the Clint Eastwood–directed movie *Invictus*).

Soccer traditionally has found its supporters among black South Africans. The national team's nickname, *Bafana Bafana*, means "The Boys! The Boys!" in Zulu. Unlike the Springboks, Bafana was not accomplished at the world level. The team qual-ified for World Cup inclusion only because South Africa was the tournament host country.

Yet, as with the rugby championship, World Cup excitement spread and intensified as the opening match drew near. South Africans cheered on Bafana and celebrated the tournament. People flew South African flags everywhere—outside their homes and businesses, on the side mirrors of their cars, even tucked into the manes of the cart horses. The tournament's theme song, *"Waka Waka* (This Time for Africa)," by Colom-bian singer Shakira and the South African group Freshlyground, played endlessly. I watched the first match with Gugulethu friends at Mzoli's, along with hundreds of crazed fans craning to get a glimpse of two television screens. When Bafana scored the first goal of the World Cup, the place went mad. Beer rained down over us like a summer cloudburst. South Africa went on to a respectable 1–1 draw against Mexico in that match. It was a thrilling time to live in the country.

For some, it could also be a dangerous time. At orphans' group, before the games began, Milly warned the children to be especially careful about taking up with adults they did not know, foreigners or South Africans. Thousands of soccer fans pouring into the country would be accompanied by a steep rise in prostitution in cities where the games would be held. South Africa had also seen a rise in sex trafficking, including trafficking in children, with inadequate attempts by the South African government to stop it.

"Don't believe anyone who offers to give you anything," Milly told the children. "Protect yourselves. Your body is your own. It's a gift from God. It's worth more than anyone can pay you for it."

Once World Cup began, rumors also sprang up that there could be violent attacks against immigrants from other African countries living in South Africa. When the tourists went home, these outsiders would be sent packing as well. Foreign shopkeepers who had opened spaza shops and other enterprises were seen as economic threats when the national unemployment rate hovered around 30 percent. In 2008, there had been xenophobic attacks in townships across the country, including in Gugulethu. Sixty-two people were killed and hundreds injured or displaced.

At Amazw'Entombi, sixteen-year-old Ayanda had written about those attacks one week for the writing prompt "The Day I'll Never Forget."

The day that I'll never forget in my entire life was the day of xenophobia. In my community, foreigners were killed by the citizens of

*Gugulethu. These foreigners were from upper Africa, from Congo,
Kenya, Zambia, Zimbabwe, Somalia, Namibia. These foreigners
were killed by other black people. I saw a Somali man being stabbed
till death. He was running away saying, I'm sorry. I'm sorry. They
stabbed him and burned his wife to death. I don't understand how
can a black person kill another black person without a valid reason. The foreigners were labeled as* amakwerekwere *[a derogatory
word for African immigrants]. I was angry when I saw this happening. I felt the pain.*

After Ayanda read that day, a few of the other girls also told
of witnessing violent attacks against African immigrants in the
townships. Thulisa made an astute observation: "These people
are coming from countries that took in South Africans during
apartheid. I don't understand why we must turn around and be
so angry with them for coming to our country now." A repeat of
that violence would be a terrible ending to the World Cup and
a further blight on South Africa's international reputation, one
that the country was trying hard to redeem with its moment in
the limelight.

I expected that some girls would not come to Amazw
'Entombi, what with all the excitement and competing activities around World Cup. Some would also be traveling to Eastern
Cape to visit family during this extended school break. But I
planned to keep it going over the month. The first Saturday of
the tournament, I arrived at J. L. Zwane as usual, fifteen minutes before our 3 p.m. starting time. The Men's Guild was meeting in a nearby classroom, singing Xhosa hymns. Their deep
bass tones reverberated through the empty church. I arranged
ten chairs in a circle, brought out the girls' notebooks and pencils, took a seat, and waited for them to come sauntering in.

No one showed up. I sat alone, listening to the rumbling voices of the men next door. I opened a window until the wind grew chilly, and then closed it again. No heads popped round the doorway to check to see who was here first before they entered. I walked outside and around the perimeter of the church. Recorded music that I could not identify blared from a crackly sound system at the nearby Gugulethu Sports Complex. I checked my phone. Early on, I had given the girls my number. Many had cell phones or access to them, usually the kind where minutes are purchased as you go along. Everyone constantly ran out of airtime minutes and had to wait to buy more when money became available. Now there were no SMS texts, no voicemail to tell me anything. Silence. I waited an hour and then returned home to Pinelands.

I hated that I took their absences so personally. In general, I was feeling far less isolated than I had been when Amazw'Entombi began. I had made some friends in Cape Town and had World Cup events of my own to attend, though I had not met anyone to date. Wherever I lived or traveled in the world, I seemed to meet and befriend amazing women. I was grateful this pattern was finally repeating itself here, but many days, these nascent friendships did little to alleviate those other wells of loneliness.

Annasuena had also gone radio silent in recent weeks. I had tried to call her on a number she gave me, which might have been Phelo's phone, or maybe Aunt Lillian's, but I never reached her or anyone else to leave a message for her. I was still learning Gugulethu's confusing streets and could not remember where she stayed, so I couldn't stop by and hope to find her. Mel—now returned home to America—had told me that in the eighteen months she'd known Annasuena, she regularly disappeared for weeks and months at a time. I did not want to lose touch with this girl who flitted from one place to another, by necessity or by choice, but I wondered whether it would fall to me exclusively not to let that happen.

Around 11 p.m., I crawled into bed with *Reading Lolita in Tehran*, lying on top of my new electric blanket, a wise purchase from Woolworths. My family back home found it hard to believe that the weather could really turn cold in Africa. Suddenly my phone, lying on the nightstand next to my reading light, pinged with an SMS. I had to read it out loud to comprehend all the text-speak:

> hi kim. i want 2 say that im realy srry 4 not informing u that most of us will not be able 2 attend 2days class as we have been involved in a programe at church from thursday til monday. the programe consists of 5 seminars. even 2moro we are attending. 2day we spent the day in George. i just came home 30 minutes ago. im realy realy srry. u must have been disappointed with us. safe sleep and gudnite. luv, ntombi

I replied to Ntombi to say thanks for letting me know and that I wanted to hear more about the weekend. I wished her sweet dreams.

As I stood outside the office at J. L. Zwane speaking to Johanna, two arms encased in soft fleece were suddenly flung over my shoulders from behind. When I turned, Ntombi launched herself into me with a fervent embrace. It was cold this day, and she wore a woolen knit hat pulled down low over her head, with the ends of her hair pressed against the side of her neck.

"I didn't know you'd be here!" she yelped. I told her I sometimes helped out with orphans' group. We excused ourselves from Johanna and went into the office to have a quieter place to talk.

"Look at you, all bouncy," I said. She let out the first genuine laugh I had heard from her in many weeks. I asked why she was at church on a Tuesday afternoon. She said that she and Sharon were to meet with *umfundisi* and give him a report on the youth retreat weekend. Her faced sobered a moment as she said, "I really am sorry no one told you we'd be gone on Saturday."

"That's all right. I did wonder how I lost *everyone* the same week." She laughed again. It seemed clear she was laughing not because I said anything particularly amusing, but simply because she remembered how. "If I'd known about the retreat, I might have tagged along. You said you went to George?" George is several hours away along the Garden Route, on the Indian Ocean.

"Yes, it's the farthest I've ever traveled from Cape Town."

"Exciting! So tell me about the retreat."

It was difficult to fully follow Ntombi's torrent of words about their weekend. The retreat was called UCAN, led by an Italian man named Davide, for the youth of J. L. Zwane. There were team-building games, such as falling backward blindfolded into the arms of your peers and trusting them to catch you. There were talks about how to communicate, how to build relationships and change the relationships you already have, if they're not working for you. There was a lot to learn about the ways to change yourself, when you cannot change your life circumstances. She spoke without pause, one recollection leading into another, until she had to stop and catch her breath.

"I really should have gone," I said. "I need to learn all of that. Shame, man!"

She cackled. "You're beginning to sound like a proper South African!"

"And you're giddy!"

"*Ja*." She abruptly fell silent and then said, "Do you know what I did? I came home after the whole weekend was over, and I told my aunts that I hated how they treated my mother. They neglected her when she was dying. She was their sister! That hurt her, I know it did. And it hurt me. I'd never said that to them but now I have."

"How did they respond?"

"I think they were shocked, to hear that from me. I hardly speak to them anymore. I just don't. They didn't say much then. But later on, one of my aunts came into my room and told me they didn't know how to take care of her when she was ill."

"Did that help to hear?"

Ntombi considered the question a moment. "It did. Some. At least she can acknowledge it."

"Your aunts failed your mom and you both. People will do that, I suppose."

"They will. But you can't blame others, even if they've failed you." She grew animated again. "Davide talked about that, too. You have to find the places and ways that you can take responsibility for your own life."

"*Sisi*, you are so jazzed about this," I said. "You know what I'm going to tell you."

"What?"

"You have to lead Amazw'Entombi and share all these revelations."

"*Sjoe*! I don't know about that." She leaned back in the chair and clamped her mouth shut, as though suddenly realizing she'd said too much.

"I do. I'm not giving you a choice. It's your turn." She pondered, started to speak, reconsidered, and chewed on one fingernail before deciding on an answer.

"Okay. But with Sharon and Portia, too. They were both there. I can't remember everything we talked about all by myself."

"That's all right, you can give highlights. Was Annasuena or Olwethu there?"

"No. I haven't seen them in a while."

"Shame. I think it would have been good for both of them. From the looks of you, it would do anyone good. You're glowing from within. You're sitting up straight, not hunkered over and looking sad. You're beautiful."

"Last night, I slept through the night for the first time in six years."

"Six? Really?"

"Yes," she nodded, her eyes shining with tears.

We had to celebrate Ntombi's transformation. The next evening, I had two tickets to see a show put on in conjunction with World Cup events, *African Songbook: A Musical Tribute to the Life of Nelson Mandela*, performed by the Cape Town Opera at Artscape Theatre in the city. A friend had to back out of attending with me. It felt a bit unfair to offer to take only one girl to a show like this when I couldn't afford to take everyone. But I wanted to honor what Ntombi was doing, the corner she had turned. That she could finally sleep once again, and laugh. That she was a strong young woman who was finding her voice—scratchy though it might be—to speak her truth aloud to those who needed to hear it.

So we went to the performance together, took pictures of one another standing in front of the billboard advertising the show. South Africans and many outside the country call Nelson Mandela by his clan name, Madiba, a sign of respect and affection. He looked down at us from the billboard with squinting eyes and a kind smile. We both loved the performance, which covered Madiba's life in three acts: his boyhood in Eastern Cape; the days in jazzy Sophiatown, in Johannesburg, in the 1950s; and his later life as a statesman. In the lobby during intermission, beaded baskets held slips of paper and pens to write a birthday message to Madiba, who would turn ninety-two the following month. Both of us wrote our greetings; Ntombi helped me with my Xhosa.

> *Min emnandi kuwe* (Happy birthday to you), Madiba!
> You are an inspiration to the whole world. *Enkosi* (Thank you). Blessings on your life and on your family.
> —Kimberly, American and honorary
> South African in 2010

> *uThixo Akusikelele* (God bless you).
> *Min emnandi, Tata, Mkhulu* (Happy Birthday, Father, Grandfather).
> It is because of leaders like you that we are able to call ourselves Proudly South African.
> —Ntombizanele

Ntombi managed to persuade Sharon and Portia to share leadership duties on "UCAN day" at our small Saturday gathering. Because it was during the school holidays, Sive was home from boarding school. She joined us for Amazw'Entombi and brought her friend Phola, another talented young writer whom I knew from my visits to the school.

"Didn't Olwethu want to come along?" I asked. Sive hedged, then said Olwethu had been out a lot lately.

"With her boyfriend?"

"*Ja.*"

"Same boyfriend?"

"*Ja.*" Sive sighed and looked away, as though she was betraying her sister's confidences.

Mandlakazi and Ayanda were there, too, and Xolelwa for a little while, though she had to leave early to walk home before it grew dark, because walking at night was especially unsafe where she lived. All the girls dressed for winter now, in jerseys (as South Africans call sweaters), scarves, and hats. Buildings are not heated, so layers are mandatory. Sharon looked casual, as she always did, in a purple turtleneck and fleece vest. She also wore, for the first time that I'd seen, rectangular eyeglasses in a shade of royal blue that popped out against her complexion. Portia was dressed in a gray sweater and leggings with a long strand of black beads that fell to her waist, knotted in the middle, flapper style. Ntombi wore jeans, a bright yellow top, and a black scarf draped around her neck. As the three conferred among themselves before getting started, I realized how much older they suddenly appeared from when I had first met them only months earlier. Huddled together in front of the whiteboard at the head of the classroom, they looked almost professorial.

Ntombi led off with the "Blame Game." Girls paired off and one had to describe a simple drawing to the other so the second girl could try to draw it exactly to match. This was a test of communication skills—listening to the other, asking questions when uncertain rather than making assumptions and then blaming the partner if the picture turned out to look vastly different from what was described. When things go wrong, Ntombi emphasized, it did no good to blame others in your life.

Portia explained "Give and Take," another game to understand how you come across to other people. Everyone walked around the circle and, after studying a girl's face, declared her primarily a "Giver" or a "Taker." Honestly, I didn't fully understand this one. It felt more like an exercise in snap judgments. It was intended to help the girls understand how they present themselves to the world, and the control that they can exercise over that, and also that there are times to be a Giver and times to be a Taker. It's not good to be solely one or the other.

Switching pairs, Sharon asked us to talk about our dreams and fears, and about how this partner could offer support in achieving those dreams or conquering fears. "When you tell other people your dreams, you make them real, hey? And you force yourself to find people you can trust, to open up to. Now, the other person has a choice, too: to offer support, or to laugh at those dreams."

Which is easier to do, Sharon asked rhetorically, support or laugh? What harm comes from that kind of laughter? How does that tear another person down when she's bravely placed herself in a position of vulnerability? Put yourself in someone else's shoes. "Maybe she only wears old clothing. But maybe there's no money at home. That's out of the person's control. What do you say to her when you laugh at her for that? We *all* remember being laughed at some time, and how that made us feel. No one forgets that." The girls listened to Sharon in rapt attention, Sive in particular. She sat forward literally on the edge of her seat.

Then Sharon summed up what UCAN was meant to teach. Instead of laughing, you can support. Instead of blaming, you can come up with different solutions. Instead of letting others make decisions, you can make your own. "We all can. We *have* to. We all have to find our own way in life, even when we take a wrong turn, hey?"

She explained what happens when you use a GPS. You program in your final destination, where you want to end up, and the GPS tells you how to get there. But maybe you decide to take a different route, or maybe you make a wrong turn. What does the GPS say? Sharon asked. None of the girls knew the answer.

"It says, 'Recalculating.' It's not a dead end. It's a different way to get where you're going. We won't all reach our destinations at the same time. And maybe the place we find there isn't really the place we wanted to be after all. But what can we do then?" She waited for a response.

Sive stared in awe at Sharon and said, her inflection rising into a question of her own, "We recalculate?"

"*Yhuu!*" Sharon clapped her hands and plopped down into her seat. "Our work here is done."

When it came time to write, Portia and Sharon claimed exhaustion from teaching, so we gave them a pass. I made the prompt freeform, anything the girls wanted to write about what had been said this day.

Today we played a game called Give and Take. A game whereby it was kind of hurting because almost everyone said I'm taking. I'm not taking it personal. Sharon told me I just need to watch how I set my face. Today I was feeling very motivated and proud to be a youth. And that's thanks to all you guys. Today I got a chance to see what are my weaknesses and strengths. The activity really helped me to see or look at what I want in life. With Amazw'Entombi I feel like they are my sisters. I really appreciate it. And not forgetting uMama Kimberly.

—Ayanda

How many times do we blame people for what we go through in our lives? Really think about it. You blame your parents for not going to university because of your family's financial instability. Same applies to the mindset of youth today. You fall pregnant and you blame your friends because they told you that sex is a good thing to do. We as the youth need to be in control of our lives. We need to take charge of our lives and we have to be responsible in order to succeed. And sometimes to be able to succeed we need to be able to trust.

—Mandlakazi

To me, what I learned today was so fully imparted. It gave me a chance to look inside myself and evaluate what sort of impact I have made in other people's lives, and also what I can do for myself. I love the fact that I got to meet you guys. I'm so glad to see young African women, independent, determined to lift up the youth's spirit, and challenging the stigma around what we have based ourselves on. So I would like to say thank you for this day.

—Phola

UCAN! I thought that this was a great experience. I learned things that I never thought of. I never realized how we always blame people for our mistakes. This for me was eye opening because sometimes we do this to people and we never think about how that person will feel. I just realized that keeping quiet won't take you anywhere cause people won't know what your dreams are. It will be impossible for them to help you unless you open your mouth. Then you will get some help and encouragement. It is important to make your own decisions and not allow people to make decisions for you. Cause they won't be there for you when things are bad. My belief is never let anyone influence you into doing what they want you to do. When people laugh at you, just take it as a step to make you strong and more confident. I would like to thank you guys for opening my eyes cause there are many young people who don't know what you have taught me today.

—Sive

When we sit and talk about issues affecting one another, we can actually reach an understanding and better communication. Talking and listening are something that we hardly ever do. By that we can find out how we all walk around looking for the same things in life, while really we can offer one another those same things. We all want love, support, empathy, understanding, to be listened to, cared for, and adored.

—Ntombi

Before we all left for the day, Portia, Ntombi, and Sharon left us with a new definition written on the whiteboard:

<u>Beautiful</u>
Be You to the Full

Halfway through World Cup month, I received a phone call from a number I didn't recognize. Traffic and background noise garbled the first words of the person at the other end of the line. I finally heard, "Kim, can you call me back?"

"Wait, who am I speaking with?"

"It's Annasuena! Don't you know my voice by now?"

Annasuena had not appeared at Amazw'Entombi or orphans' group for weeks. None of the other girls had seen her around Gugulethu, either. Now she sounded miffed that I didn't recognize her immediately. I felt annoyed that she'd disappeared without any contact.

I called her back, so the charge would apply to my phone and not the one she'd borrowed from a friend, which was about to run out of airtime anyway.

"Hey, stranger, where have you been?" I tried to keep my voice light, but I knew, after I spoke, that the question came across as needling.

"I went to Johannesburg for my eldest brother's funeral."

"Oh, Annasuena, I'm sorry. I didn't know."

"*Ja*, I'm sorry too. I wanted to call you before we left. I drove with my cousin-brother and with my other brother, and I didn't take your number with me. There wasn't enough money to bring his body back to Cape Town and bury him near my mother. We didn't even have enough for a funeral. It was just a burial on a Monday at the graveside."

Twenty years older than Annasuena, Clive died from complications of AIDS. He left behind a six-month-old daughter living with her mother in Johannesburg.

But Annasuena had some happier news to share. Her little sister, Naledi, whom she had not seen in four years, had come to Cape Town for a visit. Naledi had been only five years old when Anneline died. She had continued to live with her father, Vuyisile, in Port Elizabeth. Now he had also died in the last year. His girlfriend kept Naledi on, raising her along with her own children.

Annasuena wanted me to meet her sister and already had plans in mind for us. "Could we have a sleepover at your place in Pinelands?"

I picked up the girls at NY 46. Naledi met me at the car with an unrestrained hug. She wore a gray-and-red knit jacket that resembled a ski sweater, the fur-trimmed hood pulled up over her head. Tied together under her chin were strings with pompoms hung from the ends. She was thirteen, taller than her sister, and gangly, as though she and her body were still getting acquainted. Naledi called her sister Anna, giggled a lot, and spoke in a voice so quiet I had to ask her to repeat what she'd just said several times.

I surprised the girls with a plan to go see a movie, *Toy Story 3*, before landing for the night at my cottage. On the drive to the cinema, Annasuena coughed repeatedly, a hoarse rumble, harsher than the ailment she'd had when I was first getting to know her.

"How long have you had that cough?"

"A while. It's getting better, though." Another coughing fit seized her just as she spoke.

"Have you been back to the clinic?" She was supposed to return to the Hannan Crusaid Adolescent AIDS Clinic at the end of May, to be evaluated and started on ARVs.

"No, they made my appointment for the week I was writing exams and I couldn't keep it."

"So you haven't started . . . "

"No, I haven't. I know I need to schedule another appointment. I'll do it. People don't know."

"You know you need this cough looked at. Illnesses can affect you more severely."

"Yeah. *People don't know.*"

I looked over at her. Annasuena fixed her eyes on me and tilted her head toward the backseat, and I realized then what she meant. Naledi did not know her sister was HIV positive.

"Got it," I said quietly, glancing up into the rearview mirror. Naledi stared out the back window and hummed to herself, as Annasuena often did.

We arrived at the mall with enough time before the matinee began to grab lunch at Nando's. I asked the girls to order whatever they'd each like, but they grew timid and deferred to my choice. So we got three spicy peri-peri chicken sandwiches and chips, Fanta Orange drinks for them, and a Coke Light for me. After Annasuena and I had both dived into our chips, I saw Naledi close her eyes and bow her head before her untouched food. Her lips moved but no sound escaped. When she opened her eyes, she looked up to find me watching her.

"Sorry," she said, her voice so high-pitched she nearly squeaked.

"Don't be sorry. I wish I remembered to say grace more often," I said. She looked embarrassed and ducked her face behind her sandwich before taking a bite.

As Annasuena ate, her eyes drifted around the food court and down the rows of shops, where several groups of teenagers gathered. Laughing, flirting, hanging out, being seen. "I used to come here after school," she said, as though recalling a dream from the previous night that had only now come to mind. For a brief while, after her mother died, when there was still money available for her education, her aunt sent her to a private Catholic school near here. She made friends, as Annasuena will, and spent afternoons in the mall with them.

When we walked into the movie theatre, an attendant handed out plastic 3-D glasses with blue frames. Annasuena wrinkled her forehead and held the glasses at arm's length.

"What are these for?" she asked. Naledi twirled hers absent-mindedly in one hand, between her thumb and index finger.

"Have you ever seen a 3-D movie?" I asked. Annasuena shook her head. "Naledi?"

"Sorry!" She looked up, startled.

"I was just asking if you've ever seen a 3-D movie."

"Never."

"Oh, we're gonna have some fun, then," I said.

A day earlier, to prepare for the sleepover, I'd gone shopping at Pick n Pay. I bought avocados and brown bread, a bag of juicy *naartjies* (tangerines), yogurt and granola for the next morning's breakfast, almonds and microwave popcorn for late-night snacks, and two large Cadbury chocolate bars to share among us. When I saw the Old El Paso box, I knew what I'd make for dinner.

I put Aretha Franklin on my laptop—Annasuena liked classic soul—and we danced around my small kitchen as we made dinner. The girls had never eaten tacos, and the shape of the crunchy shells tickled them. They chopped the lettuce and tomatoes and grated the cheese. Concerned that tacos alone would not suffice, Annasuena found a box of macaroni and cheese in my cabinet and insisted on preparing it as well.

"You're a great cook, Kim," Naledi said, resting one hand on my shoulder as I opened the spice packet to shake over the mince already sizzling on the stovetop. She had an eagerness to please, and a fear of causing offense, that seemed diametrically opposed to her sister's temperament. Annasuena rarely held her opinions back and did not worry if what she said ruffled anyone.

The dining table had only two chairs, so we sat on the floor to eat, with blankets thrown over our legs for warmth. After Aretha finished, Annasuena asked what else we could listen to. I remembered that I had found and downloaded "Paradise Road." I pulled it up then, without naming the song or the singer.

Annasuena recognized it immediately. She leaned back, closed her eyes, and began to bob her head.

"Who's this?" Naledi asked, and Annasuena's eyes popped open.

"It's Joy! Mom's group."

"Oh, right. Sorry."

We listened, and when the chorus came on, I asked, "That's her, right?"

"*Ja*, that's her. She had the best voice."

"She had a *big* voice," I said. "She didn't hold back."

"No, she didn't." Annasuena closed her eyes again and listened to her mother singing.

A few days earlier, I'd been in town with friends at the World Cup Fan Park, a free gathering spot for everyone to celebrate the tournament, tourists and Capetonians alike. A stage at the far end of the park featured live performances. As we were leaving, I caught the opening lines as a female singer crooned, "Come with me, down Paradise Road . . . ." I'd never heard the song until I met Annasuena. Now it felt familiar, almost intimately so, in a strange way. I'd listened to it many times, trying to imagine what it might have been like to know Anneline, how much her daughter might reflect her.

"Do you remember much about your mom, Naledi?"

"No, I can't remember her at all."

I'd found a couple of photos online of Anneline and now asked the girls whether they wanted to see them. They agreed, though Naledi seemed more eager than Annasuena. One photo, taken when she was ill, showed Anneline in profile, her head wrapped in a brightly colored scarf. The photographer caught her as she was speaking, and the effect, coupled with her gaunt appearance, made her look severe and pained. Deep vertical creases ran down her forehead between eyebrows drawn in with pencil. Her lips glowed pink.

"That's some great lipstick she's wearing," I said.

"*Yhuu*!" Annasuena shook her head. "She *hated* to be caught out without her lipstick."

Naledi peered closely at the screen while Annasuena hovered behind her.

"You look like her, Anna."

"You think so?"

"You have the same mouth and eyes."

"*You* have her complexion, Naledi. You're lighter than me. My father must have been very dark." Annasuena stared another moment at the screen. "She was really beautiful. Before she got sick. I can't see how we look alike, though." Nevertheless, she looked pleased.

In the morning, Annasuena's cough rattled in her chest again. She thought that taking a hot shower might help, but when she emerged it hadn't. She still sounded ragged. I told her again that she needed to visit the clinic.

"I *know*."

She threw me a look that told me to shut up and gestured discreetly toward Naledi, who sat within earshot, reading from one of my books. I barged into the bathroom where Annasuena was getting ready and shut the door behind me.

"Why won't you tell her?"

"I don't know! I just can't."

"I think you should give her a chance to be a support for you. You need people who can do that."

"I know I do. But I don't want her to worry and think I'm going to die like our mom did."

"That's why you should tell her. So you can teach her about the disease, too. Remember the whole disclosure thing?"

"I remember," she sighed, too wearily for the beginning of a day.

Disclosing one's status empowers the person living with HIV, educates the community, and chips away at the stigma that lingers against people who are positive. But Annasuena's previous experience with disclosure had not gone well. After she told her aunt, Mama Lillian, that she was positive, the news traveled among the neighbors. They offered stares and whispers rather than a functional support system she might rely upon.

"Okay, yes. I'll tell her." Annasuena began to sound more resolved than resigned. More like herself.

"Do you want to do it now, while I'm here, or later when it's just the two of you?"

Naledi knocked on the bathroom door. "What's going on, guys?"

"Coming out!" Annasuena called. "Yes, I want you here." A rare moment of exposed vulnerability.

When we emerged, Naledi was shuffling about in the kitchen, twisting one long, thin braid around her finger. "What's the matter?" she asked nervously.

"Nothing's the matter," Annasuena said, then took a deep breath, which made her cough. "I want to tell you something."

"What is it?"

"I want you to know I found out two years ago that I'm HIV positive." Annasuena spoke in a steady voice and looked her sister in the eye. "I got infected when I was young. When I lived with our uncle and aunt, he raped me."

"Oh." Naledi's hand that had been twirling in her hair dropped down to her side.

"But I'm all right. I'm well, mostly. And I'm going to take care of myself so I'll stay well."

"Are you really all right?" Naledi asked.

"Yes! I didn't want you to have to worry about me. But you're my sister and you should know this. I don't want to be ashamed about it, either."

"You shouldn't be!" Naledi shifted forward as though she wanted to touch her sister, but she held back. "I'm glad you told me."

"I probably need to start taking the tablets."

"Will those help keep you well? Do they really work?"

"People say they do. Guess we'll have to see."

"It's different now," I said to Naledi, "than when your mom was sick. The medications are better and they're available when people need them. They're not so expensive. Your sister just has to take them properly." I narrowed my eyes and gave Annasuena an exaggerated threatening look.

"I will!" Her smile returned and then faded quickly. "But I am scared of the side effects. I don't want the tablets to make me feel worse. But I will start taking them. I promise."

She nodded once to Naledi, a gesture that suggested she wanted to end the discussion now.

"I'm really glad you told me, Anna."

Naledi moved then to embrace her. Annasuena closed her eyes and clasped her hands behind her sister's back, anchoring herself.

Annasuena and I packed up the leftover food for the girls to take home with them. Placing it in the shopping bag, I joked that I had no idea what *naartjies* were when I first came to South Africa and heard that word.

"Don't you have them in America?"

"We do, but we call them tangerines, or clementines. Though I think, technically, those are two different fruits."

Annasuena picked up one of the small, dimpled globes, closed her eyes as she pressed it against her nose, and inhaled deeply from the citrusy scent. "I *love* these things."

"I guess you do," I teased. "Naledi, do you *love naartjies* as much as your sister does?"

She was sitting on the lounge chair across the room, flipping through a copy of *People* magazine that an American friend had left behind after a visit, and did not respond.

"Naledi!" I called out again.

"Sorry!"

This verbal tic had begun to rattle me a bit. "You know, Naledi, you say 'sorry' a lot. You don't have to do that. You have nothing to apologize for."

Annasuena made a scoffing noise. "You do that too, Kim."

"*I* do?"

"You say 'sorry' all the time!" Sometimes her laugh took on a harsh edge, bordered on mockery, as it did now.

"Huh. I thought that was something I used to do but didn't do anymore. Guess that's why I noticed it with Naledi." I offered this with a shrug of one shoulder, and Annasuena's smile softened. Despite differences in cultures, upbringings, and life experiences, we all struggled, as girls and women, to claim our space in the world. Now here was Naledi, open and sensitive, lacking her sister's sharp edges and protective posturing. I wanted her to learn early that she could speak without apology.

When I drove the girls back to Gugulethu, Annasuena sat up front and sang along with whatever came on the radio. She sang regardless of whether she knew the words, switching to a hum if she did not.

I asked where things stood with her boyfriend, Phelo. She had not mentioned him at all overnight. She said they were still together, but she had set him straight. He could not be jealous or possessive when she was out on her own. He could not show up at her aunt's house at one in the morning to make sure Annasuena was really sleeping there, as she said she would be.

"It's disrespectful to my aunt to do that."

"It's disrespectful to you, too," I pointed out.

"It is!" she exclaimed as though the idea were new to her.

School was her focus right now, she claimed—or it would be when she returned after this break ended. She was eighteen, in Grade 9, and knew she needed to do well, to receive a good end-of-the-year report. A minute later, though, she spoke of needing to get a job, to make some money of her own, so she didn't have to depend on her aunt or Phelo to give her anything. I wondered how long she would last in high school, whether she would see it through until the Matric exams.

As tenacious as Annasuena could be, she was often mercurial with visions of her future. She wanted to work in tourism, learn new languages, and travel abroad. She could start in hospitality locally, work in restaurants or hotels, though she was convinced her short stature worked against her. She'd never seen a short hostess seating people at one of the nice restaurants at the Waterfront. Or maybe she could go into public relations or communications. Amazw'Entombi had reminded her how much she enjoyed writing, that she was good at it. Yet all these plans required her to earn her Matric or to enter FET (Further Education and Training) college, to take vocational courses. She could choose this route upon completion of Grade 9, but she insisted she wanted to finish Matric. Another three years might feel like an eternity, though. If she found she *had* to get a job and earn wages of her own, she would do what she had to do.

As we drove out the N2 highway, from the backseat Naledi asked, "Do you have a boyfriend, Kim?"

"I don't now, doll."

"Do you want to get married ever?"

"Sure. I'd love to get married."

"What? No, you wouldn't." Annasuena corrected me as though I had given the wrong answer on a pop quiz.

"What are you talking about?" I asked with a laugh.

"You're independent. You don't want a man."

"Don't you think a woman can be independent and still want a partner?"

"But you never speak about it!"

"Well, now you know. So find me a good South African guy."

"Any man would be lucky to be with you."

"Thank you, Naledi. That's sweet of you to say."

Annasuena pressed on. "But if you want to be with someone, why aren't you?" Her voice now sounded less shocked and more accusatory; at least, that was how I heard it.

"I don't know. Because I haven't found the right guy? Because I want to be with the right guy and not just any guy? It's not a decision you can make all on your own. You know?"

Annasuena looked entirely unconvinced, but I did not want to continue this conversation. I had faced that question—"Why are you still single?"—most of my adult life. I was growing weary of it, wearier still of asking it myself.

After a few minutes of silence, Naledi asked, "Are your parents still living?"

Her question startled me even more than Annasuena's reaction to my desire to marry. I hesitated for a moment and then answered, "Yes, they are."

"Both of them?" Her voice rose in surprise.

"Yes, both of them."

"You're very blessed," she said.

Hot tears rose up in my eyes then, and I was thankful to be wearing sunglasses. I was three times this girl's age, yet losing my parents remained my biggest fear in life, and an inevitability, one she had already faced. Yet Naledi's voice held none of the tones I could imagine for speaking that sentence. It was not envious, or sarcastic, or bitter. It was only pure.

11

And Guess What? I'm Still Alive

The World Cup concluded with Spain victorious over the Netherlands. I watched the final broadcast live from Johannesburg on giant television screens at the Cape Town International Convention Center, along with friends and hundreds of others. I expected this crowd, which was predominantly "coloured," to root for Spain, given that the Dutch were South Africa's first colonizers and the ancestors of those who established apartheid. In fact, it was the opposite. Many took great and boisterous glee in cheering on the Netherlands. I pointed this out to my friend Lynn, expressing my surprise at the South Africans' chosen loyalties.

"I suppose all is forgiven," she said with a wry smile. "But why shouldn't we cheer for the Dutch in the finals? We share that heritage, too."

The World Cup also ended in triumph for South Africa. There were no catastrophes, no waves of violent attacks on tourists, nothing beyond the petty crime that can be found at any large sporting event anywhere in the world. The threats against African immigrants after the final match did not materialize either. The country breathed a collective sigh of relief tinged with exhaustion and a great deal of pride at how South

Africans had banded together and presented their country to the world.

One particular moment before the final championship match thrilled the crowd at Soccer Stadium in Johannesburg. Nelson Mandela made his first in-person appearance at the World Cup, driven around the pitch on the back of a golf cart with his wife, Graça Machel, sitting beside him. A week shy of his ninety-second birthday, he was dressed against the winter chill, with a black overcoat, leather gloves, and a black fur hat. Tufts of gray hair peeked out at his temples, above the deep creases radiating from his eyes as he smiled continuously on the loop around the stadium, waving to the adoring crowd with one shaky hand. It was to be the last public appearance of his life.

The Nelson Mandela Foundation established a way that people could celebrate and honor Madiba on his birthday each year. Throughout his life, Mandela followed three rules, constructing his character and his struggle from this triad:

Free yourself.

Free others.

Serve every day.

In 2009, his birthday, July 18, was declared Nelson Mandela Day internationally, following a unanimous decision of the United Nations General Assembly. On that day, everyone is encouraged to spend sixty-seven minutes performing community service, to commemorate the sixty-seven years Mandela devoted to the liberation and leadership of South Africa. Since Mandela Day fell on a Sunday in 2010, the Amazw'Entombi girls and I decided to celebrate by holding a sixty-seven-minute session of the writing club for anyone from the J. L. Zwane

Presbyterian Church congregation who wanted to join us after the Sunday morning worship.

Wanting to stoke Ntombi's newfound leadership skills, I "volunteered" her to help me make an announcement about our plans at J. L. Zwane on the Sunday morning a week before Mandela Day. She panicked and said she would have to consider it. But Sharon and Portia egged her on, and reluctantly she agreed. That morning, I could not find her in church and thought she might not show up at all. As I stood in the sanctuary, trying to sing along with the prelude songs in Xhosa, I felt a hand grasp my shoulder. I turned to see Ntombi standing there in a bright yellow top and black cardigan, black beaded jewelry draped around her neck, and holding a sparkly clutch purse. She looked beautiful and terrified, breathing hard and audibly.

"You'll be great," I whispered in her ear. "It's a friendly crowd." It was also a sparse one, as another cold winter rain drummed on the church's metal roof. This Sunday, the church was holding another fundraising drive, this time to collect money for a celebration of Reverend Xapile's twenty-first anniversary as pastor. Members from the winning zone in the previous fund drive carried in their trophy, holding it aloft and trading it among themselves as they danced in the center aisle and in front of the altar. Once again, every church family was asked to contribute as much as they could spare, to give their pastor a proper commemoration over a weekend in August. Twenty-one years seemed a curious anniversary to acknowledge in such a lavish manner. Reverend Xapile was present for the dancing and the pleas to donate, though he stepped away from the sanctuary when the collection was taken.

When he returned, he preached a sermon based on a passage from the Gospel of John, when Jesus encountered a man paralyzed for thirty-eight years at the pool where people gathered in the hope that the water might heal them. Jesus asked the man whether he wanted to be healed. "What a ridiculous question!" Reverend Xapile jeered. "Who asks that question, when a man has been lame for thirty-eight years? 'Do you want to be healed?' Of course he does! Anyone who needs healing wants to be healed." The greater question, said Reverend Xapile, is, What are you willing to do to be healed? What will you do to change your own life circumstances? "If your mother is a domestic," he asked, "must you be a domestic, too? Every one of us needs to take responsibility for his or her own life."

During our announcement, Ntombi's voice sounded steady and sure, and louder than I would have expected. She said she was grateful for the trust and sense of support that the participants in Amazw'Entombi had built among themselves. "Now that I put my thoughts down into words, I feel like I can begin to change my own life and to change my community." She said writing is something that does not have an age limit. Anyone can do it. For sixty-seven minutes next week, she announced, this would be Amazw'Entombi's way to give back to the community.

I had grand visions of a sizable gathering in the fellowship hall for Mandela Day, church members of all ages eager to hear from their girls and to tell stories of their own. In fact, we had only six participants: Johanna; a grandmother of one of the girls; a couple of the church elders and a member of the women's guild; and Reverend Xapile's daughter, who attended university in Cape Town. I did not want to feel disappointed that the turnout seemed paltry. Perhaps the activity felt intimidating, too much like school, something many of the older members of the church would not have had the opportunity to complete.

Maybe people simply had too much to do after church, too many other ways they needed to spend their Sundays.

The girls did not seem bothered by the size of the group. A dozen stayed after church to participate, including some who had been in and out of Amazw'Entombi yet seemed eager now to associate themselves with it. Gugu and Xolelwa offered an introduction and explained how the club worked each week. We had prepared a list of writing prompts, which Mandlakazi read aloud before putting copies of them at the writing tables where people sat. To offer an example, before the session Gugu had written a piece about Gugulethu that she now read aloud. She wore a cherry-red bomber jacket. Everyone else seemed dressed to match the rainy weather, clad in blacks, whites, and grays, save for Ntombi's sunshine-yellow top. When Gugu moved about the room, she caught everyone's eye like the flash of a neon sign.

"This is called 'Gugulethu, Our Home,'" she began.

Gugulethu, our home. Home to our grandparents, home to our parents. Home to us. To our brothers, sisters, friends, and boyfriends. Gugulethu, our pride. Where boys play and check out them girls, and where girls check out those boys. We gossip, make friends and enemies. Gugulethu, land of our grandparents, who gave birth to our parents. Where they shared good times and bad. Where we had small fences and could borrow from a neighbor like a best friend. Now, years since then, what has become of our home? Is it still something we can have pride in? There's too much fighting, killing, gangsterism, shooting, murder. Nothing or nowhere is safe anymore. Our land has become a place where you have to grow up to learn to take care of yourself. Because each corner you turn, you have to look behind you, over your shoulders. Today boys as

*young as ten are gangsters and girls as young as twelve are moth-
ers. Gugulethu's mothers go to bed every night crying, missing their
dead children, or wondering if the living ones will be coming home
that night. What has it all come to? We don't know. But some of us
still have hope that one day, we will take back what is ours. Take
back our home. Take back Gugulethu. Take back our pride.*

When she finished reading, everyone applauded, and Gugu
laughed with awkward pleasure.

Johanna especially enjoyed the exercise. She chose to write
about her memories of the day Mandela was released from prison.

*On the day Tata [Father in Xhosa] Nelson Mandela was released
from prison, I was very very excited. It was my birthday month. It
was summer and a beautiful day. After hearing about him for so
long, I was at last going to see him. It was a Sunday and me and
my friends were getting ready to go to the Grand Parade in Cape
Town. Transport was no problem for everybody was in a happy
and forgiving mood. You could even get free transport to town.
When I got to our main street in Gugs, taxis were overflowing and
people were going to the train station in big numbers. We were singing freedom songs and rejoicing for our nation's father was coming
back. When we got to Cape Town the throng of people going to the
Parade from the station were so thick that my feet did not touch
the ground and I had to be careful not to fall for I would have been
trampled to a pulp. More people were coming in by bus, train, and
taxi, and the Parade was already overflowing. What a happy day!
I had never before seen a gathering of that multitude.*

She grabbed my arm and pulled me down into a seat beside
her. "Kimberly, after you write about the girls, you must help

me write my book." Johanna needed a book about her life. I did not know her very well, but, other than the girls, she was probably the person I knew best in Gugulethu, from helping with the orphans' group and occasionally seeing her around J. L. Zwane during the week, although I was spending less time there now. Many days I found her dear; other days, she proved trying. Sometimes at orphans' group she seemed to compete with the kids when it came time to collect donated food or secondhand clothing. She took these items to others in need in the community and often she took them home for herself. When Milly once spotted her holding up a shirt and sizing it against her torso, she called her out. "Johanna! Your boobies are too big for that blouse." It always seemed a complicated calculation in Gugulethu—who needed what basic material items the most, who was deserving, who decided.

Johanna told me once that she had never married. "Why would I want a husband? Someone to tell me, 'Do this! Do that!' *Sjoe!*" But she spoke about her son, a young man in his twenties, and I assumed he was her only child. I later learned that he was actually her nephew. As a teenager, this nephew had stabbed Johanna's birth son to death in his bed after an argument. He went to prison, briefly, and then was released. His parents were dead and Johanna took him into her home, considered him her child now, called him "son."

In Gugulethu, Johanna and I had attended a short dedication for the new marble memorial that had been erected to Amy Biehl, the American Fulbrighter who died not far from Johanna's home. Present at the dedication was Linda Biehl, Amy's mother, who had attended the Truth and Reconciliation Commission hearings for Amy's killers, had forgiven them publicly, and had given one a job at the Amy Biehl Founda-

tion. Afterward, I asked Johanna how she had been able to forgive her nephew, her son's killer. How had she lived through
that? Where did she find the strength to pardon what feels
unpardonable?

"I knew God walked with me through that time," she said.
"He never gave me more than I could bear. I've been forgiven.
God forgave me for my sins. How could I withhold forgiveness
from this boy who's my blood, too?"

No one else from the church, besides Johanna, wanted to
read aloud what they had written. The girls wanted to read,
though, and now took turns standing up at their tables, turned
toward their writing peers and the small audience.

Thulisa chose the writing prompt "It is time that I . . ."

*It is time that I be who I want to be and live in happiness. I tend
to hide my true personality, who I am. I tend to focus on the past
than on the future. It is time that I become proud of being an African, show my appreciation to those who have dedicated their time
to me. I want to forgive and forget, focus on what should be my
priority. People when they see me or when I express myself will try
by all means to drag me down. This time I've learned that it's not
about who I am. It's about what I do that molds me into the person
I am. It's time I did something good for those who were beside me
in times of sorrows. This is the time to say thank you for showing
me the way.*

Mandlakazi chose the same prompt.

*It is time that I learn to appreciate myself. Time that I ignore the
things that I cannot change. It is time that I focus only on things
that I can change. It is time that I appreciate the way that God*

has created me. Time that I love myself for who I am and not who I was before or who I want to be in the near future. It is time that I did something constructive about my life. Time that I learn to make my own decisions, for I don't know when abazali bam *[my parents] will leave me. It is time that I stop living in the past but live in the present. Time that I stop saying someone else is beautiful but saying instead I am beautiful. It is time that I forget who I was ten years ago but focus on who I am now and what I want to achieve in life. It is time that I ignore what people have to say about my life because everything that they say is sometimes very negative. It is time that I change. It is time that I live in the minute, hour, day, week, month, year that God has given me.*

Gugu wrote again, prompted by this question: "Who has been the hardest person in your life to forgive?"

When I think about this person it doesn't really make sense at all because the person that I'm thinking about is actually six feet underground. He's lying there peacefully, with no sadness and tears, and isn't going through all the problems and ups and downs of this world no more. This person, on the 13th of January in the year 2009 took on the journey of life into eternity. Who am I talking about? My dad. The one person I could speak to about anything and everything and never feel ashamed about it. The person I could take long walks of silence with and yet not feel the slightest weirdness. But he left just like that. With not even a goodbye. When I sat on a chair at his funeral feeling the mixed emotions that I had, I tried to turn my anger into gratitude to the Lord above for giving me the 16 years that he granted me with this man.

Like Ntombi, like Mandlakazi, like too many of these girls, Gugu was still grieving the loss of a parent—masked, in her case, by a childlike personality overflowing with an exuberant zest for life. Perhaps that was her attempt to reclaim her childhood.

Portia was preparing to leave soon for her months of volunteering in Mozambique. She wrote about a disappointment she'd had in life that actually turned out to be a blessing in disguise. She had missed deadlines to apply for further study at CPUT after she finished Matric and instead was forced to take her current gap year off from studies.

I have to say, life has its own ways of turning out even if you have planned it. Last year, I was in Matric and I was doing well. I am a very ambitious person, goal oriented, and I know what I want to achieve in my life. I never thought that I could not be studying this year, and everybody thought so too. But you cannot control everything. Here I was without a school and I was so disappointed in myself. I saw all my friends getting ready for tertiary [post-secondary study]. I really hated myself for that. Five months down the line, I get the opportunity of traveling and experiencing a different culture, meeting new people, gaining personal growth, and seeing myself in the eyes of others. I'm proud and honored knowing for a fact that I'm submitting myself for service not expecting to receive material gain but something more powerful than that—KNOWLEDGE—that no one can take away from me. This is a foundation that will keep building higher and higher. I've set myself a platform that not only benefits me but those around me as well. It has been a blessing in disguise and I'm beginning to find myself as an individual and a young woman. I'm digging a little deeper, finding so much more in life.

While Gugu was reading about Gugulethu at the beginning of our Mandela Day session, I noticed Sharon staring at the table as she listened, wearing the smile that I had originally taken for a smirk before I got to know her. The piece she wrote seemed to be a response to counter Gugu's perception of their community.

Gugulethu, Gugulethu. What a township! Over the years Gugulethu has transformed just like everything else in life. Gugs has changed and so have the people in it. As you may have heard or know, our township has become a place of violence, of hatred, a place where you fear for your life. Yes, it has. That is one of the many ways that the place I call home has changed. However, Gugulethu has come a long way. We as a people tend to look and focus on the bad and negative things in life. I guess that is why I chose this topic. It gives me a platform to appreciate the place I call home. iGugulethu, ilakishi, ikasi, the ghetto. It is where I was born and where I have spent twenty years of my life. And guess what? I'm still alive. See, that's the very thing I like about Gugs. You always have a choice. Anywhere, any place, any time you face challenges like crime and drugs. It doesn't only occur in Gugulethu. It's just that you as a person decide to fall into the trap, into those challenges. In my township, I appreciate the noise, the honking, the taxis, the laughter in the streets, the loud talking, even the harmless arguing amongst friends. You might find it strange that I say this, but for me it shows me that even behind all the violence and hatred, people are still capable of laughing. We still have hope. Most importantly, we are still unified and we have each other.

Ntombi patiently awaited her turn to read. Before she began, she took her customary deep breath and looked up. Her eyes darted around the room. She seemed to have forgotten that others were there, adults even, besides the girls of Amazw'Entombi, but she bravely continued with her reading.

"I wrote about 'What does it mean to be a Born Free?'"

Having been born in 1992 when apartheid was not ended yet has brought wonder and much more questions within myself about what kind of life I would have lived if I was born earlier, maybe in the 1980s. I do regard myself to be a Born Free as the experiences I have had growing up were in a democratic country. To me, being a Born Free means I can live my life without having to be suppressed by other people. It means I can be able to raise my voice and be heard. I can bring change to others and also to my surroundings. I can climb mountains of our beautiful creation, I can dream what is said to be impossible. I can travel the world and be with many cultures and religions. I choose what is said about my identity. I can label myself in every way that I want to and be of any color that I want to be. I'm extraordinary cause I'm born free and the world is mine. It is within me as a Born Free what I make of it.

We finished within our scheduled sixty-seven minutes and thanked Nelson Mandela for his example and inspiration. I read one of his quotations aloud, from the closing speech he gave at the International AIDS Conference in Durban, South Africa, in 2000: "It is never my custom to use words lightly. If twenty-seven years in prison have done anything to us, it was to use the silence of solitude to make us understand how precious words are and how real speech is in its impact on the way people live and die."

Johanna took a group photograph of the girls and me to mark the day. As we were tidying up the space afterward, Ntombi had news to share. She had decided to enroll in a jewelry-making course at the College of Cape Town, which has a small campus in Gugulethu. It was a yearlong FET (Further Education and Training) program for which she qualified, having completed Grade 9. "It's not really what I want to do, but I have to be out of the house. I can't stay home and do nothing. It's driving me mad."

"I think it's a great idea. Look at you, getting out and making things happen for yourself!" I swatted her playfully on the shoulder and she giggled.

"And Sharon told you about UCT?" she asked.

"No. What about UCT?"

Ntombi called Sharon over and commanded, "Tell Kimberly about UCT."

"Shame, there's nothing to tell. I just applied, that's all."

"*Applying* is something to tell." They laughed at the emphasis I gave the word.

"*Ja.* I don't know." Sharon fidgeted nervously in a way she rarely did. "My mom wanted me to apply, so I did it. But I don't know if I'd even go if I got accepted."

"You don't have to know that right now. Applying might give you options. What program?"

"Social work."

"Perfect."

Sharon always struggled with competing loyalties that she held equally dear. She knew she had family responsibilities she was expected to fulfill. More than any of the girls, she also wanted to take concrete action to improve the lives of people in Gugulethu, especially its youth. The UCAN retreat solidified this desire within her. On top of everything, she wished to direct the course of her own life, rather than letting circumstances do so. The University of Cape Town would be lucky to have this girl.

As I continued to work with the girls of Amazw'Entombi, I searched for inspiration for my own writing efforts and belatedly discovered a wing of Cape Town's literary community. The Center for the Book, an outreach effort of the National Library of South Africa, promotes a culture of reading, writing, and publishing, especially in local languages. The center is housed in the City Bowl in an enormous domed Edwardian building on Queen Victoria Street, one block up from St. George's Cathedral and across the street from the lush Company's Garden, a park originally created in the 1650s by the area's first European settlers.

I found an informal writers' group called Out to Lunch, held at the center on a biweekly basis. They organized these drop-in sessions as we did with the girls' club, giving a prompt and time to freewrite before reading our work aloud. The gatherings I attended were very small, sometimes with only two or three of us, but it helped me immerse myself in my writing during a time when I was not conscious of the girls and their efforts. The sessions were held in the main hall, a round structure lined with glass-fronted bookshelves, with white pillars that climbed to a yellow ceiling. Its shape and scale reminded me a bit of the Library of Congress back home in Washington.

When I met Nelisa, the center's staffer who ran Out to Lunch, I told her about the girls in Gugulethu. She seemed astonished that such a group existed there. "Eh? Amazw'Entombi? *Amazw'Enbombi!*" She repeated it with such force that I worried I had been mispronouncing the name all these months. She thought it was a wonderful idea and asked to meet the girls. I wanted to bring them to the center, to hold a session of Amazw'Entombi in this grand space. I wanted them to see a

place where words and books were revered, to see them take their places as writers in such a setting.

We would have to travel as a group into Cape Town. I didn't fully trust the girls to get themselves into town on their own on time. I also didn't want them to have to incur an expense with train or taxi fare. J. L. Zwane had a van that would hold at least a dozen of us, along with a driver employed by the church. So I approached Reverend Xapile in his office about taking the van into town with the girls on an upcoming Saturday session.

"I'm sorry, Kimberly, that will not be possible," he said, sitting behind his desk, below a row of closed-circuit television screens that showed different views of the church and the community center building, a security measure. I had not expected this to be a problem, so I was taken aback by his quick response.

"Is the van being used already that day?" I asked.

"No, but we must watch our expenses," he said slowly, as if searching for his words. "We do not have the money budgeted for a trip of this nature."

"Even if it's just going into town and straight back to Gugulethu?"

"That's right."

I had yet to develop any camaraderie or easy communication with Reverend Xapile. He had a somewhat haughty manner that intimidated me, reminding me that I was the outsider here. He had been welcoming to allow me to base my Fulbright project at the church, even encouraging about a program specific to girls. But I would be gone soon, back to America in a matter of months, as so many volunteers had come and gone through the church. I wanted to ask about the money that had been raised back in February for programs that the church's community center sponsored. Surely Amazw'Entombi counted? Petrol was

expensive in South Africa, but if this was a program benefiting young members of the church, it seemed a legitimate expense. I had the feeling that he refused my request because he could. I did not challenge him, but I wished that support for these girls was more forthcoming. I wished that the efforts they were making and the progress we were all witnessing, individually and collectively, could be valued and affirmed by their community. I wished *umfundisi* could acknowledge the ways that they were doing what he exhorted in his sermon: determining the direction of their own lives.

Thankfully, Nelisa agreed to come to Gugulethu on a Saturday afternoon, along with two other writers I had met at Out to Lunch, Primrose and Ravayi. Primrose was South African and young, in her mid-twenties, I guessed, not much older than the girls. Ravayi introduced herself as Zimbabwean by birth, Capetonian by choice, and German by marriage. Mandlakazi found that description hilarious and made her repeat it. We had a larger gathering that day, about ten girls. We talked first about writing, where their inspirations came from, what they enjoyed writing. Ravayi talked about how, in Zimbabwe, she saw too many people writing "letters" from rich white ghosts, hoaxes claiming that money had been buried. After she had said this, she apologized to me for the remark, and the girls and I laughed. I said I would *not* be leaving behind a note like that. But it was the only moment when I became aware that I was the sole white person in the room and how little that meant, in this context, with these relationships we had built together.

Nelisa read a short story she had written in Xhosa. I understood none of it but instead sat and watched the girls' faces as they listened. The way they observed her body language, the places where they laughed, the audible responses they pitched back to her. After she'd finished reading, Nelisa told them insistently, in English, so I could understand, that they must also read and write stories in isiXhosa, to keep the language alive on the page as well as in speech. She had already gently but firmly corrected me when I called the language Xhosa: "We must be precise. We must call it isiXhosa."

After the women read their writing, as we talked within the circle, I saw Sharon, Ntombi, and Gugu leaning toward one another, whispering. When there was a pause in conversation, Sharon asked, "Kimberly, do you have our notebooks here? Could we read from them?" I scrambled up to get the bag of notebooks I brought along each Saturday and handed them out to the gathered girls. They took a few moments to flip through their pages, choosing a piece to read back to these visiting writers. Each girl read her own words with pride, without hesitation, sitting up straight, pulling shoulders back, and speaking in a strong voice. They read as peers, as artists in solidarity with the sisters who had come to greet them. It was my favorite moment of the year.

I missed Annasuena's presence at both Mandela Day and the day the women writers visited Amazw'Entombi. After Naledi went back home to Port Elizabeth, Annasuena disappeared again, dropping contact, skipping Amazw'Entombi and orphans' group. This was her pattern, for whatever reason. It made sense, in a way, that she would be so elusive. Annasuena had spent her entire life moving, or being moved, from place to place, without people keeping close tabs on her whereabouts. She expected chaos in her living situations and it found her.

Olwethu had also made herself scarce for weeks. I had not seen her since the day I accompanied her to the clinic. When

I walked into the classroom for orphans' group on a Tuesday afternoon, it took me a moment to recognize the girl sitting in the chair across the room. I was shocked—not only by her presence but also by her appearance. Her head was shaved, her face gaunt. Milly saw me walk in and halt in surprise. She came over and said in a low voice, "He ripped clumps of her hair out. That man she's been staying with." With her back to the circle of kids, Milly mimed the assault, yanking her right arm with her fist closed around Olwethu's imaginary long braids. "Pinky said she had these big bald spots and they just had to shave the whole head. But she's back home now, praise God."

Olwethu spotted me walking in her direction and turned her head away. I stopped behind her chair and squeezed her shoulders gently, and she looked up toward me then. "I'm glad to see you here today, doll," I said brightly.

"Ja, I'm glad, too."

She did not look glad. She looked deflated and drawn, and years older than nineteen. I could not speak with her then because Milly summoned the children into the circle to begin with a Bible reading. After her Durbanville church donated paperback Bibles for the children at J. L. Zwane's orphans' group, Milly had started reading portions of scripture out loud to the children each week, beginning with Genesis. She would interrupt the reading to explain unfamiliar terms or concepts, and she brought it round to how the passage could be applied to these children's lives today. This week she read from the story of Isaac and Rebecca, how they came to be married after the death of Isaac's mother, Sarah. How his father, Abraham, prayed for a suitable wife for the grieving Isaac and sent his unnamed servant abroad to find her. How Rebecca offered the servant water from the well after his journey, demonstrating that she was the one. How Rebecca agreed to go with the servant and to marry Isaac, who loved her and was comforted.

Milly removed her reading glasses, placed them on her head, and said, "It's a beautiful story and it still happens today. If you lay your needs before God and if you trust God, your prayers will be answered if you have real faith. Listen, please!" Some of the children always grew restless during Bible study. "Really listen to this. If this is a serious need—I'm not talking about praying for the lottery numbers," she dismissed that prayer with a flick of her hand. "If you have a serious need on your heart, he will listen to your prayers and answer them. If you seek God's wisdom, he will send you the right husband and the right wife just for you, as he did with Isaac."

I suspected that Milly was tailoring this lesson to Olwethu's current circumstances. I knew she had the girl's—in fact, all these children's—best interests at heart. Yet I cringed to hear her make such a commitment on God's behalf. I knew that assurances such as these were not guaranteed, that husbands and wives were not always doled out like a requested Christmas gift from Santa. I knew all too intimately about unanswered prayers for a partner and the way those prayers raised questions rather than answering them. Were my needs frivolous? Was my faith lacking? Did God not hear, or listen? I wondered how many of these children had prayed, fervently, with their bodies and with their whole pure hearts, even if they could not form the words, for their mothers to live. Where had those prayers gone?

After the group finished and the food was distributed for the children to take home, Milly asked Olwethu to wait around so she could speak to her. She gestured to me to join them. Milly pulled up a chair across from Olwethu and I sat next to the girl. I did not want her to feel as though she were undergoing an interrogation. She sat with her shoulders slumped, staring at the floor with vacant eyes.

"Pinky says you don't want to go back to school," Milly began. Olwethu remained quiet. "I'm sad to see this, as sad as if my own daughter had left school. What do you think you're going to do now?"

Olwethu raised her eyebrows, shrugged one shoulder, and kept her eyes on the floor. "Get a job, I suppose."

"Where? What are you going to do? Work as a domestic? Wash dishes in a restaurant?"

Silence once more. Then, "I don't know."

Milly reached out and shook Olwethu's forearm lightly. She looked as if she wanted to shake her harder. "Do you love this man, with what he's done to you?"

"No." She said the word with a tired shake of her head.

"Do you think he'll care for you when you're sick?"

The question brought a rueful laugh from the girl. "No."

Tears pooled in her eyes until Olwethu squeezed them shut and swiped at her cheeks. She said nothing further. Milly looked at me over Olwethu's bowed head and gave her own head a fierce shake. I sat there, quiet and grateful that Milly could do the talking. Rather than arousing compassion, her muteness and the defeated posture of this girl angered me. Anger at her, for the stupid choices she made and the reckless ways she handled her own life. Anger at myself, for my growing impatience with her struggles, my waning empathy for her failure to recognize her own intrinsic worthiness. She elicited an almost physical reaction in me. I wanted to shake her, too. More than that, I wanted to see Olwethu herself get angry. At her mother for the poor choices she made in her own life; at

God for taking her parents away; at the man who hit her, and who did it again and again; even at Milly and me for meddling in her life. Anything but this vanquished, hollowed-out girl who sat beside us now.

"Well," Milly said, throwing her hands in the air, "when you're ready to do something different with your life, we'll be here to help you. Until then, I don't know what else to say to you."

Olwethu nodded, swiped at the tears on her cheeks again, and gathered up her bag of groceries. I did not offer to drive her home.

12

Make the Choice to Live and Not Just Exist

As 2010 wound down, everyone got busy. Beyond their involvement in Amazw'Entombi, Sharon and Ntombi began to lead the youth group at J. L. Zwane that grew out of the success of the UCAN retreat. One of the participants, a girl named Athini in her late teens, started attending the writing club as well after Ntombi and Sharon talked it up. I teased Ntombi about her expanding responsibilities, the way she was adding organized clubs and activities to her life.

"You remember telling me at the beginning of the year that you don't *do* clubs and almost didn't come to the writing club?"

"Yes! I don't know how this happened. It's Sharon's fault." She cast blame on her friend without conviction. Ntombi clearly loved her new roles and the skill sets she was discovering within herself. The jewelry course at the College of Cape Town seemed to thrill her less. It was not especially stimulating for her mind, she told me, not much to think about, just rote work with her hands and a lot of repetition. But it kept her days filled in a way they hadn't been for a long time. She was still studying mathematics and physical science on her own time as well. Ntombi was determined to pass Matric and planned to take the exams again. Now that Sharon had applied to UCT, Ntombi was thinking about varsity herself. She wanted to go to the University of the Western Cape to study communications, something that would lead to a career, and a subject that would allow her to use her writing skills.

When they took the time to peer into their imagined futures, the girls all had vivid plans for their lives, as we discovered one week when I announced a new writing prompt: "Picture your life in the future. Pick an age. What does it look like at twenty-five, thirty-five, forty-five, or seventy-five?"

"*Seventy-five?* That's mad!" said Mandlakazi.

"Hey, it's not so mad for *me* to imagine," I protested. "Some of us are closer to that decade than others."

Her eyebrows shot high and she pressed her lips together, sucking in a grin. Teenagers anywhere have a difficult time picturing themselves as old, but in South Africa, old ladies, and old men, are growing extinct. By 2010, life expectancy had fallen to fifty-two years. The country ranked 180th out of 198 countries on a United Nations list. Seventy-five could easily seem a mythical age to these girls.

I remembered how quiet Mandlakazi had been when we started, how long it had taken her to feel comfortable reading and talking with the rest of us. Now when she spoke, it was often an aside, and usually to Gugu, because whenever the two of them sat side by side, there was no stopping the fits of laughter. But she had also grown freer to offer her opinions to the whole group, with the belief that they would be heard and valued in this company.

"Mandlakazi, you're reading first, since you made fun of old age," I said.

"Ha!" said Gugu, nudging her in the side. Mandlakazi started and said, "*Yhuu!* Ohh-kay," stretching out the word to buy herself time.

"When I'm 65, I'll be living in a . . ."

"Slow down!" I said. "Take a breath. Start over. I want to hear this."

When I'm 65, I'll be living in a small beautiful house alone because I don't picture myself having a husband. I'll be living my life to the fullest because I would be having almost every thing that I've ever wanted in life including owning a business. I would have two children, a son and a daughter. My daughter will be married but as for my son, he'll probably be searching for "The One." I'll be living in the suburbs, greeting my neighbors every morning while taking a walk. I'll forget about the past, I will not worry about the future, but I will live in the present because life gives you one opportunity which is the present.

"What kind of business do you own?" I asked. She shrugged and said she wasn't sure.

"I just want to work for myself. I don't want to have a boss I have to answer to. I want to feel free." She put on a silly smile and stretched her arms out as if they were wings and she could take to the air at any moment.

Gugu came next. She always read slowly and, when the occasion called for it—as it did now—dramatically.

It is the year 2018, and I'm 25 years old. I've just completed my degree and I'm working on my masters in medicine. I've just finished my community service and my intensive and now I'm working as a junior doctor at the Western Cape Hospital in Cape Town. My life, well, it has just begun. I'm renting a flat in Camps Bay and I'm driving a VW Golf. I don't do much partying because of my busy schedule, but I do go out now and then. I'm in a relation- ship with this guy of four years and we're pretty serious because we've moved in together.

I have a little sister who is attending a private school. I'm also working towards buying another house somewhere peaceful because she definitely needs it. I'm still adorably short, but a little longer than I was eight years ago. I'm still a size 30, thank God. I still have short hair and I still wear a size 3 shoe. I have lost a lot of friends, but also made new ones, too. I still love ice cream and chocolate. They're still my weakness. I still love reading, even now more than ever. I still love strong, black, sweet gentlemen. What can I say? I like my coffee like I like my men.

"Thank you, ladies, thank you," Gugu interrupted her read- ing to take a bow from her seat in response to our hoots of appreciation for her good taste. Then she continued.

Speaking about men, his name is Lungisa, and he's the most sweet- est, loving, caring, and definitely one hot young brother. He treats me like a queen, respects me, and loves me because I can see it in his eyes. Well, my life is not perfect, but it treats me well. I don't complain. I have a loving family, partner, and the job I've always wanted. What more could a girl want?

Although Athini was new to our group, she volunteered to read before she was asked. Maybe she knew Sharon would have insisted that she read.

I see myself 30 years into the future being a professional lawyer. I see myself being independent and re-designing the house I used to

live in, which is my grandmother and grandfather's house. Being
a role model in the community. Satisfying my family's needs and
some of their wants. Being happily married to a business man and
living with our son. Passionate about our lives and making money
like there is no tomorrow. Doing our cultures and traditions proud.
I see myself having shares in mining companies. I own a Maserati
and the latest BMW. Getting involved in building ikasi *[township]*
community. Helping children get bursaries [scholarships]. I just got
the feeling I will be on top of the world. I will travel the world and
I will be myself to the full. I will take my son to Disneyland for the
first time. I will be a loving, caring, and understanding mother,
wife, and friend. I will not let money change the way I am. I will
always reach for the stars and still learn more.

"You have some expensive taste in cars, *sisi*," I said. Athini
leaned back against her chair, crossed her arms, smiled, and
looked to the center of the circle as if she were waiting for every
fabulous thing she had pictured to materialize before her eyes
right there in the classroom.

Ntombi went next. She opened her mouth to read, then
paused, tilted her head, and said, "I had a hard time getting
started with this one, because I couldn't choose what age I
wanted to be and then, well, let me just start."

How hard can it be, imagining myself as a much older version of my
life? It can be easier for me to tell how I imagine my life when I'm 19
or 20, but let me look to 50. What can I say? Quite a lot. But why
does it seem so difficult? Being 50 does not look like the best age to
be but I can appreciate what I have achieved and not entertain my
hot flashes. My beautiful twin daughters Mona and Maya have
left for varsity, but they still think my life revolves around them.

How much harder can it be for my hormones to handle? But I have to say, it was not easy seeing them leave home and I have accepted that it does not help me anyhow to still treat them like my little angels. I don't know how my husband expects me to understand his middle age issues when he seems clueless himself. He's thinking of retiring so early to spend more time on his golf game and it doesn't look like a good idea to me, as the twins have just entered varsity and we must pay. How can I forget my sister? She's 52, but she still thinks she's my mother. I still have to finish my fourth novel but my best friend Monique thinks the only thing I should spend my time doing is having conversations all times of day. Everything demands my attention right now. I have to say, I love each and every corner that makes up my life.

"*Yhuu*, your husband sounds like a lot of work." Sharon shook her head and shuddered.

"I love that you're writing your fourth novel," I said. "Can't you all see a girl in Gugulethu lying in her bed reading books by Ntombi that she got from the library?"

"I hadn't thought like that," mused Ntombi.

I watched her picturing the scene, wrapping her mind around the idea that her words could entertain and keep someone company, as others had for her.

Then it was Sharon's turn. She had started out being the first one to read for so many weeks, but now she held back and let others go first. While so many of the girls had made great strides in their writing over the year, Sharon still wrote the most complete pieces during our sessions, wrapping a topic around from beginning to end in a solid draft of a personal essay. She did it again this day.

Mmmhmm, first of all, I'm already stuck thinking about the age I should be, let alone what I will be like. But then again, the future can be even in the next 2 minutes, or tomorrow, next week, next year, or at the age of 75.

In my future, I see myself living the life. Not the high rollers life, but a life that I will be content with. I see myself living alone in a 2-bedroom apartment with bright furnishings in the lounge, lazy rugs on the floor, small pictures hanging intimately on the walls, bean [bag] cushions in a vast array of colors from lime to orange. I see a light wooden table, a glass stand with a 32-inch TV right in the center of it. Nothing big or fancy, just a little of my personality in it.

In my future, I see the ocean from my balcony—

"Camps Bay!" Ntombi interrupted her friend with a creak in her voice, her low register rising as much as it would allow.

"You *know* it, darling." Sharon held her notebook down and raised one shoulder in a saucy gesture. I said, "If you and Gugu are both living in Camps Bay, we're having an Amazw'Entombi reunion there one day." Agreement all around, and then Sharon continued.

I see the ocean from my balcony. I see peace and tranquility. I see me being beautiful, free, and living. I see me alive, hustling and bustling around in my home. I see me in my kitchen with tall chairs, marble floor, tile walls, black and metallic appliances and silverware. In my future, I look at myself in my mirror and love what I see. I see light flooding my home, I feel alive, I see me feeling the energy flowing through my body.

In my future, I see a short lady who has all she needs at that time. I see a body who is content with her 2-bedroom apartment with blue walls, mirrors everywhere, just so that this lady can see how beautiful and how far she has come. In my future, I see a powerful independent woman, with a dog or 2. I see a powersuit. I see success and inner peace.

In my future, I see love. And don't get me wrong, I'm not talking about love as in husband love. I see me loving myself like I have never loved before. You might find it strange that I'm saying this about my future but ask yourself this: How can you expect to be loved when you don't even love yourself?

So I say it again. IN MY FUTURE, I SEE LOVE. I see me just being. I see my mom and my family living far away. I'm just joking! In my future, I see me with my family every weekend. I see me with my nieces and nephews playing outside, running and playing as if tomorrow will never come.

You might find it strange that in my future I haven't mentioned what I will be pursuing as a career. Well, the future is unpredictable. In my future, I can do anything and work anywhere. Just as long as my future has me alive and healthy, with my independence, my knowledge, and the people who love me the most.

When is this future, you may ask? Well, I answered that already. The future I wrote about for me is in the next 2 minutes, tomorrow, next week, next year, and at the age of 75. It is my future, after all.

When she finished, we all applauded—for Sharon and for the lives that each girl would lead. I told her, "Well done!" and asked how it felt to write that. "*Ja*, it felt good. It's a good life I've got there." She nodded once and smiled with contentment.

Later on, back at my cottage in Pinelands, I read Sharon's piece again.

Just as long as my future has me alive and healthy . . .

That phrase sounded so painfully conditional. Even at twenty, an age where a long future, immortality even, feels like an entitlement, Sharon knew better than to assume any guarantees. For the Born Frees, a healthy future—a future that finds them alive at all—might well elude too many. I thought of Olwethu and Annasuena, who again hadn't made it to the meeting. I wondered how they pictured their futures, if they did at all, or whether a venture like that seemed too risky, too tempting of fate. With the ongoing progress in treatment, living with HIV as a chronic illness is possible for many years, maybe for a lifetime, maybe until a cure is found. But they have to take their medications, and stay away from boyfriends who could harm or kill them. They have to choose to live.

These girls imagined their futures in such similar ways. Each wanted to feel a sense of accomplishment, however she defined that—from Ntombi's novels to Athini's cars. They assumed they would have relationships in their lives, with boyfriends, husbands, children, sisters, nieces and nephews. Their descriptions looked strikingly similar to my own imagined future when I was their age. Maybe I saw myself traveling more widely, but the fundamentals lined up when we were all sixteen, eighteen, twenty. We all wanted to be known, understood, appreciated for who we are, loved.

Only Sharon paid attention, in her writing, to the one relationship each of us was guaranteed. Unabashedly and without apology, she loved herself. Her future shone in vibrant shades, in lime and orange and blue. She saw the pictures on her walls. She hung *mirrors* in every room so she could admire herself. How I envied this girl who was only half my age. How I wished I'd stumbled upon a quarter of her self-possession when I was twenty. Maybe Mandlakazi had been right. Imagining my life at seventy-five seemed an exercise in madness. But life expectancy is more than a chronological number to reach. There might be a greater madness to be found in holding on to unfulfilled expectations. Maybe my life—any life—needed fewer expectations, and more recalculating.

During Annasuena's latest and longest disappearance, I received a phone call from Naledi, who was visiting Cape Town again for the December holidays. She wanted to see me, and I wanted to see her as well. I had grown afraid, too, that I would not see Annasuena at all before I left the country. When I inquired about Annasuena, Naledi said her sister had been back in Johannesburg again, which seemed strange when she should have been attending school.

The next day, she called. When I answered my phone, there was extended silence on the other end, and I thought the call had dropped. I said hello once more and then heard, without greeting, "It's Annasuena."

"Hello." I said the word with a sigh, without meaning to, and I knew she heard it.

"Naledi told me you're looking for me."

"Yes, she called me when she got to Gugs. She said you've been back to Joburg. What's been up, *sisi*? It's been a while."

"*Ja*. I've been back and forth, staying with my other aunt. I just needed to be away from here." She sounded tired but then brightened suddenly. "Guess what? My CD4 count is 350, which means I don't have to start on ARVs right now. I'm just taking vitamins and trying to eat well."

"That's great! Wonderful to hear. We need to celebrate, when I see you. Because I am going to see you, yes?" She laughed my favorite laugh. Every time Annasuena called me out of the blue after weeks of silence, and this time more than two months, my irritation with her lack of contact quickly dissolved. Whenever I heard her voice, that clipped and proper pronunciation coupled with the silly laugh, I always realized how much I had missed her.

"*Ja.* I really want to see you, too. I'm sorry I haven't been round." Another long pause, and then, "I found out I was pregnant."

"Oh." I sucked in a breath and held it, my lungs growing tight as I waited for her to speak again.

"I just couldn't do it. I decided to have an abortion."

"Okay." It was my turn to go silent, because I had no idea what to say to her. "Did you find out when you went to the clinic?"

"*Ja*, it was then."

"When was this?"

"End of October." The last time I'd heard from her had been early October.

"I really want to talk with you about this, if you want to, but not on the phone," I said. "Can you get together tomorrow? Maybe you and Naledi and I can go to the beach for a bit. I'm running out of days to enjoy the beach." I said I would pick them up at J. L. Zwane the next morning around eleven.

Naturally they ran late and the phone numbers I tried to call did not reach them. I hoped they would show up. I could not imagine leaving Cape Town and returning to the States without seeing Annasuena. I sat in my sweltering car in the church parking lot, windows cracked open on a rare breezeless day. People were firing up the *braais*. On warm days, Gugulethu always smelled like grilled meat. As I waited for the girls, I wrote a list of errands I had to run and people I needed to see before I left. Recorded jazz music blared from a house across the street from the church. Every few minutes, I looked up from my notebook to watch for the girls. On one of those glances, I saw a man open the door at the home where the music played. He stumbled outside, out to the sidewalk that ran along NY 2. He stopped, turned his back to the street, and relieved himself against a low brick wall that enclosed the house's small front yard. Then he zipped up and slowly began to make his way up the sidewalk, away from the house, stopping every few steps to brace himself with one arm against the wall.

A woman wandered down the sidewalk toward the man, looking into the distance beyond him. She wore a yellow tank top, jeans frayed at the hem, and flat sandals. She was not young, but probably twenty years younger than the man. As she drew near him, he lurched forward and tried to kiss her. She shoved him away, her face showing irritation mixed with disgust, and walked into the middle of the street to escape another clench. He staggered on along as though nothing had interrupted his morning stroll, continuing in the opposite direction, I hoped, from where Annasuena and Naledi would be coming.

The girls finally showed up, dressed for the hot weather in short summer sundresses, Naledi's hair in long braids, Anna-suena with her hair short and spiky. She looked the same as the last time I had seen her, though she seemed hesitant to greet me. She hung back behind her sister when Naledi lunged at me for a hug. Then I embraced Annasuena, let go, and pulled her back again for a second hug. I could feel her stiffness give way as she hugged me full-on.

The girls also brought along their three-year-old cousin, Tumi, whom they had been tasked with watching. "It's like

I'm the creche this week, I guess," Annasuena said with her standard eye roll. I panicked when I saw the little boy. "I don't think we can take him along. I don't have a car seat for him." Annasuena looked incredulous and then laughed at my stricken expression. Then I realized that I'd never seen a baby or a child strapped into a car seat in Gugs. "Fine. But Naledi, make sure you hold on to him carefully in the backseat."

We drove out along the peninsula in the direction of the Cape of Good Hope. First to Muizenberg, to eat *slap* (pronounced "slup") chips—thick, greasy French fries—along the edge of the crowded beach as we watched surfers crash through the waves in False Bay. The scene was postcard perfect, with the mountains to our backs and a row of beach houses painted in rainbow colors stretched out to one side. We took pictures and dipped our feet in the water, taking turns holding Tumi because he cried if the ocean lapped his toes.

We drove on a bit farther. I wanted to take the girls to Boulders Beach because they had never seen the colony of African penguins living there. As we walked along the boardwalk that protects the birds' nests and out over the enormous boulders, penguins waddled by along the sand and between the large and spiny aloe vera plants. Their beady eyes were rimmed in red as though they suffered from allergies. Tumi was as unimpressed by the penguins as he had been by the ocean. It took much coaxing from Naledi to get him to stand for a photograph with penguins in the background and waves crashing against the boulders.

Annasuena did not mention her pregnancy. When we were back in the car returning toward Gugulethu, she ranted instead about her family. Her aunt had told other family members that

Annasuena was HIV positive. "It's disgusting that she would do that. I don't want people to know unless I choose to tell them. People look at me differently now, and I know they know. Now she's also saying that I wasn't raped by my uncle, that I came on to him."

"She said what?" I looked over at Annasuena to see whether I had heard her correctly.

"*Ja*, I know. My uncle's wife got her to believe that. She said I seduced her husband and got him to sleep with me." She spat the words out. "She said she doesn't want me in her house now because of that. It's where Naledi is staying, so I can't even go over there to see her."

"You were a little girl. You were *eight*, right?"

"*Ja*, I think. Maybe seven. I can't remember exactly."

Suddenly I felt so angry I could barely see to drive the car. "A little girl doesn't seduce a grown man. She can't. That's evil to even suggest."

"It's awful," said Naledi quietly from the backseat.

Before I thought about it, before I had even formed the words in my head, I told Annasuena then that one of my own uncles had molested me.

"Oh no, Kim!" Naledi cried.

"He didn't rape me," I added quickly. "But he touched me in ways he shouldn't have. And it went on for a long time."

"Yeah," Annasuena said softly, in a voice that understood everything I did not have to say.

"I was eight, too. And I thought it was my fault. For *years*. It wasn't. It couldn't have been. But it took me a long time, too damn long, to believe that. Do you understand that what happened to you couldn't have been your fault?"

Annasuena blew a loud puff of air through her lips. "Oh, I

know that." In spite of my outrage, she made me smile at her refusal to even entertain the idea.

"Naledi, do you know that too?"

"Yes, I know."

I had not intended to talk about my sexual abuse, with Annasuena or with any of the girls. She was the only one who had told me this happened to her, though I knew, by sheer statistical probability, that other girls would have been abused as well. To bring up my experience earlier with Annasuena would have felt like shifting a conversation that needed to be directed toward her. To raise the issue spontaneously with any other girls might open a wound I knew I could not treat appropriately. What happened to me occurred so far in my past, years before these girls were born. It was not something I thought about often anymore. Except when a grown woman would rather accuse a girl-child of seducing her husband than take that girl's word for what happened to her own body.

Hearing Annasuena say that, I remembered eavesdropping on my mother and grandmother as she visited us during a summer when I was in high school. My grandmother wanted to know why I did not wish to see my uncle anymore. Just as families everywhere hold on to their secrets, my mother had never told her mother about the abuse, although she always believed that it happened, from the time I told her when I was eight. Now she informed my grandmother, who refused to accept that her son could harm his beloved niece. It was easier for her to believe that I had lied. "How do you know she isn't making the whole thing up?" she asked. "Kim always was a good little actress."

Sexual abuse, especially when perpetrated by a relative, destroys a child's trust that people in a position to protect her will do so. It can also shatter her trust in herself. The seed of doubt planted by my grandmother's disbelief grew into a strangling vine that knotted around my perceptions of myself, my faith in my own voice and in my right to use it. How many lives, families, nations could be changed the world over if girls and women were heard, and listened to, and believed?

"People are just stupid everywhere, is what it is." With one hand, Annasuena waved away the stupid people in the world as she turned to look toward the backseat. "Tumi! What have you got there?"

Tumi had been too restless to sit next to Naledi and instead crawled onto the floorboard. He had found a cap from an empty Coke Light bottle and had begun to chew on it until Naledi took it away, to his loud protests. To appease him, we stopped off at a McDonald's for ice cream cones. Driving out to the peninsula earlier, Naledi had taught him to say a line from a song on the radio, "Who loves ya, baby?" He babbled it over and over as we sat in the restaurant, and the girls and I laughed at him and spoke no more of the stupid people in the world, the uncles who abuse, the aunts and grandmothers who refuse to hear and believe. As we drove into Gugulethu, Annasuena asked, in a low voice, whether we could drop Naledi and Tumi back at their aunt's home and then go to my cottage to talk.

She was uncharacteristically quiet driving to my place. At my cottage, I poured glasses of guava juice and we sat on the floor in the lounge surrounded by boxes I had begun to pack, things to give away, and items to take back home. I let her take the lead with the direction of our conversation.

She said she knew she wanted an abortion right away, as soon as she found out she was pregnant. "I just couldn't handle it, on top of everything. I knew I couldn't bring it up. Phelo would help with money when he's working, but it would all fall to me." She said she went to GF Jooste Hospital in Manenberg, rather than to a doctor who advertises the procedure on a flyer. The flyers are posted all around Gugulethu, on streetlights and at taxi stands: SAFE. QUICK. 4 HOURS. CALL CELL NUMBER. . .

"So I didn't take any chances. But it was hard. . . ." Her voice trailed off.

"I'm glad you were safe." I paused, unsure whether I should say what first came to my mind when she told me on the phone about the pregnancy, then I plunged ahead. "Speaking of being safe, are you using condoms every time you have sex?"

"Yes." She rolled her eyes at the question.

"I have to ask that, if you got pregnant. You've said it yourself, you don't always do what you should to take care of yourself. And that's one thing you have to do."

"I do! The condom broke, Kim. I couldn't control that."

"All right. That happens. But just so you know it would be irresponsible to have unprotected sex even if you weren't positive."

"I *know*." She shut the topic down.

We sat in silence for a while, then I asked, "How are things with Phelo?"

"*Sjoe*, I don't even know." Her voice traveled, in five words, from bitter to sad.

He had cheated on her again, and they had parted for a couple of months. She was tired of the way he did not trust her, that he didn't like her friends. He wouldn't be happy for her when she got good marks at school. His mother still hated her and had told two of Phelo's ex-girlfriends that they were both better for him than she was. But now, at the moment, she was back with him again.

"Honey, can you tell me why? When you seem so unhappy with him?" I tried to ask the question as gently as I could, given her previous reaction. I really wanted to understand, from Annasuena's perspective, what kept this girl in this relationship.

"I know, Kim, but it's complicated." She was propped up against my small lounge chair and now dropped her head back onto it, to stare at the ceiling.

"What's complicated? Tell me."

"There are things I still like about him. I've been with him so long, nearly four years. I've told him before when we need time apart, but I don't know if I can break it off entirely. If I do that, I won't have someone in my life if I need them. I heard my aunt say to one of my friends, 'If Annasuena gets sick, she needs to call Phelo. I'm not wiping up her shit.' I worry I won't have any family to take care of me."

"Is that why you stay with Phelo?"

"Yeah, I think it is," she said quietly. "He's the one who takes me to the clinic. It's difficult not to have anyone. And I can't trust my family. It's everyone for himself there."

She sat up straight, agitated now. "Do you know what happened? I was talking with my cousin-brother late one night, the one who's supposed to be my guardian. And he came on to me! I said, 'What the fuck are you doing? Are you dreaming? Do you think I'm your girlfriend?'" Her face twisted in disgust. "And the last time I saw my oldest cousin-brother, my aunt's eldest son, I was so happy to see him and *he* tried something funny. I ask myself, what do they see in me? Was I adopted by my mom? Am I not family to them?"

Annasuena held one hand out as she spoke, palm up, her fingers curling almost into a fist. Her young face creased into a genuinely bewildered look.

"It's not you," I assured her. "I don't understand why so many men in this country treat women, abuse them, the way they do. But it's *not* you."

"I just don't know why we do the things we do to each other. It's like they're total strangers to me. I only have one cousin who seems to care about me, my cousin-brother Gerald. He told me if anyone, my boyfriend, *anyone* hurts me, I should tell him. This is the youngest son of my uncle who raped me."

"Really? Does he know what his father did to you?"

Annasuena shrugged. "I don't know. Maybe he's heard about it. I don't know if he's going to turn into a monster, too, but he's told me he'll be there for me. I needed to hear someone say that."

"Did you tell him about the other two cousins?"

"No. I just didn't want to think about them anymore. I wanted to pretend it didn't happen." She rubbed her face hard with one hand and began to cry, for the first time in my presence. "I'm tired, Kim. I just get strained. I know I'm supposed to be responsible for myself. I can't expect others to take care of me. But sometimes it just gets to be too much. I get depressed. That's probably why I haven't come to Amazw'Entombi. I know I'll feel much better and I'll meet up with people I like there. Sometimes I feel stupid because that's a place I go and I feel great about, but I still can't get myself there."

"When you're depressed, it's difficult to do things like that, even things you want to do. That's why I'm surprised Ntombi has stayed with it. That girl was pretty damn depressed when we started."

"She was. How's she doing now?"

I told Annasuena about Ntombi's rejuvenation, how she had become a youth group leader and begun the program at the

College of Cape Town. "Good for her," she said with a nod and a small smile.

"That could be you, too," I told her. "If anyone has the spirit to fight depression, it's you."

She chuckled and sat there for a moment, contemplating whether or not she believed this to be true. "I know I can be irresponsible sometimes. I know I make excuses for myself. And I do blame myself for what happens to me at times. Like now. I want to keep studying, I want to get my Matric, but I need to get a job and earn money, too. I *hate* having to ask people all the time when I need things. I hate having to stay with Phelo if I don't want my aunt's boyfriend falling over me in the middle of the night. I need my own security and privacy."

"But how can you get a job that pays enough to support yourself without an education?"

"Do you think it's wrong, me wanting to work?" She asked the question in a curious, rather than challenging, tone of voice.

"It's not wrong. I understand why you do. If I were in your position, I'm sure I'd feel the same way. But I think it's a short-sighted solution."

"I know it is! But what else am I supposed to do?"

I had no answer for her. I could offer an argument for why this bright girl, who would probably pass Grade 9 now and would be turning nineteen in a month, should stay in school for another three years to earn her Matric. But it was a weak case when offered against her dependence on a family she could not depend upon. I could not urge her to dump the boyfriend who made her so unhappy when she had no one else, when she felt so alone. I could not assure her that I would accompany her to her clinic visits; I was about to leave the country. I hoped to return to Cape Town, but I had no idea when that would be, whether it would happen at all. I had no idea how I could offer Annasuena support from half a world away.

I also could not answer the questions she never asked, at least not to me: Why her? Why did these tragedies and afflictions befall this one girl? What more could happen, before she even turned twenty? Why hadn't life beaten her yet?

The day had turned to evening and I needed to drive Annasuena back to Gugulethu before it grew too dark. When we stopped and parked in front of Phelo's family home, I had to swallow a lump in my throat before I said goodbye to her. "I know you're tired, but please keep taking care of yourself. Because I'm selfish and I love you and your crazy laugh that makes me laugh. And I want you to be here when I come back to Cape Town."

She laughed then, that *kee-hee-hee* that came from the back of her throat and lit up her radiant face even in the dark. We hugged for a long time and I kissed her on the cheek. I drove away, praying that God would bless Annasuena and keep her, that God's face would shine upon her, that she would be granted peace.

I wanted the year of Amazw'Entombi to culminate with the girls giving a public reading of their writing at J. L. Zwane in December. Until that time rolled around, I hadn't realized that South Africa closes down and goes on holiday for most of December until well into January. And why not? It's summertime; Christmastime for most people, as the majority of South Africans are Christian; schools let out; the weather turns warm and beautiful. The Atlantic is colder around Cape Town than the warm waters of the Indian Ocean at Durban, yet many still flock to the city and its beaches. Many people from the townships also leave, including Mandlakazi and Onele and other girls who traveled by bus back to the Eastern Cape to spend Christmas and New Year with their immediate or extended families.

We held the reading close to December 16, the Day of Reconciliation. This was another of South Africa's public holidays that had been instituted after 1994. During apartheid, December 16 was considered a religious holiday, known as the Day of the Vow. It commemorated the Afrikaner Voortrekkers' victory over the Zulus at the Battle of Blood River in 1838, when 3,000 Zulus were killed and only three Voortrekkers wounded. The Voortrekkers took a vow: If God would help them secure victory, they would always set aside this as a holy day of remembrance. On the other side of things, after the 1960 Sharpeville Massacre, where police opened fire on a crowd protesting the pass laws and killed sixty-nine people, the African National Congress decided that it could no longer limit itself to nonviolent protest. On December 16, 1961, the ANC launched its military wing in the anti-apartheid struggle, *Umkhonto we Sizwe* (Spear of the Nation), with a series of guerrilla attacks against government installations and electrical stations. The post-apartheid government chose December 16 as Reconciliation Day to acknowledge the importance of the day to both Afrikaners and those in the liberation struggle, while also striving for national unity. Now it also semiofficially kicks off the holiday season.

It was not, however, a wise time to schedule a Friday-night reading. From the church, we drew only Manilisi, a young leader at J. L. Zwane now working with Sharon and Ntombi on the UCAN youth group, and two girls around the age of ten or eleven. I had no idea where they came from. None of the girls' family members attended. I asked the girls—Sharon, Ntombi, Gugu, and Mary-Ann were there to read—whether they had even told their families about the reading. Everyone said they had.

"People just don't come out for things like this very much, and especially around the holidays," Sharon said. Poor planning on my part.

The largest portion of the tiny crowd were friends of mine, because I had made many good friends in Cape Town by now. I finally realized that, beyond the girls, I was not finding the community I craved at J. L. Zwane. The language barrier played a large role; I could not understand the Xhosa that made up so much of Sunday-morning services. So I had begun to attend an English-language church in the City Bowl, a wonderfully welcoming, interracial congregation. At J. L. Zwane, even when individual church members embraced me on a Sunday morn-ing, or collectively as on Mother's Day, I always had the feeling of being set apart as a foreigner, someone who had come to the church temporarily to help. Fair enough; that's who I was, and J. L. Zwane had seen plenty of Americans and Europeans like me come through its doors. With the girls, though, I felt a genuine camaraderie and bonds forged from our year together.

So, in that spirit of solidarity, after I introduced Amazw' Entombi, I kicked off our event by reading my own writing. "This is called 'When the Time Is Right,'" I began.

When the time is right, I will risk looking foolish. I will not focus on how I sound, look, act, trying to see myself through another pair of eyes. How could I do that anyway? I have only my eyes, my experi-ences, my moments of ridiculousness and, Oh no, did I really say that? These quirks are all mine, all the time.

When the time is right, I will jump, though first it might be a baby jump, a bunny hop. A leap, when it's required . . . I know I can do that, but first I have to remember how to bounce. Remind myself that I do bounce. I always wonder: With a leap of faith, which comes first? The leap, or the faith? I hope I know which it is when the time is right for leaping.

When the time is right, I will look inside myself and try to figure out what I want, truly want, not what I think I should want. I won't listen to others telling me the time. I'll look at my own watch, check the time and see. Maybe my watch is in a different time zone than anyone else's. Maybe that's okay.

When the time is right, I will pray for grace, for understanding. I'll more likely need this from myself than from another person. But that time is right, is right now. How can I say things to myself that I would never say to someone else? That time's over.

When the time is right, I will risk my heart. Offer it up—to whom, I'm not quite sure yet. To someone who has time, and knows it's right, and wants to leap with me. But in the meantime, at this time, the time is right to love as much as I can. The girls of Amazw'Entombi, the beauty of South Africa, God, my family, my friends, my life. The time is beyond right for that.

The girls all chose the piece of writing they wished to read. Sharon wrote something new; Gugu and Ntombi revised previously written pieces. Mary-Ann, the baby of the group, who barely spoke above a whisper, read after I did. I guessed that she was reading a poem she had not written herself. She struggled with writing, and her words were often difficult for me to read and comprehend. But I kept these thoughts to myself and praised her bravery to read aloud.

Sharon read next, a piece she titled "Just My Opinion."

A question was once posed for our congregation to share their thoughts: "What is it that makes our children (black youth) throw their babies in drains or kill them?" It was a controversial topic and one which was hard on the ears of the female youth. Out of all the responses in the church that day, one stood out to me and not because it was correct but because it angered me. It fueled a fire in me yet I said nothing. This woman called us stupid. Now don't get me wrong, I don't mind being told I'm wrong, but to call me stupid. . . .

Since I was a young girl, I refused to be a statistic in Gugulethu. I didn't want to be a drop-out due to pregnancy and have to struggle for the rest of my life. My mom sent me to multi-racial schools and since then I have observed something. I am not trying to make any excuses for myself or the youth, but the way we are brought up has a lot to do with how we end up. I once heard someone say that in the black community we are not given the opportunity to soar to great heights and be great. We are shielded from so many things out of fear, things that shouldn't be hidden from us. The excuse is that they are trying to protect us but what good does that really do? Black people have the highest fertility rate. They say knowledge is power, yet they refuse to give us their life lessons. We could learn so much more from parents than we could from a book, but we are not even given a chance to. Conversations between mother and child have become redundant because you always tell the child what not to do and how stupid they are instead of asking what's on their minds and advising them.

Times have changed, values and morals have changed, even technology has advanced yet the ways of parenting remain stagnant. What have parents achieved by doing this, huh? Blessed with more and more grandchildren instead. What good has shouting and beatings done? We are often compared to Western culture, white people in other words, the main difference being commu-

nication. At school my friends used to talk about how their parents listen to them. The operative word being LISTEN, something which is not normally done in our culture. It frustrates me to no end what I see happening, especially when I hear comments the elderly make.

All kids need is just a platform to voice out their opinions and be heard. Not to be told they are stupid. To me, saying that just seems like the coward's way out.

I really wished Sharon's community had been gathered to hear from this formidable, articulate young leader in their midst.

Gugu went next, and once again she paired her joyful spirit and effervescence with heartbreak in "I Wish Someone Had Told Me."

Time and time again people had told me to stop worrying, stop crying, kuzolunga, it's going to be all right. That night when I was told my dad died, that was all they could say. It's going to be all right. It'll be okay. Everything happens for a reason and it's going to be okay. So I stopped crying, I stopped worrying. I stopped feeling the hurt. I stopped feeling the pain and for weeks I stopped doing just about anything. I stopped laughing. I stopped talking for weeks to months on end. I stopped thinking and feeling. Feeling what I wanted to feel, thinking what I wanted to think. I pushed all my emotions back so that it wouldn't be so hard to do what I wanted to do in the whole world.

Because of that, I eventually forgot what my father even looked like. Forgot his eyes. Forgot his smile. Funny, huh? Because that smile of his was the only thing that would lighten up my day. I didn't do what I really wanted to do. Because I didn't cry, because

I didn't feel the hurt, feel the pain inside, I almost forgot the one thing that my father had left me: the memories. His eyes. His smile.

Because of that, I really wish that someone had told me that it was okay to cry. It was okay to feel the hurt, feel the pain. But you know what I really wish someone had told me, so that I could always remember his face, his eyes, his smile? I really wish someone had told me that it was okay to miss him.

Finally, Ntombi revisited "I Need to Find a Place," the piece she had read so reluctantly when she read aloud for the first time. Starting from a raw place, this piece had only gotten stronger when she worked with it, just as her voice had, heard loud and clear this evening.

I'm not sure if it was after my mother's death or before when I started dreaming and longing to find a place of my own where it can just be me and nobody else around. Where there will be peace and quiet and I didn't have to worry about the next minute or the next year, where I wouldn't feel the need to pretend and act OK when thunder strikes or I'm just not feeling in the mood to talk. In this place, I seemed to be very happy, like this was how the world was supposed to be. When I woke up I realised how all this time I had lived in a dream filled with anger, hurt, blame, tears, pretence, and sleepless nights. But I kept on saying that I needed to find the place. I didn't know the place I needed to be was already in me, but I had decided to look the other way around. I just needed to go back within my heart and soul and look for the deserted land. When I went back to this place, all the things that I thought I had lost were still waiting for me, like love for myself, the blessing of waking up on a beautiful Sunday morning and appreciating God's love for me, the sweet message from a friend telling

me how blessed she is to have me in her life, the hope that was still
blooming, showing me I was one of many and not on my own.
Now as I look back and remember, I know that being the person
that I am today and achieving everything that I have achieved
and am still going to achieve has taken me to make the choice to
live and not just exist.

After the readings, I presented each girl with a certificate
naming her a founding member of Amazw'Entombi, Gugulethu, South Africa, 2010. We took photographs to commemorate the moment and, naturally, ate the snacks that I had
brought. I introduced the girls to my South African friends,
who were surprised, I thought, by the level of talent the girls
demonstrated. I puffed up with a staggering pride for what we
had created together.

Sharon had been accepted to the University of Cape Town;
now she had to decide whether or not to attend. Ntombi
would keep on with the jewelry-making course. She had also
decided, for certain, to attempt the mathematics and science Matric exams once more. Now that she had seen what
she could accomplish, she knew she wanted to study further,
wanted the opportunities an education could open up for her.
I hoped this young woman's determination proved stronger
than her depression. I wished everyone could have been there.
I missed seeing Mandlakazi leaning into Gugu, giggling side
by side in their chairs. These girls would be continuing on in
high school the next year, and I expected them both to do
well. For Olwethu and Annasuena, also absent this night, my
prayers were simple. I prayed that each girl would stay alive,
and stay healthy.

The girls knew from the beginning of the year that I hoped

to write a book about them, and they were excited about the idea, in a vague sort of way, as I was. I had told them I had to return to America, because my Fulbright year was ending, and I had no way to support myself to continue living in South Africa right now. I wanted to return, but I wasn't sure when, or what I might be doing besides writing a book, in Cape Town or in Washington. My own future felt more up in the air than at any time since my early twenties. I wanted to feel exhilarated by the possibilities, but really, after the end of this amazing adventure I had fought to have, the instability suddenly terrified me.

On New Year's Day 2011, a few days before I returned home, I texted all the girls for whom I had phone numbers, to wish them a happy year ahead. Some of them had already sent me texts at the stroke of midnight, wishing me the same. Ntombi responded immediately. As with all their texts, I had to read it out loud in order to understand the hieroglyphics she wrote from her phone:

> happy New Year 2 u 2 dear!! may God bless u in evry way possible nd I rily thank him 4 bringing u into this year. i jst wnt u 2 leave evrythn into his handz nd stop worying abt wht wil happen in ur lyf. u'l definatly c his work when u believe. CRAZY LUV . . . mwa!

I had come to realize that Ntombi's intuition and close observation of people extended to me. Alone among the girls, she always knew when I was stressed. We rarely spoke about God directly; few of the girls did. But there were moments where I glimpsed deep wells of faith in many of them, an assurance that their lives were cradled in a caring embrace, as Ntombi envisioned for me. I didn't know whether it was belief or hope. I didn't know whether naming it mattered.

Rereading her text, I tried hard to hear it in Ntombi's throaty tones, so I could carry that voice home with me. Then I sent crazy love back to her.

PART THREE

UBUNTU IN
ABUNDANCE:
GUGULETHU, TWO
YEARS LATER

13

As Old or As Young
As Democracy

I had forgotten how well you can see Table Mountain from a seat by the picture window at KFC. The tablecloth floated above its flat top, the cottony layer of cloud that settles over the mountain when the southeasterly wind blows. Also in my sight lines as I stared out the window were two signs. A large billboard announced: GUGULETHU, YOU'VE COME A LONG WAY. LET'S GO EVEN FURTHER. I thought at first, from the phrasing, that the sign had been sponsored by a social-change organization. It was actually an advertisement for Metropolitan, a financial services company based in Cape Town. The other sign was much smaller and affixed to the side of a garbage bin sitting near the street: an advertisement for an herbalist to "cure your bad luck." It promised services for court and divorce cases, penis size, restoration of power, and reversal of spells cast by enemies.

When I returned two years after I had left it, Cape Town looked as beautiful as ever. While the city no longer buzzed with the excitement the World Cup had brought to 2010, Cape Town Stadium still glowed as it sat beside the sea, underused, losing money. An official South African government report revealed that the country had spent $3.9 billion to host the

World Cup, including $1.3 billion on stadiums alone, including this one. The report touted the "intangible legacy" of pride and national unity the tournament had left behind. Beyond some road upgrades, tangible benefits were harder to identify; most of the 130,000 jobs created had been temporary construction or service positions. For the majority of South Africans, poverty and unemployment remained deeply entrenched. As I drove into Gugulethu, the only thing that looked different was the street signage. NY 1 had been renamed Steve Biko Drive, in honor of the Black Consciousness leader and anti-apartheid activist killed while in police custody in 1977. This was a first effort to rename the "Native Yards" streets of the township.

I had hoped to return sooner to Cape Town, to live here for another year and continue to work with the girls in the writing club as I wrote this book. Circumstances and finances had rendered that plan impossible. But now I had returned for a shorter span of time, to see the girls and catch up on their lives. While back in Washington, I had stayed in touch with several of them through Facebook. Many could access the Internet on cell phones now; after America and Europe took to smartphones, BlackBerries flooded the South African market. As I sat waiting at KFC to meet up with some of them, I had no idea who would show up, just as occurred with our Saturday gatherings. But there were other reasons for their elusiveness now, as some of the girls were living in places other than Gugulethu, and I had yet to track down some who were not on Facebook. I hoped I could find them now that I was in the country.

I sat hunched over my notebook, making a list of friends to call, until I heard a low voice say, "Hey, Kim," beside me. I looked up at a young woman in a purple cardigan with a deep V-neck, a magenta scarf tied around her head with a bow on the top to hold back her long, thin braids. Her cheeks grew rounder as her mouth opened into a wide smile, and then I recognized her.

"Oh my gosh, Mandlakazi!"

I jumped up and attacked her with a hug. She laughed and I squealed and we nearly lost our balance and fell down into my chair. The restaurant's other customers and the servers at the counter stared at our reunion in undisguised curiosity. I pulled back from our embrace to look at her. I always pictured Mandlakazi as one of the younger girls in the writing club, dressed inconspicuously in a gray hoodie or a conservative sweater that looked slightly too old and stuffy for her. She often looked as though she wanted to disappear into the background, which was why her sly asides and humorous commentary, as she grew more comfortable in the group, were surprising and hilarious. Now this young woman positively glowed.

As we sat down, I asked her whether she was doing Matric this year, or whether she was in Grade 11. "No, actually, I'm at varsity, at UWC." My mouth dropped open as I realized she was a good two years older than I had remembered her.

"But you were such a little girl in the writing club and now look at you!" I held up my hands and brandished them around her—from her bow-tied head to her toes clad in stylish flats. Mandlakazi had burst forth in Technicolor, her appearance catching up with her lively personality. She looked beautiful and happy. Her face suddenly grew serious and she said, "I've developed a very bad habit." I raised my eyebrows in a question. "I *love* clothes."

Then Gugu arrived, with more squeals and stares and hugs. "You're here! You're really here!" she said. I could have picked Gugu out of any crowd in an instant. Still tiny, still ebullient.

We ordered our standard—chicken twister sandwiches, chips, cooldrinks—and settled in to talk.

Both girls were attending the University of the Western Cape, in Bellville, a suburb not far from Gugulethu. The university was established in 1960, during apartheid, for "coloured" students only. It was designed as a "bush college" for training in lower- and middle-level positions in education and civil service. Through the 1970s and 1980s, it had been a hotbed of student activism, and black students began to enroll there before the end of apartheid. Mandlakazi was studying psychology and Gugu was enrolled in the nursing program, doing a foundational first year to build up her study skills and increase the likelihood that she would finish the program.

The girls, both eighteen now, picked right back up with a running banter about their lives. "At varsity, we're called students, not learners," Gugu informed me. "And we don't go to class, we go to lectures," added Mandlakazi. They confirmed what I had previously thought—they had not known one another before Amazw'Entombi began, and their friendship started during our Saturday gatherings. When they found themselves frequently riding the same taxis to UWC, the relationship strengthened. Now they called one another "comrade," in a mocking display of political solidarity that they'd been exposed to at varsity. They riffed on a pretend radio-show appearance, with Mandlakazi playing firebrand former ANC Youth League leader Julius Malema and Gugu taking on the role of Helen Zille, leader of the Democratic Alliance, premier of the Western Cape, and prominent white anti-apartheid activist. I laughed at the two of them until my sides ached.

Now that they were studying and exploring different aspects of themselves, the girls had added layers of ambition to their plans and dreams. Gugu wanted to be a midwife, but she still wanted that flat in Camps Bay overlooking the ocean. She had also decided she wanted to own a nice, expensive car.

"You know midwives probably don't make a ton of money, right?" I asked, taking a drink of my Coke Light. "You might need to make a choice. Why are an expensive car and a Camps Bay flat important?" Gugu tilted her head and pondered the question.

"Those are things that would show the world that I've made a success of my life." As she said this, she made a fist with her hands as if grabbing for the life she wanted, as if she could pull it closer to her.

"But wouldn't being a midwife show the world you're doing something important? It's helping to bring babies into the world."

"Yes, it *is* important," she responded, "and that's why I want to do it. But those aren't the things people really value in this country anymore. It's about what you *have*, what you can show to others."

If this was the profession she chose, I hoped that Gugu, as she made her way in the world, would find people who valued *her*. And I hoped that she could somehow still find a way to have that ocean-view flat in Camps Bay.

"How about you, Mandlakazi? Psychology is an ambitious field. What do you want to do with that?"

She planned to become a counselor and wanted to work with young people, especially with girls who have low self-esteem. "Is that something you think has been an issue for you?" I asked.

"It has. I always struggled with the way I looked and just wanted to be quiet, didn't want people to see me."

"That's how I remember you at first, too, until you started developing your comedy routine." She and Gugu cackled at that.

"*Ja*! You know, I have this darker complexion, and that's how my family has always thought of me, as the dark one. And that was how I thought about myself as well."

"Was that a bad way to think of yourself? As the darker one?"

"It's not . . ." She paused, smiled uncomfortably, as though trying to carefully select her words—for me or for herself, I wasn't sure which. "It's not a bad thing, exactly. But I knew it meant I was less attractive. And that was how I thought of myself, and I didn't want others to notice. So I dressed in black a lot of the time."

"Well, you're sure not dressed in black today. You're colorful and gorgeous."

She scrunched her face into a disbelieving but pleased expression. "Thanks, Kim."

"So, clearly you want to be noticed now. When you're at UWC especially, I'd guess?"

"Oh yeah. That's exactly what I want!"

Mandlakazi said that she had not wanted to come to Amazw'Entombi to begin with; her aunt, with whom she stayed when she moved to Gugulethu from Eastern Cape, pushed her to go. When she showed up and realized she was going to have to talk and read out loud, she almost decided never to return. Then she did, and she kept coming back. "I started to really like it. I liked to hear the sound of my own voice." As we reminisced about 2010 and the writing club, she brought up Ntombi's voice, and her reluctance to read aloud as well. Gugu said, "I could never hear her at first. I had to listen so hard. But then I got used to it, and now it's just her. Just Ntombi's voice."

Before they left, I asked the girls to write brief introductions of themselves, how they saw their lives now, what they might want a stranger reading about them to know. Here's what Mandlakazi wrote:

Mandlakazi, a name that means power. I got this name because when I was a day old, I fell and could have died. But luckily, I didn't. Mandlakazi is a very hyperactive, short, sweet, dark-skinned lady from the Eastern Cape but currently lives in Cape Town. I have three siblings and a loving mother. I am 18 years old. I am as old or as young as democracy. I am doing my first year at the University of the Western Cape, doing a BA course in psychology. I chose psychology because of what I went through in life. I lost my father when I was 14 (on 24 September 2008). In January 2009, I moved to Cape Town. Between my exams, farewell, and family ceremonies, I didn't have time to mourn for my father. Then I had to deal with a total change of lifestyle, moving from a small town, if you could even call it that, to a big city. The worst part of it was that I left my family behind. Don't pity me, though, because I made the best of my ordeal. I grew a thick skin and I got to know myself in a way I never thought possible. My name means power and I used all the power vested in me to become the person that I am today.

And here's what Gugu wrote:

I'm short, big eyed, brown hair, bubbly, always smiling and laughing. I'm witty and opinionated and outspoken. I want people to know that I am what I write. I surround myself with happy things and positiveness. I am a second born, I love food, and adore writing. I want people to know that I'm a girl who has big dreams and aspirations, a girl who isn't afraid to show people what she is made of. I'm a big believer in God, a higher source, and my ancestors. I believe that to be big you have to start small, and that things are tough first then get easier. I also believe that everything happens for a reason. Oh, and for some odd reason, I believe that one day I am going to be a star. Everybody is going to know my name. I love people, I love talking, I love making friends. I don't like being serious all the time. I love my family, my mom and sister, and I love clothes, and everything that makes me happy. I am a girl who believes that South Africa will overcome its challenges of poverty and HIV/AIDS cause with education everything is possible. I am a nursing student. I have big plans for that as well. I am a person who appreciates friendship and I don't take anything for granted. I try to count my blessings every day and give thanks for them as well. I am a Leo, I am sugar and spice and all things nice. I am Gugu.

Of all the girls in Amazw'Entombi, Ntombi always hit a tender spot within me. I had been grateful that she trusted me enough to confide about her depression. I knew the Sisyphean effort it took to begin to address that, even to crawl out of bed some mornings. I had watched her in awe, throughout 2010, emerge from her darkness and discover places of light and hope within and around herself.

She had left her aunts' home and was now living in Eerste River, a Cape Town suburb about thirteen miles from Gugulethu. She had begun to live in a Reconstruction and Development Program (RDP) house there. The RDP was established by the new ANC government after 1994, to address the socioeconomic problems and shortcomings in social service needs across the country. While she was alive, Ntombi's mother, Ncikazi, had applied for an RDP house for herself and her children, so they could move out of the home she shared with her sisters. Ten years later, years after her death, Ncikazi's house was finally ready and her daughter moved in. It was a simple concrete structure, with two small bedrooms, a lounge and kitchen area without any appliances, and a bathroom. The only furnishings in the home were two folding chairs and Ntombi's single bed. Some RDP houses come without ceilings; occupants must provide those. She was living there alone; her sister sometimes stayed with her, but it made for a long commute to her job. Ntombi the introvert did not mind staying in the house alone. A few doors down lived a friend of her mother's, a woman she could call on if she had any needs.

Twenty years old now, she looked—and sounded—exactly as I remembered her on her best days. She had completed the one-year jewelry-making course at the College of Cape Town's Gugulethu campus. She had retaken her Matric mathematics and physical sciences tests again, and once again failed to pass. This setback would not deter her, she decided; she would try yet again. In the meantime, to keep busy and to keep learning, she enrolled in a business administration certificate program at Stanford Computer and Business College, a for-profit college in the City Bowl. She hoped this effort might earn her a spot at TSiBA (The Tertiary School in Business Administration), a private not-for-profit institution located in Pinelands. Students there are previously disadvantaged South Africans who, for academic and financial reasons, would otherwise be unable to access higher education. Students at TSiBA are not required to pay for their education monetarily but rather to "pay it forward" by transferring the knowledge, skills, and resources they gain at the school back into their communities. Until she qualified for TSiBA, she would study at a place that would accept her, paying for the program with student loans and help from her sister.

While Ntombi was pleased with her studies and her level of perseverance, she had another story she more eagerly wished to tell me. She had found her father's family. Ntombi had no memories at all of her father. Her sister, two years older, would sometimes try to prompt her memory. "Can't you remember the time . . . ," but she could not. It felt as though she had never met him, and never would. She knew, though, that she had an aunt in Eastern Cape, and maybe, if she still lived, a grandmother, her father's mother. She could not remember meeting these people either, though she thought perhaps she had, at one time. Ntombi carried a box of her mother's letters with her to Eerste River and thought she knew which ones came from her father's family. She wrote a letter to that address, reintroducing herself and including her phone number. Her aunt called as soon as she received the letter and insisted that Ntombi come visit the family in Eastern Cape, where her grandmother indeed was alive. She traveled by bus from Cape Town to East London, a fourteen-hour overnight journey, and her aunt and grandmother greeted her at the bus station. They had not seen her since she was a baby.

"My gran kept crying and saying, 'Zanele, Zanele! Is it really you?'"

"Is that what they call you?" I asked.

"*Ja*, they call me Zanele," she said, fondly recalling her family's adoption of the latter half of her full name.

They traveled on then to their home in Mdantsane, the township outside East London. On this, Ntombi's first visit to Eastern Cape, the girl who grew up in an urban township braced herself for a view of rural Xhosa village life. "I thought

I'd be sent out to watch the cows or something. But my gran had DSTV [satellite television] and so we ended up watching TV all day and eating. It wasn't all that different from Gugs!"

Ntombi found one striking difference during her time in Eastern Cape. She discovered a family that welcomed and embraced her. Her grandmother showed her photographs and told stories of her father. She took the girl to visit his grave, where Ntombi stood in silence as her grandmother spoke. "She said, 'I've brought your daughter here to see you.'" I asked Ntombi whether the experience felt strange or comforting to her.

"It felt a little strange, just standing there. I didn't know what to do. But I think it brought comfort to my gran. She cried while she talked. So *ja*, I think it was good for me to be there with her."

Her grandmother had lost three of her four children; only Ntombi's aunt remained living. Ntombi also learned she'd had an elder half-sister, another daughter of her father's, who had grown up in this area with their grandmother. She died several years earlier as well, as a result of AIDS, the same way Ntombi's parents had died. Visiting with her granddaughter for the first time after so many years, her grandmother seemed to mourn anew all these lost family members. A mother is not supposed to bury her children or her granddaughter, she told Ntombi. She is supposed to watch them grow up and older before she finds her own rest. Ntombi found herself consoling her grandmother as she grieved. "I just listened to her, let her speak."

She herself had remained in an emotionally strong place the last couple of years, a dramatic turnaround she traced back to the UCAN retreat for the J. L. Zwane youth that had affected her so profoundly. Ntombi always remembered exactly what Davide, the retreat leader from Italy, had said to her. She was holding on to so much anger in her life. Nothing's going to work for you, he had told her, you won't find peace until you let that go. Forgive them, the people who have hurt you. Your mother is gone; that can't be changed. It has already happened.

"He told me I was more or less dead myself then, that I wasn't living my life. So I went back home and told my aunts I hated how they treated my mother, that I thought they brought her death on sooner, because she had no peace in the house."

"I remember your telling me about that, how good it felt to say."

"It did. Then, later on, I said to them, 'I forgive you. I need you to know that. And I'm not doing this for you. I'm doing it for me. So I can move on.' And then," she closed her eyes as she told me this story, took a deep, cleansing breath, opened her eyes, and continued, "I just felt relieved after that. I felt *lighter*."

I told her that was exactly the change I had witnessed in her from that point in 2010. I was thrilled she had been able to keep herself in a healthy space, where she could thrive. It was a privilege to watch her go from a depressed girl to a young woman who now offered emotional strength to her own family members. When Ntombi received praise, her expression altered and she look a moment to absorb it. Now she smiled in quiet satisfaction, as though she were having a hunch of hers confirmed.

My name is Ntombizanele. I am 20 years old. In my life right now, I am currently busy with finding a career path that will help me reach my goals and dreams. I am a student at Stanford College doing business administration. I won't say that I gladly joined this field of study but it's a step in the direction that I want to take. I see myself as a successful business woman in the future who is proud of the person and choices I have taken. I care about myself and all those people I have chosen to be family.

Sharon had indeed enrolled at the University of Cape Town, in spite of lingering guilt that she should be earning money by now to help support her family. When we caught up during my visit, she was two years into a program studying social development, a discipline that focuses on the social and economic conditions that enable people to improve their overall quality of life. After living at home her first year, she moved into a residence hall in Mowbray. The res, as it is known, is a large, impersonal boxy building, as dorms usually are. She still loved Gugulethu, but it was easier to study and complete her work when she stayed by herself in res than at home with a house full of family. She also felt safer in Mowbray. There had been new waves of crime in her section of Gugs, with increased gangster activity. Her phone had been stolen out of her hand more than once. She worried about her mom and her grandmother, now living in a house full of women, but her mother told her to stay put and focus on her studies.

Nestled against the foot of Table Mountain, UCT's ivy-covered brick buildings evoke daydreams of idyllic university days. It is referred to as the Harvard of Africa, the best institution of higher learning on the continent. Taking her place as one of its students had done nothing to lessen Sharon's level-headed and wry approach to life. "People talk about, oh, UCT, it's the most *amazing* place. Only brilliant people go there! It's really not. Once you're in, you see that the people who do all right are the ones who work hard. And they're still stressed out and panicking."

From the time I got to know her, Sharon always had seemed more like a young woman than a girl, mostly because of her age and her position as the eldest in Amazw'Entombi. But I think

Sharon was always an old soul, in a wise rather than a world-weary way. It was great to see that she retained her in-on-a-secret smile. She was wearing her hair long and unbraided, with her natural curls sitting atop her head like a towering crown. Settling in at varsity had taken some time. She had begun to make friends at res now, but at first, the size of UCT made her feel disconnected. I asked whether she had seen any of her classmates from Camps Bay High School. Since it was one of Cape Town's best high schools, presumably there would be other students from there at the university.

"Oh, I see them," she laughed. "The question is, do they see me?"

She remembered faces and names better than her classmates seemed to do. If she identified herself to them, they did not even attempt to conceal their surprise. "I think they're shocked that I'm actually here. They ask, 'You study here?' *Yesss*, I do. 'Since *when*?'"

Sharon enjoyed her social-development studies, though she felt the program overemphasized theoretical concerns over practical applications. "We have to take these theory classes. They teach us how South Africa is supposed to be working. I look at it and think it's not even close to working that way. Why are you teaching me this?" Her split life between the township and the university gave her a vantage point unavailable to many of her peers. She cited SASSA (South African Social Security Agency) as an example.

"We learn about their social grants, what they're intended for, who they're supposed to help. How they should be made accessible to vulnerable groups of people. But I go into Gugs and I see people queued up around the SASSA building at six in the morning every day, hours before it opens. Now, that right there tells me something's not working properly. So why teach us the ideal? Why not get more practical and get at what's wrong?"

I asked whether she wanted to get a job in government to help fix these problems after graduation, and she dismissed the idea outright. "Even if I want to, I won't be able to. Getting a government job is all about politics and who you know. Your CV isn't enough even if you're qualified. I hate politics. The ANC government has never done anything for me. My mom had done all the work to get me where I am. Only thing I can credit the government for is my student loan for UCT, and I'll be paying that back." She had completed a practicum at a refugee center in Cape Town, working primarily with women from the Democratic Republic of the Congo (DRC), and she enjoyed that work. Sharon was still deciding where her career might take her, though she had already begun to worry that her progress was too slow. She was nearly twenty-three now, would graduate at twenty-four, and assumed it would take her a while to find a job. She wanted to be financially stable by thirty; but first, she had to help out at home. When she talked about this now, it sounded less like an expectation from her family and more like a contribution she truly wished to make. Her mother had been paying school fees for years, for Sharon and her sister. Primary school. High school. She had only just paid off Sharon's business degree at Damelin College. Sharon wanted to return that support as soon as she could.

"But remember, you've got a long life ahead," I told her. "It doesn't all have to happen by the time you're thirty."

"*Ja*, I know. I'm just so tired of studying and being in the same place. I don't need a nice car and flat, but I'm ready to see real progress in my life."

As committed as she was to her studies and her future, Sharon also found time for fun. She and three friends from Gugs had formed a musical group, Blackroots Marimbas. A small, Minnesota-based organization that works in South Africa through J. L. Zwane Presbyterian Church helped the group purchase their own marimbas. They played their first gig in 2012 at the Table of Peace and Unity, a fundraising luncheon held on Table Mountain. Since then, they have performed at weddings, street festivals, even a luncheon at Parliament, with a versatile sound they describe as ranging from background atmospheric music to energetic stage performances.

Like Ntombi, Sharon also took a trip to Eastern Cape. She went to see her father, who was still living. He would call her sporadically and unpredictably, and she would chat with him then. Nothing too deep; they did not have much of a relationship still. But Sharon had grown concerned because she had never had *imbeleko*. This Xhosa ritual to introduce a child to her ancestors is traditionally performed in childhood, but just as often nowadays it is held for young adults. Her father would be the one to conduct this ritual.

"Apparently you're supposed to have quite a few problems in your life if you haven't had this ceremony. People had started to ask me if I'd had it done. When I said no, they said you can't *not* have it done. You'll go crazy." She smiled a little sheepishly. "Our people are very superstitious, Kim."

So she traveled to Eastern Cape. Her father and her brothers, his sons, slaughtered and cooked a sheep as part of the ceremony. Sharon had to consume one leg of it. Then she stood beside her father in the field as he spoke to the ancestors, told them she had come to be introduced. Please protect her, he asked, as your daughter. Keep her safe. Bring her good luck. Give her a long and happy life. After this brief presentation, the sheep was served to her extended family and to neighbors who had gathered for the ceremony, and the rest of the day was spent eating and drinking.

"And that's it. It's done now, so I won't worry about it, at least."

"Did it make you feel closer to your father, doing the ritual?"

"No, not at all." She shrugged. "I'm not used to him. Why make a hullabaloo about one ceremony when he's just going to disappear again? I know that. *Ag*, shame, it is what it is." She chuckled, then said, "If this is our culture and tradition, though, who am I to say no to it? Let's try to avoid bad luck by any means necessary!" Her chuckle deepened into full-throated and sustained laughter.

My name is Sharon and I am currently in my third year at University of Cape Town studying social work. I grew up in Gugulethu in Cape Town and have lived there since. I am very outspoken, especially about issues that are close to home. I love talking and debating. Future-wise, I hope to venture into motivational speaking. But my real passion lies in starting a community-based organization in Gugulethu for youth. I think I can make a very big contribution to South Africa as a young person. I am very hopeful about the future of South Africa. This country has a lot of potential and most of it is locked in the youth. I hope to help in unlocking that potential as I was awarded the same opportunity by youth groups and by Amazw'Entombi. Everyone has the potential. Others just need help in realizing it themselves. When that happens, I think South Africa would be at its best and keep growing from there.

14

Still Trying to Find
My Way Through

A s they began to reach adulthood, the Born Frees suddenly and collectively commanded attention. The year 2014 would bring the twentieth anniversary of South Africa's first democratic elections, along with the first presidential election when they were of voting age. They were entering the job market, or, more likely, they were not; the unemployment rate for those age fifteen to twenty-four remained above 50 percent. Driving in Gugulethu one day, I spotted a poster hanging on a lamppost, its headline taken from a story in the *City Press*: BORN FREE OR FREE FALL? The story was a preview of a special report on what it called the nation's "lost generation" and its impact on the country's future, about to be released by a company called Flux Trends. Based in Johannesburg, Flux Trends identifies and analyzes "macro trends, everything from politics, religion, youth culture, media, entertainment and technology" that affect social dynamics and South Africa's business interactions.

I flew to Johannesburg to attend the report's launch, held at the Protea Fire & Ice! Hotel in Melrose Arch, an area promoted as a "hot lifestyle precinct," the place to be seen in Johannesburg. The swanky hotel featured an old Hollywood motif, decorated with poster-size glossy head shots of such stars as Audrey Hepburn, Marlon Brando, and Marilyn Monroe. The report—*Born Free or Free Fall? South Africa 2030*—promised to explain why young people made headlines for all the wrong reasons, and why now was the time to intervene, especially in light of the country's extreme youth bulge, with 60 percent of the population below the age of thirty.

The trends the report identified echoed what I had seen among the girls of Amazw'Entombi. A breakdown in the family structure, with parents absent by death or desertion, and in particular absent fathers. A "bottom of the class" educational system where only three out of ten Born Frees completed school through Grade 12 and passed Matric. A culture of violence, especially rape and sexual abuse, perpetuated by an intransigent patriarchal society. "Stressed and depressed" youth suffering from mental health issues and post-traumatic stress disorder, who lack a social support system and treatment options. The consequences for a disenfranchised, uneducated, unemployed (and unemployable) generation could be a powder keg of unrest, a crisis waiting to explode, as had recently been seen with an outbreak of protests in Egypt, Turkey, Brazil, and elsewhere. The report also warned of the dangers of South Africa's "welfare state," where a small workforce supports a large, dependent base. Currently there is one taxpayer to every three beneficiaries of social grants, a situation that Flux Trends called a culture of dependency and an unsustainable model. All these trends would contribute to the hardships of the Born Frees and of South Africa in the absence of clear and early interventions.

Here the report faltered, offering vague and cursory advice rather than any specific plan of action. It suggested supporting

mothers and mother figures as the key to resilience. A wor-
thy admonition, but only if mothers are alive and present, or
mother figures are willing to embrace children not their own
who might well have been thrust upon them. No mention was
made, either, of how to engage those absent and much-needed
fathers. The report cited that overquoted African proverb, "It
takes a village to raise a child," and encouraged communities
and religious bodies to rediscover a spirit of *ubuntu* now missing
in too many townships. Business leaders and concerned individuals were urged to support one of several NGOs regarded
as doing effective work. Instead of providing handouts, South
Africans needed to "build up indigenous leaders, individuals
who have triumphed despite their circumstances and prepare
them to go back into the communities they came from to lead
and inspire their friends and families to achieve their own
dreams." The country needed people willing to be catalysts for
real and meaningful change with this generation.

While the launch featured a PowerPoint presentation on the
main findings, Flux Trends would provide a link to download
a PDF copy of the full and comprehensive report to anyone
interested—for a fee of R1,850 (about $167 in 2014 terms). It
pitched the report to businesses in particular, especially their
corporate social investment departments, which South African
corporations are widely encouraged to establish to contribute
to "the village" and help address the country's myriad problems. Given the high price Flux Trends charged consumers, I
had expected an expansion of the material with reference to
original research and deeper scholarship on the societal issues.
I hoped to see Flux Trends pushing an action plan for interven-
tion to break the vicious cycles embroiling this generation and
South Africa. None of these appeared in the report, a scant

thirty-page document riddled with typos and grammatical mistakes and peppered with YouTube links.

Flux Trends report launches usually conclude with glasses of champagne for all in attendance. Given the sober nature of this report's subject matter, such a festive beverage seemed inappropriate, attendees were told. Instead, we were served mugs of mulled wine. After all, it was June and wintertime. As I left the event, a stylishly dressed young woman handed me a small swag bag as a thank-you gift; it contained pricey brands of sunscreen, lip balm, and hand lotion. There was not a trace of irony in the flashiness of the way this report was presented, the struggles of this discarded generation bemoaned beneath shimmering chandeliers and dire predictions served up alongside warmed wine. Flux Trends did not indicate whether any of the money it made from this report would be used to identify and equip those indigenous leaders it wanted to boost as role models for impoverished communities. Rather than groundbreaking, this report on the Born Frees felt, to me, like a profit-making enterprise undertaken on the backs of those who would never set foot in a place like the Fire & Ice! Hotel.

When he launched the Nelson Mandela Children's Fund in 1995 in Pretoria, Mandela said this:

> There can be no keener revelation of a society's soul than the way in which it treats its children. We come from a past in which the lives of our children were assaulted and devastated in countless ways. It would be no exaggeration to speak of a national abuse of a generation by a society which it should have been able to trust. As we set about building a new South Africa, one of our highest priorities must therefore be our children. The vision of a new

society that guides us should already be manifest in the steps we take to address the wrong done to our youth and to prepare for their future. Our actions and policies, and the institutions we create, should be eloquent with care, respect and love.

Twenty years on, South Africa urgently needs further introspection and specific actions to create that new society with the care, respect, and love Madiba called for. South Africa's children and youth are waiting for it still.

As the Born Frees garnered attention within their own country, beyond its borders South Africa captured worldwide notice in early 2013 for another reason. Paralympian and champion sprinter Oscar Pistorius—the Blade Runner, the national hero who had fought to compete in the Olympics on his artificial limbs—shot and killed his girlfriend, Reeva Steenkamp, a model and television performer, in the early morning hours of Valentine's Day in Pretoria. He claimed the shooting was accidental, that he mistook Steenkamp, who was locked in the bathroom, for an intruder inside his home in a gated and guarded community. He was charged with her murder, though ultimately found guilty by a judge of the lesser charge of culpable homicide, the equivalent of manslaughter. The celebrity aspect of the case focused a harsh spotlight on South Africa's epidemic of violence—especially violence against women.

Less than two weeks before Steenkamp's death, another killing drew far less notice. Anene Booysen, a seventeen-year-old girl who lived in Bredasdorp, a small town in Western Cape about a hundred miles from Cape Town, was raped and murdered. This heinous act shared chilling similarities with the death of twenty-three-year-old Jyoti Singh Pandey, the New Delhi woman raped and murdered two months earlier. Both women were gang-raped and disemboweled. Booysen's aunt described her injuries to the *Cape Argus*: "Her throat had been slit, all her fingers and both legs were broken, a broken glass bottle had been lodged in her, her stomach had been cut open. . . . That which was supposed to be inside her body lay strewn across the scene where they found her." Both women later died as a result of their extensive injuries. Before they died, each gave a statement from her hospital bed to police that helped to apprehend the attackers.

Hundreds of thousands of Indians turned out for candlelight vigils after Jyoti's death, bringing attention to the horrifying levels of gender-based violence in India. In South Africa, remembrances of Anene were far fewer and more muted. President Zuma mentioned her in his State of the Nation address shortly after her death. For the first time in his presidency, he spoke about "the need for unity in action to eradicate this scourge" of violence against women. It remained to be seen whether a president who had once been charged with rape himself would carry through on this call for action. South African feminist researchers Joy Watson and Vivienne Lalu presented a paper comparing the responses in the two countries: "[What] remains significant about the response to Anene's death is that, unlike India, there certainly was no awe-inspiring moment of a people coming together to demand an end to rampant sexual violence."

In all I have come to know and love about South Africa and its people, that situation still stuns, perplexes, and angers me most—that tepid response to the violence directed against women and girls, to the suffering of so many amid the objections of so few. And why? Why do South Africans, who fought

so courageously and fiercely to rid their nation of a racist government, tacitly accept the abuse and killing of their mothers,
daughters, sisters, wives, friends? I cannot understand it.

The only examination I have heard that makes some sense to
me came from Graça Machel, the human rights activist who was
married to Nelson Mandela. While I was back in Cape Town, she
delivered the Desmond Tutu Peace Lecture at UWC; I attended
with Mandlakazi and Gugu. In speaking about the violence that
pervades South Africa, she said the nation has not taken the
time to seriously revisit the psychological and emotional dam-
age that apartheid inflicted on its men and women. It was a system designed to dehumanize people; now you have people still
suffering from the lingering effects of that dehumanization. A
person dealing with his own self-hatred is more likely to try
to destroy the humanity he sees in others, or to fail to recognize it in another soul in the first place. Machel suggested that
South Africa needs a concerted effort, equivalent to the post-
apartheid Truth and Reconciliation Commission, to offer a new
vision of how to deal with this violence the nation's people all
too often inflict upon one another. The scope of brokenness—in
both individuals and society—created by more than 350 years of
colonialism and oppression has yet to be fully understood, much
less addressed.

I know I took this issue personally because of my own abuse
as a girl, but also because I worried about the safety of the girls
and young women from Amazw'Entombi, especially those who
had already suffered from that violence. I had yet to see or hear
from Olwethu and Annasuena.

Milly had stopped leading the orphans' group in Gugulethu. There were some tensions with Reverend Xapile about

funds raised from America, how money was to be used, and who decided. Milly always appeared inexhaustible to me, but in truth, she had grown weary and needed to break with the group and with J. L. Zwane Presbyterian Church. But she had tried to keep up with many of the children and continued to help them find scholarships for studying. From Milly, I learned a little about Olwethu and Sive, her sister. Sive had continued at Bridges Academy boarding school and was now in Grade 12, her Matric year. Olwethu had not returned to school to finish Grade 11, or beyond. I connected with Sive and arranged to see her and her sister at their Aunt Pinky's house when Sive was back in Gugs on a school holiday.

Holding a conversation with these two girls had always been an exercise in frustration; I wondered whether that would be the case now. I had thought of them all the time back in Washington, especially Olwethu. I wondered about her health, whether she was sticking to her ARV regimen, as she must. Whether she had left the boyfriend who yanked out clumps of her hair. When they first saw me outside Pinky's house, both of them hung back shyly and approached my car at a slow pace until I flung my arms out and embraced both sisters at once. They laughed at me then, Olwethu in the way she did to keep her mouth, still without upper teeth, covered.

Inside the house, the television was turned on and blaring, even though no one sat in the lounge to watch it. Sive ran into her room to gather items from school to show me. Only half-way through the year and she had already been named the top achiever in Grade 12. A second certificate of excellence commended her high marks in English, history, religion studies, and life orientation. As she posed for a photograph, holding the certificate, Pinky came home and warmly welcomed me back to Gugs.

"Did you see what our girl's done then, hey?" Pinky turned to Sive, and it was difficult to tell who wore the prouder smile.

Sive was also an elected student leader at the boarding school, a position that sounded rather like student council, where she served as a liaison between her classmates and the school's administrators, communicating information in both directions. Sive had big plans after Matric. She wanted to study chemical engineering or medicine, at UCT or at Stellenbosch University, a previously all-white, Afrikaans-speaking institution near her boarding school.

"Those are some ambitious plans, *sisi*," I said.

"I know! I am ambitious. But I'm a hard worker as well, and I know I can do it."

"I know you can, too."

Olwethu sat silently at the table as Sive bubbled over with all her news, smiling at times, mostly looking down at her phone. "And now tell me what's up with you," I said, turning her way.

"Not much. I'm working in a restaurant part-time in Wynberg."

She could not remember the name of the restaurant. She got the job through her cousin, with whom she now lived. Pinky had asked her to move out of the home for good, when Olwethu kept staying away too many nights after she quit school. At the restaurant, she cleared tables, washed dishes, and occasionally, if the cook had stepped out, prepared a breakfast. She wanted to train to be a chef, she said. As she spoke, Sive took a phone call and stepped outside to talk. With only the two of us then, I asked Olwethu another question.

"Is it hard for you, to see Sive praised for her accomplishments at school?"

"No." She said the word with the hint of a question in her tone. I decided to press her a bit.

"If it were me, I know I would be a little bit jealous, even if I loved my sister and was proud of her and what she was doing."

She insisted again that it was not hard to watch Sive's success. Even as she said these words, she began to cry. I tried to honor her silence for a while before asking quietly, "Where are those tears coming from?"

Olwethu swiped at her face and said, "I think the tears are from disappointment in myself."

She called 2010 the year everything went wrong, the time when she began making bad choices, with school, with the boyfriend. When she first met him, he listened to her when no one else did. Olwethu could not talk about any of her problems with her family; Sive was away at school. Her friends at school might listen to her, but she was spending most of her time with her boyfriend anyway—someone she thought would give her attention without judgment. Even a girl so hesitant to talk as Olwethu wanted to know that someone would simply listen when that's what she needed.

He hit her for the first time three months after she started seeing him. She had gone to a party with friends, without him, and did not return to his place that night. The next morning he was angry and hit her. She did not tell anyone. "He usually didn't hit me where I had a blue eye. He hit me on my body where no one could see it." The time I took her to the clinic, and her face was bruised and blue, was maybe the third time he had abused her. "When you're with an older guy, he manipulates you to believe it will be okay, that he's sorry and he won't do it again," she said.

She finally split from him in 2011, long after she'd had to move into her cousin's home to have a place to stay besides the boyfriend's home. Soon after she broke up with him, she met another boy, closer to her age; she was twenty-one, he was twenty-three. Olwethu said this boy helped her learn to respect and love herself, to be honest about who she really was, and to have dreams again, like studying to be a chef.

Olwethu thought she knew why life had gone so wrong for her, why she was HIV positive, why she left school, why she stayed with a man who harmed her. She had never had *imbeleko*, never been introduced to her ancestors. In her mind, her life is the string of bad luck that Sharon had hoped to avoid with the ceremony. That was the main thing holding her back. In order for her life to turn around, she must do *imbeleko*. Except Olwethu did not have any contact with her father's family, had no way to reach out to them and ask for someone to perform the ritual. Once again, she was stuck in a situation where she felt she had no control.

"Where do you think you can take charge of your own life?" I asked. "Or do you feel like you can do that in any way at all?"

She stared at the table for a long time before answering. "I think maybe I can change ten percent of my life. Ninety percent is out of my control. But I think I've kind of given up. When you have been told again and again many times that you're nothing, you kind of believe it. That you are nothing."

"Do people honestly tell you that, or do you think that's what you hear?"

"*Ja*, they do. People say, 'You're just like your mother.' I think sometimes that I inherited my mother's mind or something. Like, she also made bad decisions. So I'm going down the same path she did. I guess I'm thinking like her."

"So it feels like you don't have a choice then?"

"It does feel that way."

I asked about her health. She looked good, better than I had expected her to look. Her hair was cropped close to her head again, but her face was full and her skin brighter. She looked healthy, but she had not always been well during the previous two years. A bout of pneumonia had put her in the hospital, as TB had already done twice. She said she was taking her ARVs; I don't know that I believed her.

There was another delicate question I wanted to ask. Milly had told me that, according to Pinky, a few years earlier, Olwethu had been meeting boys at the train station when she traveled into town for high school. The two women suspected this to be the source of her HIV infection. Olwethu had been diagnosed positive in 2007.

"Do you know how you contracted HIV?" I asked.

"I really don't know. Maybe it's . . . ," she searched for words, or memories, or some answer to offer. "I really don't know."

"Were you seeing any boys before that time?"

"Every time I would . . . At that time, I only had one boy-friend when I first started to date."

"Yeah, just one can do it, I guess."

"Maybe I don't know how it happened."

"Have you wondered?" I had wondered at this question as well. How much did it matter to her to know how this disease that had killed her mother came to her?

"I have wondered, but . . . I've kind of said, so what? What's going to make any change, to know that? It doesn't make the difference."

Olwethu might have contracted HIV from an earlier boy-friend, or, like so many of her peers, she might have been raped by an HIV-positive man. I did not ask her outright; I wasn't sure I would fully believe her answer, whatever it might have been. I told her once that I thought she gave me the answers she thought I wanted to hear, rather than the truth. "Sometimes I do," she had replied with a cagey smile. If she, too, had been raped, that was, of course, not something I wanted to hear. But my frustrations with this young woman had clouded my own response to her and to her disease.

Doctors and scientists want to know how people are infected with HIV so they can study the virus, learn how it mutates, and thus try to find a cure and a vaccine. Public health workers want to know so they can attempt to curb the spread of AIDS. All the rest of us want to know so we can assign blame or absolution. A child who contracted the virus from his mother during birth or breastfeeding, a woman infected when she was raped—these people, we can proclaim, are innocent victims. But HIV transmitted through bad judgment, poor decisions, or a promiscuous lifestyle leads to a mindset that can also run rampant and viral: the belief that these individuals living with AIDS brought it upon themselves.

A wave of shame rolled through me as I realized how I had assigned guilt to Olwethu based on hearsay, her silence and earlier dishonesty, and our previous interactions. Judgments like that only entrench stigma further and are as insidious as the virus itself. She was absolutely correct. As she lived with HIV's effects, the illnesses and the stigma, it really made no difference at all in Olwethu's life to know how she acquired the virus.

I asked what she would like readers to know about her. She looked at me cautiously. "Positive or negative?"

"Either one."

She curled her lips under as she thought about it. "I want people to know I'm strong, even though I'm not strong right at this point. But I've had to be strong to go through my life."

"You certainly have. Do you think you can think of yourself as being strong?"

Another long pause. "There's a part of me that can believe in myself and know I'm strong. But every time I think that way, there's a bad or negative thing that will come up in my mind or in my life that brings me down again."

I asked once again whether she was all right with having her life, her health, her emotional struggles written about in a book. Here she did not pause at all. "Yes, I am okay."

"Really and truly?"

"I am," she insisted with a smile, without trying, for once, to self-consciously cover her mouth. "Maybe someone's going through the same thing I'm going through. Maybe she can learn something from me."

Olwethu, at last, was recognizing the courage she contained within herself. I, too, could see her bravery now, more than I had given her credit for.

None of the other girls from Amazw'Entombi had been in contact with Annasuena. No one had even seen her around Gugulethu. Given her proclivity to disappear for long stretches, this did not surprise me. She had told me before how claustrophobic Gugs felt. With aunts, neighbors, and a boyfriend's mother all prone to gossip, her business could be known so easily by so many. People on her street knew her HIV status because others could not keep the information to themselves, not because she had chosen to disclose to them.

Maybe she had gone to stay with a friend in Khayelitsha, a nearby township much larger than Gugs, and therefore more anonymous. Maybe she had returned to Johannesburg to stay

with family for a while there, or to Port Elizabeth to be close
to Naledi. These were all ideas she considered and mentioned
while I was living in Cape Town, and plausible possibilities to
explain her absence. What I refused to consider, even when the
thought nagged at me, was the chance that Annasuena might
not be alive.

When I stopped by J. L. Zwane, I saw Johanna, who also had
not seen Annasuena around Gugs. But she knew where Phelo
lived, which I could not remember, and she thought she had heard
that he and Annasuena remained together. Johanna went with
me to his house. She spoke to his mother in Xhosa and I waited
in the lounge, sitting on a sofa next to a console with another
television turned on and volume up, with no one watching.

"Annasuena will be coming just now," Johanna said. As a South
African idiom, just now could mean a long wait. I settled in to
catch up with Johanna, but just now came sooner than I expected.

I heard her laugh first, that familiar snicker, and then, "Kim!"

Annasuena stood in the doorway, looking healthy and
beautiful. Her body had curves, more woman than girl now.
We hugged three times, because I kept pulling her back to me,
and she kept laughing. Phelo's mother joined us, and I could
sense Annasuena tensing up then. She lowered her eyes and
reached one arm across her body to grasp her elbow as if to
brace herself.

"What are you doing with yourself now?" Johanna asked her
before I had the chance.

"I just started at Northlink College." She glanced at me a bit
nervously, then looked back at Johanna. "And I have a baby.
She's asleep back there."

"You have a baby girl?" I gasped.

"*Ja.*" Now she looked my way and grinned.

"Don't wake her up," Phelo's mother warned.

"I won't wake her." Annasuena angled around toward me, her face out of sight of the other two women, and rolled her eyes.

I wanted to hear everything, and I knew we could not have a real conversation with the other women present. We made a plan for me to return the next morning, so I could meet the baby. I apologized to her for my long delay in returning to Cape Town. I had told her when I left that I would be back again soon, because I had hoped I would be.

"That's all right," Annasuena said with a sly grin. "I knew you'd be back."

When a child is born in South Africa, a member of the extended family often chooses the baby's name. The decision does not always rest with the parents alone. For Annasuena and Phelo's girl, her aunt, Mama Lillian, selected a Sotho first name, and Phelo's sister a Xhosa middle name. Her first name, Nthabeleng, means "Rejoice." Siphesihle means "Beautiful gift." Everyone called the baby Nthabi.

She was older than I expected her to be, a toddler rather than a baby. Annasuena brought her out to meet me in the yard outside Phelo's shack, behind his mother's house. Just waking up from a nap, Nthabi glared at me with sleep still in her eyes. They were enormous eyes, twice as large as Annasuena's. She had a heart-shaped face and a high forehead. Tiny twists of hair, not yet long enough to be braided, covered her head. She wore a fleece hoodie printed with pink and purple hearts. Every time Annasuena pulled the hood up over her daughter's head, to shield her from the wind, Nthabi tugged it off again.

"She hates anything on her head. It's going to be like this all winter again," Annasuena sighed.

Nthabi allowed me to hold her for a brief moment, until she

pushed against my shoulders and motioned to be let down. She set her sights on a young calico cat crawling around in the yard. "Go see Kitzi," Annasuena said. Nthabi stumbled across the yard, kicking up sand with each step.

"She's gorgeous."

"Thanks. I think she is, too."

"Who does she look like, do you think? You, or Phelo?"

Annasuena answered without hesitation. "I think she looks like my mom."

I had seen only one photograph of Anneline from the time before she fell ill, the single picture that Annasuena possessed of her mother, besides those in *Drum* magazine. This photo was large and rectangular, the size of a placemat, and laminated for protection. It was a close-up shot of Anneline during a performance— mouth open, in heavy stage makeup, sequins shining on her dress collar. One shoulder was elevated—she might have been raising her arm as she held on to that final note of "Paradise Road." She was stunning and glamorous, every inch the star. Nthabi was one lucky girl. Annasuena had taken the baby to visit her mother's grave in Gugulethu, to introduce her to her grandmother, an informal moment of *imbeleko*. She asked for wisdom and Anneline's guidance in raising this child.

Annasuena had given birth at Mowbray Maternity Clinic in July 2011. "It took *forever*. I finally had to have a caesar." It took me a moment to realize she meant a Cesarean-section birth. "The baby was just being stubborn and wouldn't come out."

"So she's definitely your daughter," I teased.

"She is!"

I hesitated to ask the question that had been lurking in my mind ever since I found out Annasuena had a child. "Was Nthabi born HIV negative?"

She was. "I've been so careful with her. I kept her on the medication, because I breastfed her for six months. The clinic didn't want me to do that, but I wanted to. It's better, it's cheaper. And I've made sure to have her tested regularly."

Annasuena said she had started on an ARV regimen when she found out she was pregnant and kept to it faithfully during her pregnancy. While in labor, she received nevirapine to reduce the risk that HIV would be transmitted to the baby during delivery. After Nthabi arrived, she also received doses of nevirapine during her first month, and then she continued taking it during breastfeeding.

"And you're still taking ARVs yourself then?"

She grimaced and raised a hand to cover her eyes. "I was. It's been a couple of months since I ran out and I haven't got back to the clinic."

"*Sisi*! *What* are we going to do with you?" I shook her gently by the shoulders.

"I don't know," she said with a drawn-out sigh. "I know they'll give me a hard time when I go back there."

"Yes, they will. There are reasons for that. You need the hard time."

"I know I do."

"But it sounds like you've done all the right things for Nthabi."

She brightened then. "I hope so. I know I'm not perfect, but I'm trying to be a good mom."

"How do you like it? Being a mom?"

"*Yhuu*! It's hectic."

Phelo came home as we were talking in the yard. I had only met him a couple of times, briefly, in 2010, but he looked as I remembered him, thin and handsome, with a sleek shaved head. Twenty-six now, he and Annasuena had been together, on and off, for six years. He picked up the baby and kissed her hello. Annasuena asked him whether he could keep Nthabi then so she and I could have some time to go off and talk.

We left my car at Phelo's and wandered around Gugs. Anna-suena told me the baby stayed with Phelo during the week, and she stayed at NY 46, sleeping in the shack with Mama Lillian behind the family home still occupied by her cousin-brother and his now-wife. The responsibilities of motherhood wore on her when she had Nthabi every day of the week. "Some days I just don't have the patience to cope with her."

Annasuena had stayed out of school in 2011 while she was pregnant and then returned the following year for Grade 10, in a different school in nearby Manenberg. And then she was done with high school. She could not see it through another two years to complete her Matric. Not right now. She was twenty-one years old and she had a child, and if she was going to study, she needed it to be for something that would earn her a wage, and quickly. She received a child-support grant from SASSA for Nthabi, R300 (about $27 in 2014 terms) a month. Phelo sometimes found employment, but he was not always good about remembering to use his wages to buy dia-pers and milk and other things the baby needed. He loved Nthabi, though, and Annasuena had been surprised to see him become such a good and attentive father. But relations between the two of them were as unstable as always. She had caught him cheating on her a couple of times after the baby was born. They broke up, reconciled, repeated the cycle. Once, a year earlier, Annasuena had slept with an older man who lived near her, because he agreed to buy her diapers and food. "I know it was the wrong thing to do, and it's not some-thing I'm ever doing again. But I didn't have any other choice then." She told this to me in her straightforward way, in a tone somewhere between contrite and defiant.

Really, she needed to work, she insisted. She had just started a vocational course at Northlink College, studying civil engineering and building construction—carpentry, masonry, and plumbing. It was the last sort of work I could see Annasuena doing, and far from her first choice of study. She had wanted to do a course in public relations or business administration. But this was the only program offered by the time she submitted her late application, and she did not want to sit idle. She wanted to be doing something productive with her life.

There was another conversation I needed to have with her, to help me try to understand this girl and things she had told me. "So," I began cautiously, unsure where this discussion might lead. "When I was about to leave Cape Town, you told me you'd found out you were pregnant, and that you had had an abortion."

She looked away. "I know. I don't know why. I was freaked out. I didn't want to tell anyone."

"Yeah, I get that. But," I pressed, "why say you had an abortion? Why didn't you just tell me you were pregnant? Or not say anything to me at all?"

Annasuena whipped her head back and looked straight at me. "Because *you* told me I was irresponsible."

"When I did I say that?"

"You said I was irresponsible to not use a condom." The intensity of her anger startled me, and so did the defensiveness I felt spring up in myself.

"No. I said *it* was irresponsible to not use a condom. Especially if you know you're positive."

She threw me a withering look that said what she didn't need to say. I knew what she meant, and I knew she was correct. I was parsing words. *It* meant *she*. Annasuena understood what I was saying, probably better than I did myself. I knew back then that what I'd said had come across as a lecture. Honestly, I was fine with that. Sometimes Annasuena needed to be nagged. She'd just said as much herself in regard to taking her ARVs. She did not seem to have anyone in her life who held her responsible for her own choices. That stubborn streak often closed her off to anything she did not want to hear. I didn't want her to absorb my criticism in a way that reinforced negative beliefs she might harbor about herself. But I wanted her to use condoms. I wanted her to take her medication so she didn't develop full-blown AIDS, so she would stay alive. I wanted her to stop being irresponsible, especially now that she was responsible for this little girl.

South Africa's generation of AIDS orphans is now on the cusp of parenthood. Young women like Annasuena, Ntombi, and Olwethu have all been raised by parents who left their care to others, and then by guardians reluctant to accept the role. How does an orphan learn to be a mother? How does a girl who herself was partially parented learn how to parent?

"I'm sorry," I told Annasuena. "I should have found a better way to say what I said. I'm sorry that's what you've been thinking for two years."

"It's fine." She had turned her head away again. I stared at her, ducking my head down until I knew I could get her to meet my eyes. "It's fine," she repeated with a tight, unconvincing smile.

"Are we okay?" I asked.

"*Ja.*" I raised my eyebrows as high as they would go. "We are," she said. "We're okay."

"So now can I harass you about your ARVs?"

She then laughed the genuine Annasuena laugh that I loved, the one that made her sound girlish and not at all motherly, and we fell back into our easy conversation.

When we drew near Phelo's house again, Annasuena looked at me with a cheeky smile and said, "Do you have a man in your life yet, Kim?" I smiled back at her and said, in my best, broadest, English-speaking white South African accent, "*Ag*, shame, man! *Still* looking."

"*What?* Why?"

"Same reasons as before, I guess."

"*Yhuu*! You're too picky."

It was not the first time I had been told that, and Annasuena might well have been correct. Given the frustrations she had expressed to me so many times over her relationship with Phelo, I wanted to tell her that she needed to be picky herself. I did not say this now because her anger at my irresponsible comment still smarted, and I didn't know how she might hear it. I also didn't say it because I could not insist to this girl that it was better for her to be alone than to be unhappy with a man. I couldn't make that assurance to someone who had spent so much of her twenty-one-year life feeling alone.

Ubuntu teaches that a person is a person through other persons. Plural. Romantic movie dialogue aside, no one person completes you. No one can. No one should. If you are very lucky, if you open your eyes and your heart to it, you can find the people who expand your personhood. I could not presume to tell Annasuena where to find those people for herself. I had already wasted too much time in my own life noticing who was absent from it, rather than taking account of who was present. But I believed she would find them, because I believed in this girl's powers of resilience.

Before I went to South Africa in 2010, a friend told me, only half jokingly, that she expected me to come home with a baby I'd adopted. I did not, nor did I bring home a teenager. I didn't go into Gugulethu to rescue these girls. They did not need me, or anyone, to save them. Annasuena, Ntombi, Sharon, Mandlakazi, Gugu, Sive, Olwethu—these young women are saving themselves, making their own way through life over whatever obstacles have been placed before them, whatever shortcomings of their own have held them back. Nor did I need them to give my own life meaning, as meaningful as I have found the time I've spent with them. In Amazw'Entombi, we were all learning as we went along how to live the lives we had been given, and how to use words to, perhaps, lay new paths before us.

I asked Annasuena whether she was still writing her poetry.

"No, I haven't been. I haven't written anything, only schoolwork. I want to get back to it, though I miss it." She sounded apologetic and wistful. "But with studies and the baby and, *eish*! Just life, you know?"

I am Annasuena Malebo, who lives in South Africa, in Gugulethu. I'm a student at Northlink College, doing my first year there. I live with my aunt and cousins and my lovely daughter. I'm only 21 years of age, been through so much I'd swear I was twenty years older, but anyways. I'm like a scone who's slightly burned and brittle outside, but soft and delightful inside. Just need a touch of jam and cream. When I look at myself I see a very strong young lady whose heart is floating in tears of pain and struggle that were brought to my life. Through it, I still rise above the thunder, I still smile beautifully, I still laugh hilariously. I'm still trying to find my way through. I'm very ambitious, love singing, and I've got more to give in this world.

Youth Day

Little Stream Retreat Center hides itself away on seven acres in the hills of Constantia. Grassy picnic lawns border an oak forest that trills with birdsong. An outdoor tea garden serves the best scones and jam in Cape Town. By June, some of the trees have lost their leaves, yet everywhere you look remains lush and verdant from the winter rains. A sagging wooden bridge crosses the eponymous little stream that gurgles beside a stand of bamboo. Little Stream is fifteen miles and a world away from Gugulethu, and it seemed the perfect place for a daylong retreat and reunion of Amazw'Entombi.

We gathered there on Youth Day. On June 16, 1976, high school learners walked out of their classrooms in Soweto, the sprawling township outside Johannesburg, to protest lessons taught in Afrikaans, the language of the apartheid government, rather than in English. As thousands of students assembled, the police opened fire, shooting into the crowd. Estimates are that between 200 and 600 people were killed, and thousands wounded, over the days of riots that followed. Now June 16 is a public holiday, honoring those killed in the Soweto Uprising as well as the youth of today.

I hired a van to take the girls and me to Constantia from

Gugulethu, unsure, as always, of how many would show up.
Gugu *promised* she would come, then woke up too late, posted
on Facebook about how late she woke up, and sent me an SMS
saying she was running late. By then, the van was halfway to
Constantia and could not turn back. I had not met up with
Olwethu and Sive yet, so they were not there. But we had Sharon, Annasuena, Mandlakazi, Ayanda, and Athini. Ntombi desperately wanted to come, but she would not miss her Saturday
morning study session for the Matric exams she was still trying
to pass. She took a train and a taxi and then walked down the
long road that ended at Little Stream to join us around lunchtime for the rest of the afternoon.

The girls scattered around the gardens to sit alone and read
their notebooks from 2010. I also gave them yet another writing prompt to complete over the course of this day: "What did
Amazw'Entombi and writing mean to you?"

*Amazw'Entombi, wow! What a society! When I look back at
2010, when the group started, I was a very busy individual who
loved writing quietly on a piece of paper and I'd chuck it in a plastic file. I never seemed to struggle to find inspiration. It was like
myself, my everyday life and experiences were my inspiration.
Amazw'Entombi was full of young different girls that I'd never met
before, but I wasn't frightened, nor shy. Well, that comes naturally
with the Annasuena package. Anyways, we done some writing
together and shared each others' thoughts. Something that I'd normally do on my own, but felt wonderful, refreshing, writing with
them, and it was a new form of inspiration. We were a unity filled
with different emotions, drives, and ambitiousness. That's what
made it a strong group by voice. Some voices were very small, but*

*what they said or read was miraculous. It just surprised me what
other girls were capable of. They had the ability for once to speak
their minds, with no one to tell you no, you can't.*

—Annasuena

They caught up on one another's lives. Annasuena had not
seen any of the other girls since 2010. Now she told them she
had a daughter. The others crossed paths sometimes at J. L.
Zwane for church, or when they made plans to get together, as
Sharon and Ntombi tried to do, but not often enough. Everyone
had become busy, with their current schooling, or looking for
work. They were living in different places now. There was no
Saturday-afternoon writing club where they knew they would
see one another.

We talked—about South Africa, the education they had
received, the country they were inheriting. About violence
against women, and the violence against everyone that had
ratcheted up in Gugs. How Sharon does not even like to leave
her UCT residence hall in Mowbray to come back home to Gugs
over the weekend, and when she does, how she stays inside her
home all weekend long because it is no longer safe to be out on
her street during the daytime or the night. How Ntombi had
learned her cousin is a rapist, and the mothers with daughters
who live on his street were trying, in vain, to have him arrested
and charged. We discussed the serious and the silly. When two
hours of talking had gone by and we needed to take a break,
Sharon said, "I *miss* this."

*Today has been a day filled with stimulating debates, conversations,
and opinions. In the little time we have spent together the issues we*

have discussed are so close to home, we are so passionate about them, and I've come to realize that this was my, or our, outlet. It is the one place, or rather one of the few platforms we have to discuss, talk, and share our thoughts, ideas, and feelings about things we care about.

This has also taken me back to what Amazw'Entombi did for me in 2010. Writing in itself is an outlet, it's a way to share my thoughts, ideas, and feelings. But Amazw'Entombi wasn't just writing. It was also these conversations, it was a comfortable gathering where we could talk about anything with no fear of judgment. It was a safe space for me and it was a place where I grew mentally, emotionally, and in my writing.

I looked through my journal of Amazw'Entombi and I see the growth there. The first page of my journal is literally half a page and I see no emotion in it. It's blank and vaguely superficial. But as time went by, I see the change. I see more of myself in the writing. There is so much depth, so much meaning, so much of what I was feeling then. The writing is pieces of me growing up and talking about the feelings I had in that transition. I think that without the group I would have stumbled through the transitions I was making that year. By having that creative outlet and the platform to share completely, I think I handled my year well. I don't know how I would have handled it before, but I think the fact that my feelings weren't overwhelming or I didn't go into a panic actually says something about Amazw'Entombi and writing.

There I go rambling on. Whereas at first today I found it difficult to start writing and that is caused by the fact that I haven't been writing, aside from essay writing, of course. With all the things happening with school I find I don't have the time to write. Sometimes I type my feelings and then erase them just to get them out, but I never write anymore. I guess I don't really have a reason for it.
—Sharon

————

After we talked, we played. It was a brisk day, thankfully without any rain. To keep warm outside, the girls were draped in jerseys and scarves, leggings and boots, fashionable as always. A wide wooden swing hung on two thick ropes from the branch of an oak tree. We took turns sitting on it and pushing one another when our legs could not pump hard enough to catch any height. We traded off my camera and posed for photographs, fashion-model shots. Mandlakazi turned most creative when the camera came out. She had perfected a bug-eyed look with a comically exaggerated pout, a pose she varied with different hip and arm positions. For one photo, though, I caught her unawares as she was swinging. She was twisting sideways out of control, her mouth wide open, eyes squeezed shut, her head thrown back in joy.

On the other side of the stream, we stood in groupings with our backs against the giant stalks of bamboo. We shot multiple frames so we could switch off which girl had to remain out of the picture in order to take it. Along the curved stone stairway that leads down to the little stream, a sign is tucked into the bushes, printed with an anonymous quotation: "The only thing we take with us when we leave this world is our relationships. Have you loved and have you loved well?"

Amazw'Entombi granted me an opportunity to express my opinion about things and concepts that I thought did not matter to me. So much so that I would struggle to put my thoughts into words. Time went past, the writing got better, but thoughts were still rather difficult to put into words. As I write now, my thoughts are still jumbled up, but somehow I have gotten past that and really write down what comes to mind. My writings represent the person that I was and the person that I am now. It is quite strange how that young girl came alive just now, just by reading my old writings.

I don't write anymore. Between writing essays and updating statuses on social networks, I really don't put much effort into it. Randomly, I come across my journal. Only then do I think of writing, but I hardly get to it. I guess inspiration is the only thing that gets me writing and that inspiration is usually anger. Do I have a passion for writing? I doubt it. But do I like writing? Yes, I do.

—Mandlakazi

During our retreat day, I read aloud to the girls a portion of an early draft of this book. From the corner of my eye I could see Annasuena watching me, rapt, her mouth slightly ajar. Sitting on comfortable lounge chairs out on the veranda, I faced these young women whose distinct and vivid lives and personalities and ways of seeing the world I was trying to capture with words of my own. I felt more nervous than I likely ever would reading from the book.

When I finished, they applauded and Sharon gave her bless-ing. "It is perfect. We trust you now."

I laughed. "Didn't you trust me before?"

"We've had bad experiences, Kim," she said in a weary tone.

"What do you mean?"

"People come here, they take our picture. 'Look! Hunger in Africa!'"

Mandlakazi and Ntombi both fell back against their seats, howling. Annasuena moved to the edge of her chair and raised her voice to be heard above the laughter. She now wore that serious expression and body posture I knew well, gestures that spoke in tandem with her words to convey how passionately she felt about what she was going to say.

"What I *really* hate is someone who would write about your struggles and not look into the person you really are. Okay, *ja*, I've got this hard life. But I'm also a person with happiness and all the other stuff that comes with life. Don't just write about the problems."

"*Ja*, look at the realities, but also see the good things happening," agreed Sharon. "That's what we ask."

To me, Amazw'Entombi are like my sisters because they are goal driven, ambitious, strong, stand up for what they believe, and most of all they are beautiful. When I am with these girls I learn a lot of self-respect. I focus more on my inner being. I take myself into consideration and I just thank the Lord for meeting such ladies. I know we might not see each other much often but in our hearts we think about each other. These girls make me feel confident as a young black South African. At the moment, I have no writing and it is so sad because I believe writing is where you realize your thoughts and emotions.

—Ayanda

As we sat that day at Little Stream, Nelson Mandela lay in a Pretoria hospital. He died six months later, at the age of ninety-five. I don't know who in South Africa first christened this generation the "Born Frees." I imagine it was a name bestowed in hard-won hope. These young women recognize the irony in that name. They understand that the freedom awarded them at their birth looks different as an ideal than it does from the perspective of their daily reality.

The name they chose for themselves, though, always rang true. *Amazw'Entombi.* Voices of the Girls.

Well-meaning, compassionate people will speak of giving "voice to the voiceless." I have used that phrase myself, in earnest tones and with passionate calls for justice. The idea offers a veneer of empowerment, another loaded word. But it is power directed first toward the speaker, the advocate, the one who wishes to give the voice, who assumes that it is in his or her power to grant. These young women have always had voices. They just needed to be prompted, to have the questions asked, and for the rest of us to have ears to hear, and the good sense to listen to them.

Amazw'Entombi to me at first was a place I could run to on a Saturday afternoon just to get away from home really. Without realising I slowly opened up, had a smile on my face again, had something meaningful to look forward to at the end of the week, to share a laugh. I found myself with sisters I was free sharing with, knowing I had no fear of being judged for who I am. It's the only place I could share how I feel without being told I'm a child and had no right voicing out my thoughts and feelings. Amazw'Entombi gave me a space and encouraged me to find my voice, to write what it means being intombazana [a girl], *growing up in the township of Gugulethu in need of direction and inspiration. When I look back now, I know those Saturday afternoon gatherings were not just a place to run to so that I can get away from home. They were a place of growth for me, a transition to a better person, a willingness to open up myself and let my voice be heard. It's a place I learnt to love my God-given husky voice and mostly it's a place I learnt how it felt and what it meant to be listened to.*

—Ntombizanele

ACKNOWLEDGMENTS

"It always seems impossible until it's done." I don't know the context behind these words from Nelson Mandela, but surely he was referring to the struggle for South Africa's liberation. I keep that quotation posted above my desk, beside a photograph of Sharon, Ntombi, Mary-Ann, and Gugu, from our Amazw'Entombi reading. Writing a book is not the same challenge, I realize, as liberating a nation. But Madiba's simple, wise, and reassuring words next to those glowing faces kept me company—kept me going—through many moments when it did seem impossible.

My thanks begin with the Fulbright Program, the educational and cultural exchange through the U.S. Department of State. Their support allowed me the significant time and resources I needed to settle in Cape Town, form the writing club, get to know the girls, and conduct initial research for this book. Thanks to Ada Valaitis for first planting the idea to apply; Dr. Benedict Carton at George Mason University (GMU) for helping me to craft a stronger proposal on my second attempt; Dr. Sean Field at the University of Cape Town (UCT) for serving as my academic affiliation; Jermaine Jones, the program manager for sub-Saharan Africa, for patiently answering many emails and phone calls; and the staff at the U.S. consulate in Cape

Town and the embassy in Pretoria, for logistical support and opportunities to get to know the South African Fulbrighters heading to the United States. I am especially grateful to my GMU Fulbright advisor, Dr. Deirdre Moloney. The rejection of my first application crushed me; she told me without hesitation to apply again. The year that led to this book might never have happened without her encouragement. I hope each girl in Amazw'Entombi meets someone like Deirdre, who tells her to try again at the moment she most needs to hear that.

When I decided I wanted to go to Cape Town, Bob Schminkey knew where, specifically, I needed to go. He introduced me to Gugulethu and to J. L. Zwane Presbyterian Church and Community Center. I owe Reverend Spiwo Xapile tremendous thanks for providing the space for the writing club to meet, endorsing it within the community, and encouraging the girls to participate. I thank the entire congregation of J. L. Zwane for welcoming me as well, and for raising such remarkable young women. Besides introducing me to Annasuena and Olwethu, Reverend Mel Baars O'Malley drove me all over Cape Town before I could drive myself. I appreciate her patience and humor. Conversations with Edwin Louw, the center director in 2010, helped me begin to grasp life in Gugulethu and life for the girls. Johanna Singapi died before this book was completed. I wish I could have thanked her properly for showing me the way around Gugs, translating Xhosa into English, and coming to our Mandela Day writing session. I wish I could have helped her to write her own book.

A decade working at Bread for the World taught me about international development policy and the power of stories to move people to action. It also fueled a desire to spend a longer amount of time in Africa. Lynora Williams, Howard Salter, and

Adlai Amor are exceptional supervisors and great friends; each helped to make me a better writer and storyteller. I had a first tentative conversation about my Fulbright and book plans with Jim McDonald in an Irish pub in DC. He understood immediately why I wanted to take on this project, maybe better than I understood at that point. He believed that writing was my vocation. I thank him for supporting me and these efforts in so many ways. Jim was also a traveling companion on my first trip to Africa in 2002, along with the wonderful Asma Lateef and the unforgettable Ray Almeida. Ray passed away early in 2010, and I miss him. Sometimes I heard his critique in my head as I wrote, his booming voice almost present in the room. I hope he would like this book. I wish, too, that John Brennan could read it. He would buy me an Irish whiskey to celebrate. I'm grateful for the stellar people that Bread employs, because it gave me smart, committed colleagues to learn from, so many of whom remain good friends.

In the MFA program at George Mason University, Beverly Lowry and Steve Goodwin made me read good narrative nonfiction, which made me want to write it, and to write it well. From Beverly, I also learned solid research techniques and a question to ask, repeatedly: "What's this story really about?" I appreciate her teaching and her friendship. Many thanks, as well, go to Susan Shreve, Alan Cheuse, and Richard Bausch.

A fellowship in global religion reporting from the International Reporting Project at the Paul H. Nitze School for Advanced International Studies at Johns Hopkins University allowed me to return to Cape Town for focused research on violence against women and girls in South Africa. I thank John Schidlovsky, Melody Wilson Schreiber, and Denise Melvin for seeing the value in examining this topic in greater detail, and for their support of this book.

I could extend my time in Cape Town to catch up with the girls and fill in the blanks in their stories only through the generous support of friends and backers of this book via an Indiegogo fundraising campaign. For their extraordinary generosity, I thank Margaret Cohen, Kathleen O'Toole, Kimber Dodge, Andrew Wainer, Judy Coode, Bob Schminkey and Sara Holben, Annie Smiley and Hashim Shadan, Sandra Westfall, Lois Cecsarini, Cynthia Reeves, John and Janice Ungruhe, Amy Sullivan, Jennifer and Amy Stapleton, Julie Brewer, Rose Berger and Heidi Thompson (in memory of Solea), Julie Polter, Cynthia Ranke, Sandra Maben, Jennifer and Nathan Spande, Kathy Pomroy, Catherine Long, Sherrie Lawson, Hank Steuver, Andrew Nolan and Mickey Moran, Milt and Shirley Sawyers, Jim and Dean McDonald, Matt and Megan Newell-Ching, and Jane Letourneau.

Many people in Cape Town graciously shared their time and knowledge to help me understand the city and the country as a whole. Staff at the National Library of South Africa assisted with information on Gugulethu's history, as did the archives at the Center for Popular Memory at UCT. The university's Department of Historical Studies kindly helped me gain access to UCT's library. Freddy Nkosi Lutonadio of African Monitor identified others I should speak with about gender-based violence. At Sonke Gender Justice, Patrick Godana and Desmond Lesejane gave enlightening interviews, while Nelisiwe Ohajunwa allowed me to sit in on an *indaba* with the young men of Gugulethu. The work being done by the South African Faith and Family Institute gives me hope that religious leaders might finally take seriously the crisis of violence against women and girls. For the example they set for faith communities, thank you to Elizabeth Petersen; Fatima Ismail; Nobuntu Matholeni; staff members, volunteers, and pastors in Oudtshoorn; and the Reverend Mpho Tutu. Thank you as well to Bernadette Muthien of Engender; Ilse Ahrends of the Saartjie Baartman Center for Women and Children; Jeremy Routledge of Embrace Dignity; Jenny Arendorf of Place of Hope; and Christopher Baumann of the Imbadu Men's Project at the Center for Christian Spirituality. Nelisa Lunika from the Center for the Book honored the girls with her visit to Amazw'Entombi and by respecting them as artistic peers. Bridges Academy staff, led by Dennis and Susan Wadley, allowed me to hold writing sessions for girls at the boarding school and to spend some time with Sive out there. I thank Annasuena's aunt, Lillian, and Fanie Jason for helping me to learn details about Anneline Malebo's life. Though not a member of Amazw'Entombi, Annasuena's younger sister, Naledi, gamely agreed to appear in the book. Her presence in Cape Town was always a joy. For providing a gorgeous location and delicious food for our retreat, thanks to Little Stream Conference and Youth Development Center. Modjaji Books is a wonderful independent feminist press that publishes southern African women writers; publisher Colleen Higgs allowed me to reprint selections from Sindiwe Magona's poems. I hope we can find a way for Modjaji Books and Amazw'Entombi to collaborate in the future. From DC, Judith Mayotte introduced me to people in Cape Town I hope to get to know better on future trips; I thank her for sharing her contacts and knowledge.

I couldn't have been any luckier than to land at Inkwell Management with my agents, Michael Carlisle and Lauren Smythe. Their unwavering commitment to this book and their surplus of faith in me carried me through a particularly rough patch of writing, as did hearing Lauren's steady voice over the phone. She also helped me find my footing to tell my part of this story.

They have my profound thanks, along with Alan Cheuse for the introduction to Michael.

Deep gratitude to the wonderful team at Norton, equally committed to telling the story of the Born Frees. Alane Salierno Mason's careful edits and probing questions drove me to figure out what I was really trying to say, what this book was really about. So did perceptive feedback offered by Megha Majumdar and Remy Cawley; it thrilled me to hear how much they loved the book. Remy has also been helpful in too many ways to mention, along with Jillian Brall, Laura Goldin, and Alice Rha. A meticulous copy edit by Kathleen Brandes caught several discrepancies I made in the spelling of Xhosa names; that's a great copy editor.

I could never have written this book without the support—emotional and material—of so many friends who enrich my life beyond measure. Andrea Jeyaveeran and I have been friends since we were younger than these girls; how lucky for me. She is the best first reader, a perfect combination of tough love and relentless champion. I'm thankful for her, and for Richard Vernon, and their fabulous daughter, Esme. Molly Marsh helped me find my way to South Africa and back again, offering solidarity through transitions. Paulina Vaca endured my spikes in stress with the understanding of both a fellow writer and a compassionate friend. Rebecca J. Vander Meulen understood things others could not. Judy Coode is a great cheerleader for victories large and small; so is Jennifer Coulter Stapleton, in a different Tennessee accent. I appreciate Duane Shank's careful proofread of the manuscript, along with his quiet, steady belief. The Ungruhe family—Janice, John, Hannah, and Olivia, beloved goddaughter—offered welcome breaks and Cincinnati treats.

For early feedback, encouragement along the way, and energy when mine flagged, I thank Julie Polter, Kathleen O'Toole, Margaret Cohen, Amy Sullivan, Jennifer Spande, Racine Tucker-Hamilton, my *sisi*, Sarah Turner, Anne Wayne, Tracey Vail (for *ubuntu*, especially), Lois Cecsarini, Carlos Navarro, Hilary Doran, Ann Kaloski, Julie Gerdes, Laura Pohl, Beth Newberry, Martha McLaughlin, Stephanie Kriner, Jim Stipe and Christina Way, and Kari Verhulst. David Lewis offered website support and company in Cape Town. For Sunday night wisdom and prayers, I'm grateful to Barbara Howell, Dennis and Jayne Wood, Michelle Sinkgraven, Cosby Hunt, and Danielle Goldstone, and for memories of the mighty Leon Howell, storyteller extraordinaire. Erin Kolodjeski gave me a stick-shift driving lesson before I left DC; her reassurance that "everybody stalls" helped outside the car, too.

For what felt like a long time, I truly thought my year in Cape Town would yield more solitude than friendships. I was *so* wrong. Thank you to Mariette Steyn for the warmest welcome to her country, and to Kavita Pillay for putting us in touch. Peter and Martli Tuffins offered me a beautiful place to live and many cups of tea. Lynn Spieringshoek felt like an old friend from our first meeting. She brought me to Liandi Venter, Kerry Rademan, and Stephanie Kuhhirt; together, we enjoyed World Cup revelry and too many brownies. In Gugulethu, Ntombi Nyumbane and her mother, Elizabeth ("Like the queen!" she told me) were especially kind to me. Leigh Haynes is a Texan, but I will always picture her in Cape Town. Nicola Tipping is South African, but I'm glad she came along with Leigh to an ex-pats' club and I got to know her as well. I wish I had discovered Central Methodist Mission my first month in Cape Town. They have welcomed many sojourners into their congregation and are really good at it. I have never felt at home so quickly in any place. Special thanks to Adrienne van der Merwe, Sharon Cupido, Rene Goliath, Rutendo Dumbutshena, Gilbert and Jane Lawrence, the extended Abrahams family, vast and embracing, Sarah Young, and Joyce Ndlamhlaba. I enjoyed dinners and laughter with Brandon and Rose-Anne Reynolds, Kai and Ella, and with Roy and Rae Smith. I danced with Noel and Lisa Johannessen, with Emma and Grace, until we all dropped.

But it was hospitality and friendship above and beyond what I imagined that enabled me to finish the book, as some special Capetonians opened their homes to me for extended stays. I felt honored when Karen Cookson considered me a friend; it is not a term she employs lightly. At a less-than-convenient time for her, she still insisted on putting me up for six weeks. The additional presence of Ruth Cookson and Khanyisile Tiyo enlivened that time, while Kathy and Vuyiswa took care of us all. Likewise, Milly and Ian McQuade welcomed me into their family home. Living with Milly helped me see how she kept J. L. Zwane's orphans' group going for so many years: her stamina and faith never wane. The McQuade granddaughters, Jenna and Danica, also provided nice distractions; I believe Jenna will be a writer herself one day. Terence and Malia Parker always helped me to balance work and fun, with an equal commitment to each. Terence patiently schooled me in the South African educational system. He also read the manuscript to ensure that I made no major mistakes or incorrect pronouncements about South African history or culture. If any errors remain, they are mine alone. Malia, meanwhile, reminded me to breathe; she also made me feel deeply known. Far more than benefactors, Karen, Milly, Ian, Terence, and Malia are the godparents of this book; I cannot thank them enough.

All of these friendships have created, for me, what Dr. Martin Luther King, Jr., called the Beloved Community. I also call them family, extended over oceans and continents, over ties of affinity that began with my family by blood.

To my parents, Harry and Patricia Burge, and to my brother Kvn Burge, one of my best friends, thank you for everything, and then for even more. Your steadfast belief in me helped to quell many doubts and misgivings. Every lesson you have taught me about love and an expanded, richer definition of family can be found among these pages. And welcome to the family, Stacey Hall.

Naledi was right; I am very blessed.

Finally, to the heart of the book: My greatest thanks, of course, goes to the Born Frees, to all the girls who came through Amazw'Entombi. Thank you for trusting one another and me enough to open your hearts and raise your voices. I wish I'd had infinite time and words to tell the story of each one of you. But I'm fully confident you'll do that yourselves. I can't wait to read what you write and see where your lives go. *Enkosi* to Samantha, Nonzukiso, Connie, Keneuwe, Sivenathi, Nosiyamcela, Onele, Xolelwa, Anelisa, Nompumelelo, Wendy, Queen, Anathi, Zusipe, Zintle, Bonani, Siphosethu, Zinzi, Silindokuhle, Asanda, Zandile, Phumzile, Unathi, Yanga, Nobuhle, Thandazwa, Azile, Lisa, Zelda, Phola, Amanda, Athini, Portia, Mary-Ann, Thulisa, Ayanda, Olwethu, Sive, Mandlakazi, Gugu, Sharon, Ntombizanele, and Annasuena. *Maqhawekazi*—heroines—every one.

SELECTED BIBLIOGRAPHY

Books

Afolayan, Funso. *Culture and Customs of South Africa*. Westport, CT, and London: Greenwood Press, 2004.

Arendse, Cara-Lee, and Shirley Gunn, eds. *Edge of the Table: Fourteen Cape Flats Youths Tell Their Life Stories*. Cape Town: Human Rights Media Centre, 2010.

Besteman, Catherine. *Transforming Cape Town*. Berkeley, Los Angeles, and London: University of California Press, 2008.

Bray, Rachel, Imke Gooskens, Lauren Kahn, Sue Moses, and Jeremy Seekings. *Growing Up in the New South Africa: Childhood and Adolescence in Post-Apartheid Cape Town*. Cape Town: HSRC Press, 2010.

Carter, Jimmy. *A Call to Action: Women, Religion, Violence, and Power*. New York: Simon and Schuster, 2014.

Crais, Clifton, and Thomas V. McClendon, eds. *The South Africa Reader: History, Culture, Politics*. Durham, NC, and London: Duke University Press, 2014.

Dowden, Richard. *Africa: Altered States, Ordinary Miracles*. New York: Public Affairs, 2009.

Epstein, Helen. *The Invisible Cure: Africa, the West, and the Fight Against AIDS*. New York: Farrar, Straus and Giroux, 2007.

Field, Sean. *Oral History, Community, and Displacement: Imagining Memories in Post-Apartheid South Africa*. New York: Palgrave Macmillan, 2012.

Field, Sean, Renate Meyer, and Felicity Swanson, eds. *Imagining the City: Memories and Cultures in Cape Town*. Cape Town: HSRC Press, 2007.

Finnegan, William. *Crossing the Line: A Year in the Land of Apartheid*. New York: Persea Books, 2006.

Foster, Douglas. *After Mandela: The Struggle for Freedom in Post-Apartheid South Africa*. New York: Liveright Publishing, 2012.

Gumede, William. *Restless Nation: Making Sense of Troubled Times*. Cape Town: Tafelberg, 2012.

Hochschild, Adam. *The Mirror at Midnight: A South African Journey*. Boston: Mariner Books, 2007.

Jansen, Jonathan. *We Need to Talk*. Johannesburg: Bookstorm and Macmillan, 2011.

Krog, Antjie. *Country of My Skull: Guilt, Sorrow, and the Limits of Forgiveness in the New South Africa*. New York: Three Rivers Press, 2000.

Madondo, Bongani. *Hot Type: Icons, Artists, and God-figurines*. Johannesburg: Picador Africa, 2007.

Magona, Sindiwe. *Forced to Grow*. Cape Town: David Philip Publishers, 1992.

———. *To My Children's Children*. Cape Town: David Philip Publishers, 1990.

Malan, Rian. *My Traitor's Heart: A South African Exile Returns to Face His Country, His Tribe, and His Conscience*. New York: Grove Press, 1990.

———. *Resident Alien*. Johannesburg: Jonathan Ball Publishers, 2009.

Mandela, Nelson. *Long Walk to Freedom*. New York: Little, Brown and Company, 1994.

Mesthrie, Rajend, and Jeanne Hromnik. *Eish, but Is It English? Celebrating the South African Variety*. Cape Town: Zebra Press, 2011.

Motsei, Mmatshilo. *The Kanga and the Kangaroo Court: Reflections on the Rape Trial of Jacob Zuma*. Johannesburg: Jacana Media, 2007.

Newman, Katherine S., and Ariane De Lannoy. *After Freedom: The Rise of the Post-Apartheid Generation in Democratic South Africa*. Boston: Beacon Press, 2014.

Nolen, Stephanie. *28: Stories of AIDS in Africa*. New York: Walker & Company, 2007.

Ramphele, Mamphela. *Conversations with My Sons and Daughters*. Johannesburg: Penguin Books, 2012.

———. *Steering by the Stars: Being Young in South Africa*. Cape Town: Tafelberg, 2002.

Steinberg, Jonny. *Sizwe's Test: A Young Man's Journey through Africa's AIDS Epidemic*. New York: Simon and Schuster, 2008.

Swartz, Sharlene. *iKasi: The Moral Ecology of South Africa's Township Youth*. Johannesburg: Wits University Press, 2009.

Thompson, Leonard. *A History of South Africa*. New Haven and London: Yale University Press, 2000.

Tutu, Desmond. *No Future Without Forgiveness*. New York: Doubleday, 1999.

Wilson, Francis. *Dinosaurs, Diamonds and Democracy: A Short, Short History of South Africa*. Cape Town: Umuzi, 2009.

Worden, Nigel. *The Making of Modern South Africa: Conquest, Apartheid, Democracy*. Malden, MA: Blackwell Publishing, 2007.

Articles, Reports, Research Papers, Speeches, Etc.

Baldauf, Scott. "Class Struggle: South Africa's New, and Few, Black Rich." *The Christian Science Monitor*, October 31, 2006. http://www.csmonitor.com/2006/1031/p01s03-woaf.html (accessed October 25, 2014).

Bauer, Nickolaus. "Entrenched Inequality Threatens SA's Future." *Mail & Guardian* (Johannesburg, South Africa), July 24, 2012. http://mg.co.za/article/2012-07-24-entrenched-inequality-of-opportunity-threatens-sas-future (accessed October 25, 2014).

Bhorat, Haroon. "Economic Inequality Is a Major Obstacle to Growth in South Africa. *New York Times*, December 6, 2013. http://www.nytimes.com/roomfordebate/2013/07/28/the-future-of-south-africa/economic-inequality-is-a-major-obstacle-to-growth-in-south-africa (accessed October 25, 2014).

Boseley, Sarah. "Mbeki Aids Denial 'Caused 300,000 Deaths.'" *The Guardian*, November 26, 2008. http://www.theguardian.com/world/2008/nov/26/aids-south-africa (accessed October 25, 2014).

Davis, Rebecca. "Anene Booysen: Why India and SA Responded Differently to Two Brutal Rapes." *Daily Maverick* (Johannesburg, South Africa), November 15, 2013. http://www.dailymaverick.co.za/article/2013-11-14-anene-booysen-why-india-and-sa-responded-differently-to-two-brutal-rapes/#.U69mrxaczwI (accessed October 25, 2014).

Dugger, Celia W. "Keen to Learn, and Let Down in South Africa." *New York Times*, September 20, 2009.

———. "South African Children Push for Better Schools." *New York Times*, September 25, 2009.

———. "Partying Amid Poverty Stirs South Africa Debate." *New York Times*, February 14, 2011.

Greene, Margaret E., Laura Cardinal, and Eve Goldstein-Siegel. *Girls Speak: A New Voice in Global Development*. International Center for Research on Women, Washington, DC, 2010.

Holborn, Lucy, and Gail Eddy. *First Steps to Healing the South African Family*. South African Institute of Race Relations, March 2011. http://irr.org.za/reports-and-publications/occasional-reports/files/first-steps-to-healing-the-south-african-family-final-report-mar-2011.pdf (accessed October 25, 2014).

Independent Online (South Africa). "Zuma Confirms Love Child." February 3, 2010. http://www.iol.co.za/news/politics/zuma-confirms-love-child-1.472439 (accessed October 25, 2014).

Jewkes, R., N. Abrahams, S. Mathews, M. Seedat, A. Van Niekerk, S. Suffla, and K. Ratele. "Preventing Rape and Violence in South Africa: Call for Leadership in a New Agenda for Action." MRC Policy Brief, South African Medical Research Council, November 2009. http://www.mrc.ac.za/gender/prev_rapedd041209.pdf (accessed October 25, 2014).

Joseph, Raymond. "SA's Heartbreak of the 'Paradise' Songbird." *Drum*, May 16, 2002.

Kaiser Health News. "Mandela Reiterates Belief That Antiretroviral Drugs Should Be Made Available to All South Africans." August 19, 2002. http://www.kaiserhealthnews.org/Daily-Reports/2002/August/19/dr00012955.aspx?p=1 (accessed October 25, 2014).

Kanengoni, Alice. "Editorial," *Buwa! A Journal on African Women's Experiences* 1, no. 2 (September 2011). http://www.osisa.org/sites/default/files/buwa2011.pdf (accessed October 25, 2014).

Knoetze, Daneel. "Mom Recalls Anene's Dying Moments." *Cape Argus* (Cape Town, South Africa), February 8, 2013. http://www.iol.co.za/capeargus/mom-recalls-anene-s-dying-moments-1.1466446#.VEQpC0uczwI (accessed October 25, 2014).

Mail & Guardian (Johannesburg, South Africa). "MRC: Quarter of Men in South Africa Admit Rape." June 18, 2009. http://mg.co.za/article/2009-06-18-quarter-of-men-in-south-africa-admit-rape (accessed October 25, 2014).

———. "Toll from Xenophobic Attacks Rises." May 31, 2008. http://mg.co.za/article/2008-05-31-toll-from-xenophobic-attacks-rises (accessed October 25, 2014).

———."Zuma 'Deeply Regrets' Love-Child Pain." February 6, 2010. http://mg.co.za/article/2010-02-06-zuma-deeply-regrets-lovechild -pain (accessed October 26, 2014).

Mandela, Nelson. "Closing Address by Nelson Mandela at 14th International AIDS Conference, Barcelona, Spain." July 12, 2002. http://www.mandela.gov.za/mandela_speeches/2002/020712_aids.htm (accessed October 26, 2014).

———. "Speech by President Nelson Mandela at the launch of the Nelson Mandela Children's Fund." May 8, 1995. http://www.anc.org.za/show.php?id=3540 (accessed October 26, 2014).

News 24 Archives (Cape Town, South Africa). "Mandela Repeats AIDS Backing." August 16, 2002. http://www.news24.com/xArchive/Archive/Mandela-repeats-Aids-backing-20020816 (accessed October 26, 2014).

Pillay, Yogan G., C. White, and N. McCormick. "How Times Have Changed: HIV and AIDS in South Africa in 2011." *South African Medical Journal* 102, no. 2 (2012).

Plan International. "Girls in the Global Economy: Adding It All Up." *Because I Am a Girl: State of the World's Girls 2009.* http://plan -international.org/about-plan/resources/publications/campaigns/because-i-am-a-girl-girls-in-the-global-economy-2009/ (accessed October 26, 2014).

South Africa Info. "'Remarkable' South Africa Still Has Work to Do." November 5, 2013. http://www.southafrica.info/business/economy/development/goldman-sachs-051113.htm#.U4FyjV6czwI# ixzz32hNzKFmA (accessed October 26, 2014).

Stuijt, Adriana. "One Female Every 26 Seconds Raped in South Africa." *Digital Journal,* March 5, 2009. http://www.digitaljournal.com/article/268602 (accessed October 26, 2014).

Times Live. "Full text of President Jacob Zuma's State of the Nation speech 2013." February 14, 2013. http://www.timeslive.co.za/politics/2013/02/14/full-text-of-president-jacob-zumas-state-of-the -nation-speech-2013 (accessed October 26, 2014).

Vegter, Ivo. "South Africa: Rape—the South African Scourge." *All Africa,* August 1, 2013. http://allafrica.com/stories/201308021370.html (accessed October 26, 2014).

Watson, Joy, and Vivienne Lalu. *Rupturing the Norms: The Social and Political Response to the Rape of Anene Booysen.* Heinrich Boell Stiftung Southern Africa, Cape Town, 2013. http://za.boell.org/sites/

default/files/uploads/2014/09/rupturing_the_norms_saresponse_
to_rape_anenebooysen_1.pdf (accessed December 11, 2014).
Williams, Bronwyn. "Born Free or Free Fall? South Africa 2030: Now's
the Time to Intervene," Dion Chang, ed. *A Flux Trends Report*, June
2013.

Websites

The Coalition for Adolescent Girls: http://coalitionforadolescentgirls.org
Department of Basic Education, Republic of South Africa: http://www
.education.gov.za
Equal Education: http://www.equaleducation.org.za
The Girl Effect: http://www.girleffect.org
International Center for Research on Women: http://www.icrw.org
Sonke Gender Justice: http://www.genderjustice.org.za
South Africa Government Services: http://www.services.gov.za
South African Faith and Family Institute: http://saffi.org.za
South African History Online: http://www.sahistory.org.za
South Africa Info: http://www.southafrica.info
UNAIDS: http://www.unaids.org